Improving the Health and Well Being of Young People Leaving Care

Bob Broad

Russell House Publishing

First published in 2005 by:
Russell House Publishing Ltd.
4 St George's House
Uplyme Road
Lyme Regis
Dorset DT7 3LS

Tel: 01297-443948
Fax: 01297-442722
e-mail: help@russellhouse.co.uk
www.russellhouse.co.uk

British Library Cataloguing-in-publication Data:
A catalogue record for this book is available from the British Library.

ISBN: 1-903855-62-4

Typeset by TW Typesetting, Plymouth, Devon
Printed by Alden, Oxford

Russell House Publishing
is a group of social work, probation, education and
youth and community work practitioners and
academics working in collaboration with a professional
publishing team.
Our aim is to work closely with the field to produce
innovative and valuable materials to help managers,
trainers, practitioners and students.
We are keen to receive feedback on publications and
new ideas for future projects.
For details of our other publications please visit our
website or ask us for a catalogue. Contact details are
on this page.

Contents

List of Tables and Figures

Tables

Figures

Preface

This book sets out the research, practice and policy evidence about the health and well being needs of young people who have been 'looked after' who are leaving care or who have left care. It examines to what extent wider social exclusion, family background, and individual resilience factors determine these young people's health and well being, and it provides many examples of good professional practice and service models. The book examines what young people who have been in care say about the extent to which their current health and well being needs relate to their earlier, often abusive, lives and therefore the type of direct work and service provision most likely to be relevant to them. It draws on primary empirical research findings, and policy and practice developments to highlight best practice, and provides examples of service models for improving health and social care. The case is also put for social care staff to respond more systematically to the requirements of the Children Act 1989 (S23. 6) to first assess family and friends (kinship care) when examining placement options.

As well as setting out the detailed legislative, historic and policy framework about young people leaving care, the book draws on a range of research, user, practitioner, service models and theoretical perspectives. These include those of care leavers about the types of health and well being services they receive and value; practitioners and managers perspectives about how leaving care work is shaping up in a post-modernisation social inclusion context; and service frameworks and analytical perspectives. There are two large leaving care research and practice development studies at the heart of this book, both conducted by the author. The first is a national overview study about the work of 52 leaving care teams working with 7000 young people leaving care in England and Wales focusing on the impact of the Children (Leaving Care) Act 2000 on the health and well being of care leavers. The second is a two-year research study consisting of structured in-depth interviews with young people leaving care about their health and well being.

How this book is organised

This book is in four parts.

Part One details and analyses the rationale and content of current and recent leaving care legislation, and the links between social exclusion, care leavers, and health and well being. It provides a critical analysis of the powers and duties under the Child Care Act 1980, the Children Act 1989, and the Children (Leaving Care) Act 2000. It is argued that in discussing and assessing young people's health needs it is much more relevant and helpful to think about 'health and well being' than simply 'physical health' needs. The terms 'health and well being' and 'social exclusion' are presented as important conceptual terms, service framework indicators and practice signposts.

Part Two analyses the impact of the Children (Leaving Care) Act 2000 on the health and well being of care leavers in relation to the provision of education, employment, training, accommodation and financial services and supports. It also gives specific examples of needs assessment, pathway planning, personal advisor initiatives, and anti-discriminatory practices with black and minority ethnic young people, young parents, asylum seekers leaving care and young people with physical disabilities or learning difficulties.

Part Three presents detailed accounts of young people's perspectives on their health and well being and the impact of earlier, and often damaging, life histories on their current relationship and well being. In this part there is a strong emphasis on 'what works' in improving the health and well being of care leavers, and discussion of the young people's participation in the research. This part also includes a detailed case study of young mothers' and mothers-to-be and examples of the types of services and direct practice regarded by them as having been most relevant and helpful.

The book's final part, *Part Four: Reflections and Recommendations: Lessons From Research and Practice* contains three chapters. The first by Professor Panos Vostanis, sets out the challenges and a policy framework for meeting the mental health needs of care leavers. The second by Julie Harris, examines the health and well being issues facing disabled care leavers and contains examples of good practice, as well as challenges. The last chapter presents a wide range of good practice recommendations for health and social care practitioners, and introduces a new comprehensive policy, practice and service framework for meeting the health and well being needs of young people who have been in care. The book concludes with a series of recommendations including that of introducing a nation-wide, systematic and comprehensive system of health and well being indicators for young people and families in order to identify need, and lever in and target services.

Who this book is for

The book's applied research and development findings and practice exemplars should appeal to all those who work in or manage social care, health, education, counselling, housing, or training services which impact on young people in and leaving care, or other young people who face social exclusion.

Its empirical research and analytical base will also be of special interest to academics and students working in the childhood, social work, child welfare, health, counselling, youth studies, youth justice, social exclusion and applied social policy fields.

Dedication

This book is dedicated to the memory of Martin Flood, father, friend, husband, social activist, musician and social care practitioner, who passed away on 1 November 2004 after a 10 year battle with cancer. His energy, love and ideas live on in his family and in all those touched by his love and passion, as well as his dedication to social justice.

Acknowledgements

The inspiration for this book comes from working and undertaking research with young people in leaving care projects and with those who work with them. In 1997 I was particularly struck by the importance of young people's health and well being issues when, with Lesley Saunders, I conducted a research study about the health needs of young people leaving care. In the face of adversity the young people's positive contributions and resilience were especially humbling. It seemed important then to give a higher prominence to health and well being issues in so far as they impact on young people leaving care.

A special thanks is extended to all the leaving care teams which participated in the national leaving care research study and to the Action on Aftercare Consortium which commissioned it. Next, thanks is also extended to the three voluntary organisation projects for participating in the two year 'Improving the Health and Well-being of Socially Excluded Young People' research project conducted in partnership with *The Children's Society* (Monaghan and Broad, 2003). These were the Barnardo's Manchester Leaving Care Service, the Manchester Foyer, and the Children's Society In-Line Project, Newcastle. I am also very grateful to the young people who participated in that study and a special thank you is extended to Maddy Monaghan, the researcher on the project. A particular thanks is extended to Professor Dave Ward, Head of the School of Health and Applied Social Sciences, Faculty of Health and Life Sciences, at De Montfort University, Leicester for his continued support.

I would also like to thank the publishers especially Geoffrey Mann, Martin Jones and Clive Newton for their responsiveness, advice and helpful comments. Finally a very special thanks is extended to my immediate family, Denise, my wife and Jenny and Jonathan Broad, our children, for their enduring love and support, and understanding of the pressures of working full-time, and being an active father and husband. Their ideas about health and well being issues were also welcome.

About the author and contributors

Dr Bob Broad is Professor of Children and Families Research, and Director of the Children and Families Research Unit, in the Faculty of Health and Life Sciences at De Montfort University, Leicester.

Julie Harris is a research Officer in the Policy and Research Unit at Barnardo's. At the time of writing she was an independent consultant specialising in leaving care issues, and in particular, those affecting young disabled people.

Panos Vostanis is Professor of Child and Adolescent Psychiatry at the University of Leicester, and Consultant for a designated mental health team for looked after young people, young offenders, homeless and refugee families.

Part I

Leaving Care Legislation, Social Exclusion, and Health and Well Being

Chapter One

Young People Leaving Care: Policy and Legislation

Introduction to the book, aims and rationale

The aim of this book is to draw on research findings and policy and practice developments in the leaving care field to highlight current practice and the opportunities to further improve outcomes for young people leaving care. This book especially focuses on the health and well being of young people leaving the care system. In this book the term well being is used to describe the range of physical, mental, cognitive, behavioural and social aspects, that make up what can be called a 'good life' and are a part of the total universe of human life (see DoH, 2002: 1; Bradshaw, 2002). It also embraces the promotion and development of healthy lifestyles (often code for '*healthier* lifestyles') for young people (Children and Young Peoples Unit, 2001) and 'well being' will be examined in more detail in the following chapter as one aspect of health and well being which is introduced here.

The term 'well being', especially when set within the wider context of social exclusion, appealed to this author as the focus of a book about young people leaving care for a number of reasons.

- The term well being has immediate policy relevance, especially when associated with the government's social inclusion agenda of joint service planning, and holistic and crosscutting agency initiatives, such as those relating to education and training for socially excluded young people.
- The term is well suited as a heuristic device because it encompasses and encapsulates and captures the human condition. It immediately suggests a wide range of physical, spiritual, health and emotional aspects central to an analysis of human being.
- Heuristically the use of the term conveniently enables a full range of the social aspects of life, here relating to young people leaving care, and service provision for them, to be properly considered, in a way that the terms 'health' or 'poverty' would likely exclude. Here this

author is thinking of social aspects of young people's lives such as their 'living conditions' or 'financial circumstances' as much as levels of emotional well being or weekly income.
- The notion of well being is an 'idea of its time' both in political and policy terms. In relation to the latter for example, the raging debates and disputes in the 1970s and 1980s about 'what is poverty?' seem to have been submerged and to a degree subverted and silenced within the preferred political discourse of 'social exclusion' (a theme developed in the following chapter). It is also the case that current and past government's dislike of the term 'poverty' is matched by their ready approval given to those more ambiguous and seemingly lower-level discourses, currently about 'social exclusion' previously about 'back to basics' and 'self-help.'
- Arguably then there is a sense in which academics and policy makers can engage in debate about, and more likely undertake government funded research about 'social exclusion' and 'well being' more than about poverty. Thus Bradshaw, the editor of an impressive and groundbreaking book about the well being of children, states that whilst in the past government has not produced 'a regular, comprehensive analysis of the well being of children' (Bradshaw, 2002: xi) things are changing. In particular he cites the evidence about the growth of the Children and Young Person's Unit, government surveys, and the appointment of Children's Ministers in the UK.
- In addition the term 'health' is increasingly recognised as being not just about physical health but mental health and well being. An influential report that embraces and endorses this approach is the *Bright Futures* report sub-titled 'promoting children and young people's mental health.' That report states that it is about the well being of children and young people' (Mental Health Foundation, 1999).

The potential disadvantage of the use of the term, so far as services are concerned, is that it does not appear to fit neatly into service descriptions, or service accountability frameworks. Yet as we will see later, this is not necessarily the case in that it is more often a matter of services delivering their particular services, for example accommodation, within the context of planned, joined-up-thinking. Such thinking needs to focus attention on the needs of the whole person, here a care leaver, who is likely to have the sorts of different, pressing and simultaneous needs characteristic of other young people facing social exclusion. The crucial difference, is that so far as care leavers are concerned the local authority is the legally responsible and accountable parent, which may not be the case, for example, for a young person attending a Youth Offending Team.

There are two leaving care research studies conducted by the author which are at the heart of this book and they complement each other in terms of subject focus, the different ways they were conducted, their scope and application. The first research study (conducted over an 18-month period) presents findings from a national overview study into leaving care work in England and Wales. It evaluates the ways in which the Children (Leaving Care) Act 2000 (CLCA 2000) was being implemented eighteen months after its introduction in 2001. The second research study (conducted over two years) consists, almost entirely, of structured in-depth one-to-one and focus group interviews with young people leaving care about their well being. This second research study featuring the young people's perspectives on their health and well being also contains a case study of young women leaving care who are parents or parents-to-be. It is primarily from these two research studies, as well as other material, which this publication's practice and policy recommendations will follow.

This book does not include detailed direct practice guidance with young people leaving care since this has already been comprehensively covered elsewhere (for example, Wheal, 2002) except where new ways of working since the CLCA 2000 are highlighted by practitioners, for example about Pathway Planning. The book's focus is on young people leaving care after the point when they were looked after, in foster care or residential care, and therefore it is outside the book's brief to examine the health and well being of children in foster care or residential care. Rather, the focus is on the perceptions, described in Part Two, of leaving care services since the CLCA 2000, and in Part Three, of young people

leaving care making the transition to independence. It is primarily from these two research studies, as well as other material that this book's practice and policy recommendations will follow.

The thesis of this book, based on the evidence presented here, is:

1. The explanations for the poor state of care leavers' health and well being derive from their earlier life experiences of social exclusion, emotional abuse and the continuation of a lack of direction, funding, and inadequate services.
2. A new and comprehensive range of funded and flexible services and service strategies are needed to meet the material, emotional, self-esteem and well being needs and tackle the social inclusion agenda, as well as meeting more immediate crisis-based health needs.

Let us begin then in this part of the book with an examination of the legislative and policy context for care leavers. A chapter focusing on social exclusion, and the health and well being of care leavers will follow this one.

Background to the Children Act 1989 and the Children (Leaving Care) Act 2000

The Children Act 1989

It has been argued by Biehal et al. (1995) that there were three developments associated with the introduction of statutory changes to the leaving care legislation, which eventually became incorporated into the Children Act 1989 legislation. These were:

1. The force of the consistent evidence emerging from studies about the level of deprivation experienced by care leavers, and the problems they experienced when making the transition from care towards independence (including Bonnerjea, 1990; Stein and Carey, 1986; Randall, 1988 and 1989).
2. The ways in which the messages of young people and those representing their interests in the 1970s and 1980s, both became more vocal and formalised, especially through the medium of the *National Association of Young People in Care* (or NAYPIC), *The Who Cares? Trust*, and *Black and in Care*.
3. The contribution of the professional child care lobby dedicated to legislative reforms.

In relation to 'after care', the term then used, these included the recommendations of the *Social Services Committee Report on Children in Care* or *Short Report* (DHSS, 1984). These recommendations were amended by the *Review of Child Care Law* (DHSS, 1985) and included in the White Paper *The Law on Child Care and Family Services* (DHSS, 1987).

These three developments had social, legal and professional dimensions. The social dimension was and is concerned with the social context of the employment, housing, training, and education situation facing care leavers. Critically it is also underpinned by the desire for young people to have further legal and social rights, to services and power holders. Such an agenda is still propounded by young peoples groups, charities and lobby groups. The Children Act 1989 simply could not deliver on this three fold agenda except in so far as it attempted, somewhat weakly and half-heartedly, to emphasise corporate not departmental responsibilities. The legal dimensions and professional dimensions took forward the concerns of researchers and other academics about the shortcomings of the Child Care Act 1980 and research findings which pointed to the poor life chances of care leavers.

The Children (Leaving Care) Act 2000

Again this legislation was introduced as a result of a mixture of factors, not least of which was the political one of the arrival of a new and more welfare-state-friendly administration in 1997. As a result of constant campaigning, lobbying, evidence about poor outcomes for young people leaving care in the 1980s and 1990s, and mainly triggered by a finding of 'widespread abuse of children in care' (DoH, 1998: 5) specific new legislation was enacted in 2001. The emergence of the CLCA 2000 resulted from a specific government commitment (DoH, 1998) to implement Sir William Utting's recommendations contained in his *Review of the Safeguards for Children Living Away from Home* (Utting, 1997). The consultation document *Me Survive Out There* (DoH, 1999b) was published for consultation and the Children (Leaving Care) Bill 2000 received the Royal Assent in October 2000 and the CLCA 2000 was introduced in October 2001. It also followed three previous pieces of legislation, the Children Act (1948), the Child Care Act (1980), the Children Act (1989) introduced since the Second World War which included specific provision for

after care. It also followed the *Too Much Too Young* campaign by the Action on After Care Consortium (1996), about care leavers entitlements to housing benefit (Barnado's, 1995), criticisms of the Children Act 1989's limitations (Broad, 1997) and of its variable impact and implementation (this author, 1998).

According to the government (DoH, 2000) the main reason behind the provisions to be contained in the CLCA 2000 was to improve the life chances of young people leaving care (DoH, 2000: 2). Its main aims included countering the trend for young people to be discharged from looked after care as soon as they are 16. The government had also reported in *Me Survive Out There* (DoH, 1999b) that:

- As many as 75% of young people leaving care have no educational qualifications.
- Up to 50% of care leavers are unemployed.
- Up to 20% of care leavers experience some form of homelessness within two years of leaving care.

Other key aims of the legislation were to improve the assessment, preparation and planning to leave care, provide better personal support for young people after leaving care and improve the financial arrangements for care leavers. Local authorities became responsible for assessing and meeting the needs of these young people and removing their entitlement to non-contributory benefits. The money, which would have been available via benefits, was transferred to local authorities to help support these young people, considerably increasing local financial responsibilities and accountability, at strategic, team and individual levels.

Consultation about the CLCA 2000: Social justice meets the accountant

Whilst there were some discussions within the Department of Health and with relevant groups about the scope and extent of the legislation and Guidance there was never enough time provided to make full comments. As a member of the DoH Quality Protects Leaving Care Project Team I remember at one point, along with others, being given just two days to send in detailed comments on the legal aspects of the proposed legislation! Indeed this same pattern of token and rushed consultation also applied to the preceding formal consultation document *Me Survive Out There* (DoH, 1999b) in that case seeking detailed comments during the summer holiday period. Professional and academic advisors recommended that legislative entitlements should be clear, comprehensive and apply to everyone who had previously been looked after. In addition it was firmly recommended that funding should be attached to each child irrespective of which post-care route that child took. The department was advised of the folly of introducing the term 'relevant children' with the implication for those not meeting the criteria being described as 'irrelevant.' Such advice was ignored. There were also recommendations about prioritising the physical and emotional health of care leavers through the introduction of additional duties in the legislation and joint work with the NHS. All these recommendations were made in order to promote the principles of clarity, generosity, equity and social justice. However the group was informed that the treasury would not agree to the principle of funding accompanying each child and proposals for wider definitions of statutory entitlements were disregarded. It is also worth noting that other forces which shaped the legislation, some would say quite properly, were the views of the Association of Directors of Social Services and the Local Government Association, about what was affordable, practicable and deliverable.

Eventually when the legislation, the CLCA 2000 was enacted, it was, of course, most welcome from the Cinderella of the child care sector, always short of resources and operating in the shadow of other, child protection, priorities. However as we will see, and in keeping with previous legislation for care leavers, there were a very limited number of new powers and duties under the CLCA 2000, and considerable funding limits, although these were not fully acknowledged at the time. Perhaps this was because campaigners, academics, voluntary organisations and young people's groups were thankful and grateful for 'anything' after the paucity of attention and investment the leaving care field had received in the 1980s and 1990s. Also since government funds many of these groups, directly or indirectly, these groups probably feel constrained about the extent to which they can be openly critical.

Let us start by examining the duties, and then the powers of the three main Child Care Acts

(1980, 1989 and 2000) beginning with the duties provided under the CLCA 2000.

Duties placed on local authorities under the CLCA 2000

The CLCA 2000 did not replace the Children Act (1989) but built on and extended the duties and powers included in the leaving care and aftercare sections of that Act. Of critical importance is the Act's provision that the authority that last looked after a young person will continue to have responsibility, regardless of where that young person moves to in the country. This author would argue that it needs to be recognised that under the CLCA there is neither universal, nor comprehensive nor equitable provision for all care leavers. Instead carefully targeted care, duties and powers for different types of care leavers were introduced. The provisions of the CLCA apply only to those categories of children and young people as defined in the CLCA 2000 and Regulations.

Thus children and young people affected by the CLCA 2000 are:

- *Eligible* children – aged 16 and 17, who have been looked after for at least 13 weeks since the age of 14 and who are still looked after.
- *Relevant* children – aged 16 and 17, no longer looked after for at least 13 weeks since the age of 14, and who have been looked after at some time while 16 or 17, and who have left care.
- *Former relevant* children – aged 18–21 who have been either relevant or eligible children or both.
- *Qualifying children and young people* – aged 16–21 (or under 24 if in education/training) who cease to be looked after or accommodated after 16, and qualifying children and young people who left care before October 2001.

Duties

- To keep in touch with a relevant child (S23 B (1)) to make sure, as far as is possible, that they receive help, work education, training, or employment.
- To carry out a needs assessment of a relevant child aged 16–17 (S23 B (2)). The needs assessment will then be the basis for preparing the Pathway Plan. As a looked-after child, an eligible child aged 16–17 will already have had a needs assessment completed in order to formulate a Care Plan, and this should form

the basis for the assessment required under the 2000 Act.

- To prepare a pathway plan (S23 B (3)).
- To keep in touch with a former relevant child whether within the area or not, and if lost touch with the former relevant child to re-establish contact (S23 C (1) (2)).
- Appoint a personal advisor for a former relevant child.
- Continue the appointment of a personal advisor and undertake a pathway plan, subject to regular review (S24 (a) (b) (c) (d)).
- Regarding qualifying children and substituting existing S24 Children Act (1989)) there is a duty to carry out functions under S24A and S24B to advise, assist and befriend, and give assistance.
- Provide care leavers in Higher Education, or pursuing such residential further education courses, with vacation accommodation or the means to secure it, should this be needed (S24 B (5)).
- Care leavers aged 18–21 will have a young person's advisor, a Pathway Plan (to be reviewed and updated every six months), and the local authority must keep in touch.

Comment

In practical terms then, local authorities were given duties to undertake needs and service or pathway planning functions in much more rigorous and accountable ways. In particular they must appoint and make available personal advisors, undertake needs assessments, including financial assessments, and jointly with the young person and other agencies make Pathway Plans, identify 'suitable' accommodation, and keep in touch with the young person.

The CLCA 2000 amended the primary legislation, the Children Act 1989 and introduced new groups of young people in terms of service eligibility. The main principles underlying the Children Act 1989 are the promotion of the welfare of the child, work in partnership with parents, acknowledging the importance of families and the views of the child and of parents, and, finally, emphasising the corporate responsibility of the local authority. The Children Act (1989) placed a number of duties on local authorities, many of which concern the acceptance of legal responsibility and the provision of advice.

Duties placed on local authorities under the Children Act 1989

Duties

- To advise, assist and befriend children who are looked after, with a view to promoting their welfare when they cease to be looked after (S24) (1)).
- To advise and befriend young people under 21 who were looked after by the local authority after age 16, or who were accommodated by or on behalf of a voluntary organisation and are known to the local authority to need advice (S24(2)).
- Looked after young people who qualify for advice are those who at age 16 were either in local authority care, or were provided with accommodation, including those compulsorily accommodated (young people on remand or the subject of a supervision order with a residence requirement) (S22(1)).
- To advise the relevant local authority when a young person who they are advising and befriending moves to another area (S24(11)).
- To establish a procedure for considering any representations, including any complaint, made to them by a person qualifying for advice or assistance about the discharge of their functions under this part of the Act (S26(3)).
- It is the duty of the local housing authority to assist so far as this is compatible with that authority's own statutory duties (S27(2)).
- To provide accommodation for any child in need who has reached the age of 16 and whose welfare is likely to be seriously prejudiced without accommodation(S20(3)).
- Young people aged 16 or over may be accommodated if they agree, despite their parents' objections (S20(11)).

Comment

The Children Act 1989 only marginally extended local authority duties, because, as we will see, the local authority had just two additional statutory duties placed on it in the 1948 and 1980 legislation in respect of aftercare. Essentially the Children Act 1948 duties focused upon advising and visiting young people after care, and these were not extended under the Child Care Act 1980. Also the Children Act 1989 duties were essentially procedural as well as being concerned with the provision of advice and assistance. The extension of local authority duties towards young people leaving care as contained in the Children Act 1989 was a marginal one, with virtually no financial duties placed on local authorities. The housing duties placed on local authorities in the Children Act 1989 were dependent on other statutory housing legislation.

Prior to the Children Act 1989 the legal framework for leaving care work was the Child Care Act 1980. At the time of that legislation the social security legislation allowed 16 and 17 year olds to receive social security payments and there were not lower levels of benefits for those aged under 25. It was also left as a discretionary matter for local authorities as to if and whether they defined young people leaving care as vulnerable, under the Housing (Homeless Persons) Act 1977. However there was some improvement to the minimal aftercare provisions contained within the Child Care Act 1980.

Duties placed on local authorities under the Child Care Act 1980

Duties

- Section 28 of The Child Care 1980 stated that the local authority has a duty to advise, assist and befriend any young person who was in voluntary care, unless the authority is satisfied that this is not required. The duty only applies to young people between 16 and 18 years of age who were in voluntary care on reaching 16.
- Section 69 of the Child Care Act 1980 gave the local authority the duty to advise and befriend any young person who was in the care of a voluntary organisation unless the authority is satisfied that this is not required or they have arranged for the voluntary organisation to offer aftercare.

As one would hope and expect there are many more duties placed on local authorities in respect of care leavers now than in any previous period. That is obvious. The 'big question' that follows is what effect has recent legislation, and related policies had on the life chances and well being of care leavers? Throughout this book that key question is addressed. At this point however let me end this review of the leaving care legislation, summarising the main legislative powers as well as the statutory guidance and regulations from the CLCA 2000.

Powers and Guidance under the CLCA 2000

Powers

These need to be understood within the wider context of the duties outlined earlier, the fact that many Children Act 1989 provisions remain in place and that there is a considerable volume of guidance and regulations, which follow. If these powers are not understood in this wider legislative context they seem woefully inadequate and could give a misleading account of the breadth of the CLCA 2000. The restated powers are:

- To advise and befriend a young person known to the local authority provided that the authority considers that he needs help and dependent on where the person previously lived (S24A (2) (3)).
- To give assistance to anyone who 'qualifies for advice and assistance' and who was formerly looked after by the local authority by contributing to expenses incurred by him in living near the place where he is employed, seeking employment, or in receipt of education or training; by making a grant (S24B).
- To accommodate young people over the age of 16 up to the age of 21 in a community home (S20 (5)).

Regulations and Guidance-CLCA 2000

The Guidance for the CLCA 2000 should be read in conjunction with *The Children Act (1989) Guidance and Regulations*. In the Needs Assessments and Pathway Plan section (Regulations and Guidance, 41) young people's needs must be identified, as well as the nature and level of contact and personal support to be provided, and by whom, to the child or young person.

Pathway plans must cover the following:

- Details of the accommodation the child or young person is to occupy.
- A detailed plan for the education or training of the child or young person.
- How the responsible authority will assist the child or young person in relation to employment or other purposeful activity or occupation.
- The support to be provided to enable the child or young person to develop and sustain appropriate family and social relationships.

- A programme to develop the practical and other skills necessary for the child or young person to live independently.
- The financial support to be provided to the child or young person, in particular where it is to be provided to meet his accommodation and maintenance needs.
- The health needs, including any mental health needs, of the child or young person, and how they are to be met.
- Contingency plans for action to be taken by the responsible authority should the pathway plan for any reason cease to be effective.

There is an inadequate acknowledgement in the CLCA 2000 that care leavers who are disabled (estimated at between 10–25%) have special needs requiring special solutions and dedicated funding.

Powers under the Children Act 1989

The list of powers under the Children Act 1989 is somewhat longer than the list of duties. In respect of providing financial assistance, and until the CLCA 2000 prioritised and amended financial arrangements for care leavers, this had previously been downgraded from a duty to a power.

Powers

- To advise and befriend other young people under 21 who were cared for away from home after the age of 16: young people accommodated by a health or education authority; young people in any residential care or nursing home (for a consecutive period of three months). This will include young people with a physical disability, mental illness or handicap, and those with educational and behavioural difficulties; young people privately fostered. S24(2), S24(4), S24(5).
- To provide assistance in kind or, in exceptional circumstances, in cash, to any young person who qualifies for advice. Cash assistance may be subject to repayment and a young person or parent may be means tested unless in receipt of Income Support or Family Credit (S24 (6)) and S24 (7)).
- To provide financial assistance connected with the young person's further education, employment or training. This power enables the local authority to contribute to expenses and the costs of accommodation so that a

young person can live near a place where he or she is employed, seeking employment or receiving education or training (S24 (8)).
- Education and training grants may continue beyond the age of 21 to enable a young person to complete a course (S24(9)).
- To accommodate young people aged 16 to under 21 in a community home, provided the home takes young people who have reached 16, if they consider that to do so would safeguard or promote their welfare (S20 (5)).
- Local authorities may request the help of other authorities, including any housing authority, to enable them to comply with their duties to provide accommodation (S27 (1)).

Powers under the Child Care Act 1980

Powers

- Local authority discretion to make contributions for accommodation and maintenance to assist with education and work for young people leaving care aged between 17–21 (S27).
- Provision of advice and assistance (including financial help) to anyone formally in care for young people aged between 17–21 (S29).
- Local authority to house anyone under 21 in a community home if it is provided solely for children who are over compulsory school age (S72).

Comment

Although the Children Act 1989 produced a most welcome new legal framework for leaving care work, by far the majority of the responsibilities, and all those requiring resource inputs, had power and not duty legal status. Thereby the less scrupulous local authorities could introduce minimal changes and still act within the law. Some of the financial provisions of the 1989 legislation were virtually the same as those contained in the Children Act 1948, the Children's and Young Persons Act 1963, and the Child Care Act 1980. For many years the broader social and financial context has been one which discourages and prohibits the very financial investments in services needed by young people leaving care.

Unlike the CLCA 2000, the Children Act 1989 placed the emphasis about the provision of financial supports for care leavers on the social security system and not social services. The powers and regulations concerning the CLCA 2000 mainly concern advisory, assessment and service planning, and financial management functions. Introduced in 1999 the DoH's ring-fenced *Quality Protects* funding helped local authorities 'improve the life chances of young people leaving care', a *Quality Protects* priority. However, in relation to the CLCA 2000 there is no analysis of the cost to local authorities of implementing these duties and guidance and therefore, there remain outstanding and unanswered questions about how changes in the leaving care field can be funded on an ongoing, not short-term, special grant basis. There is also no indication elsewhere of additional post-*Quality Protects* or dedicated ring-fenced funding to lead, enable and sustain the much-needed envisaged changes.

The legislation affecting young people generally, whether about their education, housing and housing benefits, benefits generally, or youth training is designed to reinforce the financial responsibilities of parents, and reduce the role of the state in financing young people seeking and/or having to live away from home. Yet this dominant philosophy, from the early 1980s to the current time, to increase parental responsibility, does not seem to apply to the same extent to the corporate parent i.e. the state, of young people leaving care. It was an especially acute problem during the 1980–1997 period, during which both public expenditure and the role of the welfare state were reduced.

Other related developments

Disability

The Carers and Disabled Children Act 2000 enables local authorities to make direct payments, in lieu of services, to disabled 16 and 17-year-olds so that they have more choice and control over how their needs are met. Direct payments can play a useful part in preparing a disabled 16 or 17-year-old for the responsibilities of adulthood (DoH, Guidance). Where local authorities have set up a Personal Assistance Support Scheme in order to implement the Community Care (Direct Payments) Act 1996, the disabled care leaver's personal advisor will need to work with this scheme in order to support the young person to use direct payments. After the age of 18 direct payments can continue under the Community Care (Direct Payments) Act 1996 (CLCA, 2000, Guidance, para. 26).

Sections 5 and 6 of the Disabled Persons (Services, Consultation and Representation) Act 1986 are also relevant since they are designed to ensure a smooth transition from full-time education to adult life for a young person who is subject to a 'statement of special educational needs'. Their effect is to require the relevant education department to obtain the view of the SSD as to whether such a young person is disabled. This is done at the first annual review of the statement of special educational needs, or the first reassessment of the young person's educational needs, following the young person's 14th birthday (CLCA 2000 Guidance, para. 24).

Advocacy services

Since the CLCA 2000 was enacted there has been a change regarding advocacy services. The Adoption and Children Act 2002 amended the CLCA 2000 to place a duty on local authorities to make arrangements for the provision of advocacy services to children leaving care who wish to make a complaint (S24D and 26 Adoption and Children Act 2002).

Accommodation

The Homelessness Act 2002 also stipulates that local authorities must deem all 16–17-year-olds and 18–21-year-olds leaving care to be in priority need of housing. Also, so far as the *Supporting People* developments are concerned, and in the *Leaving Care Arrangements and Supporting People* guidance (2003) it states that the *Supporting People* grant does not fall within the funding of services under the new leaving care arrangements, but is available within other grant systems.

Personal advisors

With the introduction of the *Connexions* Service (phased in after 2001) there are a range of strategic opportunities for leaving care services to make appropriate arrangements in respect of the provision of appropriate personal advisors for care leavers.

Unaccompanied asylum-seeking children

Unaccompanied asylum-seeking children (UASC) are covered by the Children Act 1989 and the provisions introduced by the CLCA 2000 in exactly the same way as other children. However, they will also have an immigration status –

applying for asylum, acceptance as a refugee, granted exceptional leave to remain or refused leave to remain – which will need to be taken into account by councils providing services for them (Guidance, 15).

Strategic issues (England and Wales)

Public Service Agreements (PSA) targets and the Performance Assessment Framework (PAF)

In a constantly revised performance context the initial national priorities guidance target concerned the level of employment, training or education amongst young people aged 19 who were looked after by councils in their 17th year. This was set to be at (least) 60% of the level amongst all young people of the same age in their area. In terms of local authority responses for 2001–2002 they averaged 46% (DoH, 2002b) and this education target for 2003–04 was subsequently increased to 75% and thus posed a real challenge to many local authorities. This target was then further revised, this time downwards, following the Social Exclusion Unit's Report (2003) demonstrating that education is a continuing problem area for children looked after. Other Public Service Agreements also target the engagement of children in education as well as educational attainment levels. *The Children Act Report 2002* (DfES, 2003b: 36) points to a slight improvement, from 34% to 44% for 1999–2000 and 2001–2002 respectively, of children leaving care aged 16 or over having at least one GCSE A*–G or equivalent.

Within the document *NHS Plan Improvement, expansion and reform: the next 3 years priorities and planning framework 2003–2006* (DoH 2002a, Appendix B) there are also specific targets for local authorities for care leavers.

Under the heading 'Life Chances for Children' the document states that the NHS and local government will work together to improve life chances for children to:

- Increase to 15% the proportion of children leaving care aged 16 and over with 5 GCSEs at grade A*–C, and maintain this level up to 2006 (to be reviewed). As we have already seen this PSA target has already been revised downwards, and further revisions are also likely.
- Reduce by 2004 the proportion of children aged 10–17 and looked after continuously for

at least a year who have received a final warning or conviction by one third and maintain this reduction up to 2006.

In sum then the general content and direction of performance indicators for local authorities are concerned with:

- Ensuring each young person leaving care has a Pathway Plan that is regularly reviewed.
- Maximising the number of young people engaged in education/employment/training at the age of 19.
- Supporting young people in suitable accommodation.
- Staying in touch with young people until they are 21 or longer if they are in a programme of education or training.
- A reduction in offending.

In the longer term and set within the government's National Task Force the children's *National Service Framework* (NSF) is developing standards across the NHS and social services for children, including children in special circumstances. Within that wider strategic context it is likely that further standards and/or targets will be introduced.

Strategic issues (Scotland)

The Children (Scotland) Act 1995 places responsibilities for looked after children on local authorities in Scotland and, in respect of duties towards care leavers, is very similar to the Children Act 1989 which applies in England and Wales.

Since then the *Supporting Young People Leaving Care* (Scottish Executive, 2003) consultation paper was produced, and is similar in its aims and structure to the *Me Survive Out There?* (DoH, 1999b) consultation document which informed the CLCA 2000. The subsequent *Supporting Young People Leaving Care* regulations and guidance (2004) applies to all young people preparing to leave and having left care in Scotland from 1 April 2004. The guidance uses the legal terminology for children leaving care taken from the Children (Scotland) Act 1995 and contains very similar assessment and planning elements as are contained in the CLCA 2000. It also covers the key service areas of accommodation, education, and training, as well as others. The term 'life coach' to advise and assist young people to draw up pathways is used instead of 'personal advisor' the term used in England and Wales. As in the

CLCA 2000 there is very little attention paid to health and well being issues for young people leaving care other than stating that young people's health needs will be assessed and should be met. As with the CLCA 2000 it remains to be seen how the guidance paper's laudable aims will be funded and how young people groups will be involved in evaluating and monitoring progress.

Major research in the leaving care field

In the UK the major academic research in the leaving care field has been undertaken at York University, and this author. Research by Stein and colleagues and by this author continue to highlight the problems facing young people leaving care and the help provided by leaving care teams (for example see Biehal et al., 1995; Broad, 1994, 1998). Stein and colleagues continue to produce research evidence about good practice (for example see Stein and Wade, 2001); and this author about the health needs of young people leaving care and facing social exclusion (1999); Monaghan and Broad (2003). The practice and policy development work by *Rainer* (its National Leaving Care Advisory Service-previously *First Key*) also provides a much needed welcome source of ongoing support for local authorities (for example see *First Key*, (2001) and Stein, Sufian and Hazelhurst, 2001).

Serving to emphasise the difficulties for young people leaving care who are disabled, a *Fostering Network* research study about young people with disabilities making the transition to independence after leaving foster care concluded:

> *Disabled care leavers have to contend both with arrangements for care leavers, and with arrangements for young disabled people moving to adults' services. In both cases there are difficulties.*
>
> (Fostering Network, 2000: 3)

Research by Barn et al. (forthcoming) about issues facing black care leavers; Allen's work (2003) and, from York University, research about the costs and outcomes of leaving care services, and care leavers and resilience (Stein, forthcoming) are also making important contributions.

Research findings since the CLCA 2000

There is very little published research and/or development material about what has happened to young people leaving care and leaving care services since the CLCA 2000 was introduced.

First, and at the Roberts Trust seminar in London (Roberts Trust, 2003), one year after the Act's introduction, young people highlighted resource and bureaucratic constraints in implementing the Act. These were expressed both in resource terms such as a continuing lack of choice, flexibility and support about accommodation, education, and personal advisors: and in direct work skills terms, for example about how staff can encourage young people to stay in education. Concerns about the shortage of dedicated resources for leaving care services after the ring fenced funding arrangements end in 2003/4 were also noted, as was a recognition of modest progress in leaving care management information systems following the Act's introduction.

Next and in 2003 a postal survey of foster carers was conducted by the *Fostering Network* (2003: 5) about the implementation of the CLCA 2000. 139 foster carers responded. The results indicate a lack of information and training received about the CLCA 2000. For example when foster carers were asked if they had been given information about the CLCA 2000, 75 (54%) stated that they had still not been given any information about it and only 22 (16%) had received any training on it. The vast majority that received this training found it helpful. When asked the question 'Have you noticed any difference in response since the Act was introduced in October 2001?' only 17 foster carers or 15% of those responding (n=114) said 'yes' and 97 or 83% replied that they had not noticed any difference. Furthermore when asked if they had noticed any difference in the kind of help provided since October 2001 again only 17% said 'yes' and 83% said that it had not made any difference. It is very striking and disappointing that such large numbers of foster carers, from 102 counties, agencies and councils across England, have not received information, been trained or noticed any differences in leaving care support services for young people leaving care post-CLCA 2000. Significantly in a separate study, when professionals were also asked if they had received training on the CLCA 2000, 56% of respondents (n=135) reported that they had not received sufficient or any training (WMCCC, 2003: 23). In other words these studies suggest that for key stakeholders, here foster carers and social care professionals, and up to 18 months after the Act's introduction in October 2001, a large majority considered that they were inadequately prepared. In Hai and Williams study of eight London authorities they concluded:

> There is strong evidence that the authorities are responding to the CLCA 2000 by putting in place services which seek to be more young person centred and to meet the range of needs of care leavers. Needs assessments and Pathway Plans are being completed ... Multi-agency services, particularly those required by care leavers with a high and continuing level of need, while much more in evidence, still require greater attention ... Continuing to focus on the individual needs of young people will require that the identified improvements to services continues-and this will stretch the resources and capacity of all agencies. If the aims and objectives of the Act are to continue to be met, managers will need to find ways of ensuring that resources are retained and increased proportionate to any increase in the care leaving population and in their needs.

(Hai and Williams, 2004: 104)

The research study *After the Act: Implementing the Children (Leaving Care) Act 2000* (this author, 2003) examined how far the CLCA 2000 had been implemented across England and Wales up to two years after its introduction. This study, undertaken eighteen months after the CLCA 2000, detailed the work of 52 leaving care teams working with 7,000 young people leaving care. The comprehensive and mixed findings form the core of this book and are described in Chapters 3, 4 and 5 (also see Broad, 2005) and point to a mix of positive changes, continuing problems and mixed responses.

This chapter has described the legislative and policy framework for young people leaving care, and highlighted the key strategic, research and performance indicator issues. In the next chapter the term 'social exclusion' will be introduced as a framework for understanding and examining young people's life chances, as well as how health and well being issues for care leavers have been addressed at policy, practice and legislative levels.

Chapter Two

Social Exclusion, Health and Well Being and Young People Leaving Care

Introduction

Although this book is specifically about young people leaving care it is argued here that with the vital exception that the local authority is their legal parent thereby carrying certain legal responsibilities, care leavers needs are very similar to other young people facing social exclusion. The aim of this chapter then, is to begin to discuss care leavers outside the usual care leavers' research 'box' by analysing needs, risks and health and well being problems within the wider social exclusion context. It is useful to examine the term social exclusion in order that:

- The processes leading to all young people facing social exclusion, including care leavers, can be more fully identified.
- Policy interventions can be better understood and applied within a wider socio-economic, as well as a child welfare context.

After that section, the links between social exclusion, health and well being and leaving care are then developed and made more explicit.

Policy relevance

At the national level there are major initiatives about young people leaving care, social exclusion, homeless young people and health issues that should have a positive impact on socially excluded young people. Here the policy relevance of this research is around the work being done by the Social Exclusion Unit, 'rough sleepers' initiatives as well as the *Promoting Health for Looked after Children* consultation document (DoH, 1999c). First, in 1997, a House of Commons Select Committee concluded, 'The failure of local authorities to secure good health outcomes for the children and young people they look after is a failure of social services departments towards health agencies for service provision' (House of Commons, 1998). As we will see later in this chapter there is no specific acknowledgement of poverty of young people leaving care or the impact of poverty on health.

However, amongst the accommodation, training, education, employment and relationships sections within the main regulations there is a clear requirement (in Schedule 1) for pathway plans to 'deal with health needs including any mental health needs' including undertaking health assessments, based on looked after health records (DoH, 2001a).

Next, and in a major review and action plan about the education of children looked after, the Social Exclusion Unit (SEU) fully recognises the importance of health and well being issues. The SEU argues that one of the five major problems impacting on these children's education is that 'children in care need more help with their emotional, mental or physical health and well being' (2003). That report also confirms the significant level of unmet mental health needs amongst this group of children.

Other policy initiatives include the work of *Connexions* as well as, for looked after children, planned national minimum standards for children's homes, which includes 'health' as part of its 'quality of care' indicators. The revisions to the guidance (draft) for the Housing Act 1996 extends the priority need categories of homeless people to include 16 and 17-year-olds, and 'corporate parenting' (House of Commons, 1998, para. 265). Next the aforementioned draft consultation document *Promoting Health for Looked After Children* (DoH, 1999c) was a draft policy response to that House of Commons Report and states 'Children and young people in public care are amongst the most socially excluded groups in England' (DoH, 1999c, para. 1.1). The CLCA 2000 places additional responsibilities on local authorities to assess, plan and provide social work support for young people leaving care up to and, in some cases, beyond 21 years of age. Health does not feature strongly in that Act and where it does, it tends to point to care leavers aged 18 to 21 (First Key, 2001). The inclusion of health as one of the identified children's developmental needs within the framework for the assessment of children in need and their families (DoH, 2000b) is a recognition that 'health' requires assessment by social services and other agencies together. There are other ongoing policy initiatives that should impact on health including local Children and Adolescent Mental Health Services (CAMHS) and a range of national and local teenage pregnancy, sexual health, and substance misuse initiatives.

Also some local authorities have set up *Quality Protects* funded health worker posts or multi-agency initiatives. The *Kings Fund*, London, funded a major development project to improve the health of looked after children and First Key, the National Leaving Care Advisory Service, is helping fund the *Take Care, Take Control* health project in Lewisham, South London, in a Health Action Zone. The *Foyer Federation* has also published *Working Together* (Foyer Federation, 2001) to promote better health for young people facing social exclusion. Whilst it remains to be seen whether all these recent initiatives and wealth of guidance will produce better outcomes for socially excluded young people, there is undoubtedly a climate of heightened awareness of the various health issues facing all young people today. It is against that background then, of a rising interest in improving the health of young people leaving care, that the research project *Improving the Health and Well-being of Socially Excluded Young People* (summarised in Monaghan and Broad, 2003) took place. The key findings about care leavers health and well being issues, informed by a commitment to seeking young people's views, are presented and discussed in Part Three of this book.

Social exclusion

Agencies or organisations attach slightly different meanings to the term 'social exclusion'. For example, as we have already seen, the government's *Social Exclusion Unit* (SEU) was set up in 1997 to help improve Government action in reducing social exclusion by 'providing joined up solutions to joined to problems.' The SEU defines social exclusion as:

> *A shorthand term for what can happen when people or areas suffer from a combination of linked problems such as unemployment, poor skills, low incomes, poor housing, high crime environment, bad health and family breakdown. In the past governments have had policies that tried to deal with each of these problems individually, but there has been little success at*

> *tackling the complicated links between them, or preventing them from arising in the first place.*
>
> (SEU, 1997)

The term 'social exclusion' then, relates to those groups of people whose quality of life and ability to fully participate in society is severely curtailed. In a leading study into poverty and social exclusion the term 'social exclusion' is further analysed and regarded as having the following four key elements:

- *Impoverishment or exclusion from adequate income or resources.*
- *Labour market exclusion.*
- *Service exclusion.*
- *Exclusion from social relations.*

(Gordon et al., 2000)

The authors of that study found that 'non-availability of services' (collective exclusion) was a bigger barrier than 'non-affordability' and commented that 'Poverty and social exclusion are not acts of God, nor are they an inevitable consequence of economic and social progress' (Gordon et al., 2000, 70). They concluded:

> *High rates of poverty and social exclusion have the effects of worsening health, education, skills in the changing labour market, relationships within the family, between ethnic groups, and in society generally.*
>
> (71)

The term 'social exclusion' then is wide-ranging and can include people subject to homelessness, ageism, racism, sexism, unemployment, poverty, poor educational attainment, and exclusions based on views about sexuality and disability. Many people who are socially excluded are on a low-income level and experience the poorest levels of health. The various problems experienced by people who are socially excluded often have a cumulative and reinforcing effect. Vranken (1995) refers to three definitions of social exclusion:

- In relation to social rights and the processes by which people are excluded from those rights. Social exclusion is then analysed in terms of the denial or non-realisation of those rights.
- A gradual or sudden reduction of social integration. This process is specified through a series of stages that represent an intensification of the degree of social exclusion: integration, vulnerability, assistance and disaffiliation.
- An extreme form of marginalisation, as a situation of discontinuity, as a 'catastrophic rupture' with the rest of society. In this

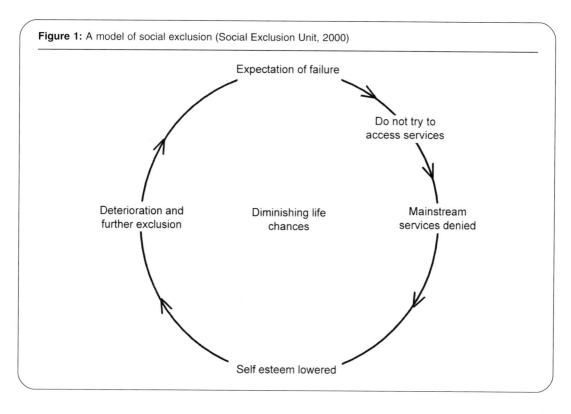

Figure 1: A model of social exclusion (Social Exclusion Unit, 2000)

Expectation of failure

Do not try to
access services

Deterioration and
further exclusion

Diminishing life
chances

Mainstream
services denied

Self esteem lowered

meaning it refers to both a specific social condition and to health as a multi-faceted phenomenon. Social exclusion, then, in matters of education is illiteracy and concerning housing it is homelessness. Similarly, then, ill health is by definition a form of social exclusion.

Boeck (1999: 6) further defines social exclusion as:

A multi-dimensional disadvantage which severs individuals and groups from the major social processes and opportunities in society such as health, housing, citizenship, employment and adequate living standards, and may be manifested in various forms, at various times and within various sections of the population.

The term social exclusion, therefore, indicates a process taking place as a result of the decisions and non-decisions of many institutions. It occurs in particular circumstances and environments, but the attack on dignity and sense of powerlessness and exclusion applies across the board. A number of issues reflect conditions of social exclusion both directly and indirectly: employment, income levels, housing, environment, education, transport, poverty and access to welfare and other support services as

well as health. Exclusion from a cluster of these resources or services implies exclusion from mainstream society (Boeck, 1999). Figure 1 illustrates the harrowing downward spiral of social exclusion.

To address social exclusion at a macro level, and beyond the individual level, wider structural changes are needed, and not simply minor adjustments to individual service delivery. The emphasis of the SEU is on both individual and macro levels, but it primarily seeks to promote joined-up government and co-ordinated central and local government departments, and other agencies, working together. It is not concerned with structural change, about reducing inequalities through the redistribution of resources and entitlements but instead focuses more on institutional change. According to the SEU at the local level the most effective strategy for addressing the complex and inter-related social exclusion issues is through partnerships between agencies, and the affected communities themselves. This has a resonance with the Labour government's community development projects (CDPs) in the 1960s and 1970s as reported by Loney (1983). At that time attempts to produce policy innovations resulted in unresolved tensions between local and central government, with the civil service criticised as being incompetent, unable to innovate, respond and co-ordinate across the key Whitehall departments, thus stifling change (Loney, 171–97).

Social exclusion's four elements of impoverishment or exclusion from adequate income or resources, labour market exclusion, service exclusion and exclusion from social relations have a direct resonance for many care leavers. In relation to health inequalities the key message from the literature is that these are caused by an unequal distribution of the determinants of health. These determinants include economic, social, psychological, environmental determinants, personal behaviour and access to treatment and care.

However, if we then ask the question about which of these determinants are most important in contributing to health and to health inequalities, this becomes complex because the determinants interact with each other. Nevertheless, the following are examples of the detailed determinants of health reported as causing and sustaining health inequalities in developed countries (Institute for Public Health Research and Policy, 2000):

Economic determinants
- Level of income relative to others.
- Money worries.
- Level of employment.

Social determinants
- Level of individual social support.
- The extent of the individual's social networks.
- The level of social cohesion within community.
- Educational attainment.

Psychological determinants
- Individual's perception of control and autonomy.
- Individual's perceptions of his or her own health.
- Level of stress-ability to cope with demands.

Environmental determinants
- Level of pollution.
- Quality of the housing environment.
- Extent of environmental hazards such as busy roads.
- Access to safe, green spaces.

Personal behaviour
- Smoking/diet/exercise.
- Level of risk-taking behaviour e.g. drug use.

Access to treatment and care
- Particularly to high quality primary care and to effective treatment.

According to health inequalities research (for example, Benzeval et al., 1995) it is not known which of those determinants are most important in contributing to health and health inequalities. It is important to remember that many people who grow up in disadvantaged circumstances who are exposed to a multiplicity of risk factors do very well and live long, healthy and productive lives. In other words although there is a 'probabilistic cascade' that growing up in disadvantaged circumstances leads to poor health, being 'at risk' of ill health is not the same as 'being destined' to poor health (Benzeval et al., 1995). Despite this important caveat there are an identified range of policy action initiatives suggested by Bartley et al., (1995) which can *influence*, though not eliminate, *health inequalities*. These are:

- Strengthening communities.
- Strengthening individuals.
- Improving access to essential facilities and services.
- Encouraging macro-economic and cultural change.

It is also worth repeating that the links between inequalities in health and deprivation are not new 'discoveries', for example these were suggested in *The Black Report* (DHSS, 1980) and indeed, about observations of poor children in London in the nineteenth century, contained in the works of Charles Dickens. In the contemporary leaving care field this author would argue that it is primarily in the *strengthening individuals* and *improving access to essential facilities and services* initiatives where social and/or health promotion care staff work with young people. These are clearly identified, familiar and important areas for intervention.

Health, well being and young people leaving care

The term well being

Well being has been defined in the following terms:

> *Well being is a general term encompassing the total universe of human life domains including physical, mental and social aspects that make up what can be*

called a 'good life'. Health domains are a subset of domains that make up the total universe of human life.
(International Classification of Functioning, Disability and Health quoted in DoH, 2002c: 1)

In other words the term 'well being' includes a range of 'physical, cognitive, mental, behavioural and emotional' dimensions, similar to those used by Bradshaw (2002, xiii). It is these dimensions which will be the prime focus of the well being research evidence presented here, as well as any evidence about the financial circumstances of young people leaving care. The term 'health' is described in relation to the other domains of well being. Well being is regarded here as a term that is set within the context of a government committed to promoting social inclusion. Thus, in relation to children and young people:

Children and young people should develop healthy lifestyles and opportunities to achieve optimum health and well being, within the context of high quality preventive and treatment services – if and when they need them. Children and young people should have the resilience, capacity and emotional well being that allows them to play, learn and relate to other people, and resolve problems in life.
(Children and Young People's Unit, 2001).

Having summarised what constitutes social exclusion, and well being, what constitutes health inequalities and ways to reduce them, let us now look at the research evidence about the health and well being of care leavers.

Identifying health and well being needs-research evidence

In the care leavers' health and well being literature the key issues that emerge are:

1. The health and well being of care leavers is often over-looked despite high needs.
2. Health and well being is a holistic concept requiring 'whole person' solutions.
3. Improvements in young people's self esteem can lead to general health and well being improvements.

Let us begin with an overview of the nature and extent of health and well being problems facing children looked after and leaving care. Unsurprisingly and as with the leaving care literature, these tend to be most prominent and marked in the looked after field in the mental and emotional health areas. McCann et al.'s study into

residential care (1996) found a significant number of adolescents were suffering from severe, and potentially untreatable psychiatric disorders that required properly trained staff to identify. Overall, and alarmingly, these disorders were reported as being at a level akin to those found in a psychiatric adolescent unit and trained staff were not available. A wider and more representative national survey of 2,500 young people looked after aged 11–17 also found high, but not such high, levels of emotional disorder:

- 37% were rated as having a conduct disorder.
- Those looked after were 4–5 times more likely to have a mental disorder than a matched wider population.
- Two-thirds of all the looked after children were reported to have at least one physical complaint including eye/sight problems (16%), speech or language problems (14%), bed wetting (13%), difficulty with co-ordination (10%) and asthma (10%).
- The children with mental disorders were four times more likely than those with no disorder to report not spending time with their friends.
- Almost all the children with a clinically assessed disorder had been in contact with at least one of the services during the past year. Frontline services were the most common source of help with 80% of children having been in contact with a social worker and 49% a teacher. Over a fifth of children had also received advice or treatment from a GP or family doctor (National Statistics, 2003: 16–26).

There is also a full review of the mental health needs of looked after children by Richardson and Joughlin (2000) which again detailed the mental health needs of this group of young people, but again did not focus on young people leaving or who had left the care of the local authority. In relation to mental health services (also see the chapter by Vostanis in Part Four of this book) the key service problems appear to be:

- The lack of a systematic focus for assessing health needs, beyond physical check-ups.
- The lack of mental health services for young people in need.
- The lack of availability of CAMHS services.
- The lack of availability of health services other than for those in crises (e.g. Someone overdosing).
- The unsuitability of CAMHS for all mental health needs of care leavers.

● Major problems for young people accessing adult services once they reach eighteen.

High levels of teenage pregnancy and, less so, substance abuse issues (mostly cannabis, rather than class A drugs use) are prominent in the care leavers literature. The National Children's Bureau has also produced practice guides for care staff working with health issues (Lewis, 1999) as well as for staff seeking to improve children's awareness of sexual health issues.

West's study of care leavers (1995) suggests that many factors affect the health and well being of socially excluded young people and what follows are specific examples of the same individual, community, family and environmental policy action initiatives flagged up earlier from the health inequality literature. These are family life, relationships, resilience, support networks, attitudes, social assets as well as accommodation and money. West (1995) concluded that improvements to young people's material circumstances, principally income, and support networks and improved public attitudes to young people who have been in care, were critical issues in meeting the health needs of young people leaving care. This study was one of the earliest to indicate that young people leaving care considered that their physical and mental health and emotional well being were inextricably linked with their material circumstances, backgrounds, care experiences, and social relationships. West concluded that a lack of basic provisions including feelings of isolation and loneliness and increased depression and risk taking behaviours, led to ill health (West, 1995).

A government report about young people leaving care (Social Services Inspectorate, 1997) also drew out the links between health, well being and other aspects of life after leaving care particularly in relation to finance, leisure and accommodation. Buchanan and Brinke (1997) examined the links between depression and dissatisfactions for children when they were looked after compared with later in life, when they were adults. Unsurprisingly perhaps, but of huge significance here, they found that children and young people who had been in care, even for a short period, had, in adult life, significantly different attitudes to family life, different social support networks and more psychological difficulties compared with those who had not been in care. They recommend that since life

satisfaction can relate to out-of-home and out-of-work activities, creating opportunities for young people to develop these outside interests, as they grow up, may *increase their sense of self worth* and indirectly protect them from later mental health problems.

In a large action research project in Glasgow about the health of young people in and leaving care conducted over several years (Big Step, 2002: 30) it was found that 45% had self-harmed and that there was a link between self-harm and levels of depression. The report concluded that a health promotion emphasis on building self-esteem and self-confidence were good starting points for tackling other problems (Big Step, 2002: 31). Mental health issues are highlighted in Allen's research study as one of several major life challenges to care leavers which further complicates and delays the young people's ambitions to make the transition to adulthood and live more independently (Allen, 2003: 31). There is also further evidence both that care leavers are over-represented in young offender institutions, and that their experiences of receiving formal supports to deal with mental health problems are often poor and at best, very mixed (Ward et al., 2003).

Young people living in kinship care

In considering the health and well being of young people leaving care another large group of young people not traditionally included in the 'leaving care research' field are those young people who have been looked after and who then move into a kinship care placement. This group of young people leaving care have also been looked after, but instead of receiving services from a leaving care team, and with the knowledge of social services, they move on to live with a member of their extended family or a friend. There is very little research on this group of 16 plus young people who have previously been looked after to live in kinship care. The reason for this is because almost all the limited UK kinship care research that has been conducted has been about children under 16 (Broad, 2001). Nevertheless what is known about kinship care placements is that according to the young people, kinship care is often their preferred choice to stranger foster care or residential care placements because it is seen as a safer arrangement compared with others (Broad et al., 2001). In one rare study about young people leaving care and the extended family the conclusion pointed to the advantages and the complexities of extended family involvement. In considering future partnerships between extended families, the child and the birth parents the study concluded:

> *The message for young people and families is that social work at this (leaving care) stage needs to be different from the 'in care' period. Greater family involvement is potentially helpful and would be generally welcomed. Helping to increase it is not straightforward, but – family members and care leavers are willing to try.*
> (Marsh, 1999: 13)

Unfortunately there has been little evidence since that study was published to indicate that extended family members are any more systematically involved in decision making and family placements for young people leaving care at 16–18. However, there is evidence of a continued growth in the use by local authorities of kinship care. The number of children in kinship care (fostered with a relative or friend) is significant. For example, in a typical year, and as at 31 March 2002, 6,900 children, or 12% of all 59,700 children looked after, were living in a family and friends foster placement (DoH, 2003). These placements are also increasing year-on-year both as a proportion of all foster placements and as a proportion of all children looked after. For example between 31 March 1996 and 31 March 2000, the numbers of children looked after increased by 13%, from 50,600 to 58,100 children (DoH, 2001, Table A: 41). Over the same period the number of children looked after in kinship care increased by 32%, from 4,800 to 6,300 (DoH, 2001, Table iv: 23). This compares with a 15% increase in all foster care placements over the same period. There are additional and largely unrecorded kinship care placements/arrangements that are supported outside the looked after system. These are mainly either children 'in need' (S17 Children Act 1989) or on a Residence Order (S8 Children Act 1989).

In this author's kinship care study about young people making the transition to adulthood 23 (or 46%) of the sample (n=50) were in the 16–17 age group and 72% were 16 or over. The young people in that study expressed the main advantages of kinship care as:

- Feeling loved, valued and cared for.
- Being rescued from/not being sent into stranger local authority care.
- Wanting to be with people who know you and you know them.

- Feeling safe from harm or the threatening behaviour of adults (including residential and foster carers).
- Being listened to.
- Sustaining a sense of who they are (identity) through maintaining contact with family, siblings, and friends.
- Belonging and feeling settled, *especially* not being moved around and subject to disruption and being cared for and nurtured.

The consistent indications from the UK kinship care research studies, and numerous American studies are that although they may experience similar health and well being needs, and that placements need regular support as well as monitoring, many children and young people leaving care feel safer, better cared for and loved in kinship care placements compared with their previous placement. It is also highly likely that the key differences between a young person living in a mutually agreed kinship care arrangement and in independent living are the former's feeling of belonging (i.e. not isolated) loved, wanted and safe.

Having highlighted the research evidence about the health and well being needs of care leavers, including those leaving care and living in kinship care, let us move on to examine the research evidence about the nature, levels and extent of specific service provision for care leavers which aims to improve their health and well being.

Identifying service provision

Research by Hai and Williams (2004) indicates that any improvements in health outcomes for care leavers are associated with leaving care staff having a link with a named health professional. Agreement on what health issues need to be addressed in the pathway plan contributed to an increased number of physical health checks taking place (Hai and Williams, 2004). Again and again the research evidence points to a lack of availability of mental health services for young people leaving care (for example, see Mather, Humphrey and Robson, 1997), and this appears to be an ongoing, largely intractable and alarming problem. Again as Hai and Williams' study states, in what is otherwise a largely positive study about the implementation of the CLCA 2000:

> *... managers and workers identified significant gaps, deficits and difficulties in some aspects of multi-agency*

working. This was particular so in respect of health and especially in access to CAMHS or other mental health services for young people aged 16–18. In many authorities CAMHS only work with young people up to the age of 18.

(Hai and Williams, 2004: 102)

One of the key questions raised is how these children's and young people's needs can be best met and whether there should be *specialist* or more *mainstream* services provided? White's research raises important questions about what the focus of such work should be, questioning assumptions about whether . . . 'looked after children are in need of specialist psychiatric services, rather than requiring a more mainstreamed and cost-effective range of support services aimed at their needs as distressed children experiencing difficult times' (White, 2004).

According to Vernon's report about London's leaving care services and in relation to health and care leavers, she concluded:

● There are missing linkages between social services departments and the health service, in particular over issues of child and adolescent mental health. These missing linkages are evident in two main respects: first in relation to child and adolescent mental health services themselves, and secondly, in relation to the transition between these services and those for adults.
● Social services would welcome more support from health and other agencies on personal and health education, and on meeting the considerable mental health needs of care leavers.
● Social services were increasing their efforts, in conjunction with others, to support the cultural needs of young people, especially asylum seekers (Vernon, 2000).

In an earlier health promotion research project focusing on the health issues facing care leavers in Northamptonshire, Der-Kevorkian (1996: 26) concluded:

In order to try to improve the health of an individual or a group, it is important to have an understanding of the context in which a person or group of people live. Therefore if statutory and voluntary services are to help young people to obtain a better quality of life, then those services have to consider the whole person. First and foremost, young people cannot be subdivided into the issues they present with at any one time, but agencies need to look at the overall picture for the

young person when providing assistance so as to offer the best and most appropriate service.

In another study, again highlighting both the holistic dimension of health and young people's perception of it, care leavers defined ill-health as associated with a lack of good accommodation, money, support, negative relationships and family networks (Saunders and Broad, 1997). In a majority of instances young people in that study equated health and well being with happiness, low stress, access to friends, ability to go out with peers, and regular income sources. The following is a summary of the main research findings about *service recommendations* from the young people themselves:

● **Physical health.** Measures to improve physical health i.e. eating, exercise and living more healthily were low on young people's life agenda compared with trying to survive, in many cases on less than minimum financial support, maintaining satisfactory social relationships and meeting the daily demands of life.
● **Dangers of being in care.** For the majority the effects of being in care were alarming, and for most of the young people, created stress and insecurity prompting various responses, including drug taking, depression, and ill health. A lack of understanding at school about their situation, combined with low expectations by teachers made this situation worse. The seeds of ill health post -care were sown whilst the young people were in care.
● **Less than healthy lifestyle to release stress.** It seems that the young people felt that the immediate short term emotional gain or satisfaction, or benefits of not living as healthily as they might outweighed and overruled their objective knowledge about the negative long term consequences of certain less healthy activities (excessive drinking being one example).
● **Isolation and unhappiness.** Isolation and unhappiness arose from living alone in unsatisfactory accommodation.
● **Improving emotional support.** Improving emotional support was seen as vital when the young people are in care, preparing to leave and after leaving care. There were many suggestions in the report about how this might be done.
● **Professional attitudes.** The combination of a relatively high proportion of young people

with a chronic mental illness or condition and the perceived unhelpful attitudes of professionals especially regarding the provision of mental health services, is of particular concern. Again there are recommendations about improvements in the report. Changing professional attitudes is not an easy or straightforward matter.

- **Professional relationships.** The fact that so many satisfactory personal relationships were lacking for this generally needy group of young people goes some way to explaining the high value some placed on some professional relationships. Consequently there was a high level of disappointment felt if/when the standard of that relationship fell short of the mark, so far as they were concerned. Concomitantly past disappointments concerning relationships with social workers also explained low expectations, and not 'opening up,' with problems remaining unaired and bottled up.
- **Social determinants of good health**. That four of the top five determinants of health are not generally considered by the young people to be health issues, and that four of the bottom five were, demonstrates the wide scale and inter-agency nature of the challenges that need to be met, from the young person's perspective.

The main *organisational recommendations* from that study were:

- To ensure that young people who are, and who have been, looked after by the local authority make a successful transition into healthy adulthood requires further commitment from the local authority to develop a corporate inter-agency strategy.
- To facilitate this process it is strongly recommended that the local Social Services Department pursue a strategy of developing joint protocols and policies with other appropriate organisations to assist and drive implementation.
- The key services involved are social services, the health authority (including primary health care, psychiatric services and health promotion) and housing. Other relevant agencies are leisure departments, youth and community services, the benefits agency, the Learning and Skills Council and the employment service.

- A willingness by social services departments to review looked after and leaving care policy and procedures.
- Establish a working group with the key agencies senior management representation to implement the research's recommendations.
- Give young people leaving care 'a real voice'.

In Wyler's comprehensive review of services to promote the health of young people leaving care he concluded:

Apart from general health promotion and education, initiatives designed specifically to respond to the health needs of care leavers are rare, and where they do exist are often new and untested. The lack of a strong practice response is most acutely felt in relation to mental health. Practice is also weak in meeting the needs of care leavers with borderline disability.
(Wyler, 2000: 28)

It is especially those care leavers with learning difficulties or a physical disability whose basic needs, including health and well being needs have far too often been overlooked, whatever the grand aims of legislation may have been. It is also the case that 'self harm' by care leavers, a long-standing problem and emotional health indicator, is slowly beginning to be discussed and addressed. In another development Essian (quoted in Douglas, 2004) points to the scale of the challenge of providing mental health resources for care leavers, concluding:

To deal adequately with mental health problems among care leavers would require a massive overhaul of social policy initiatives and independent assessment procedures in general.

Moving beyond the specific health and well being needs of care leavers, if we look more broadly at ways of improving the health and well being of young people attending Foyer projects, it is significant that the organisational requirements and recommendations are very similar to those leaving care. These include:

- *The NHS needs to take the lead in assessing and meeting mental and physical health needs of young people facing social exclusion (examples of suitable NHS outlets included 'walk-in centres' primary care, secondary care, dental provision).*
- *The NHS and Foyers need to involve users to form service partnerships so that health promotion and illness prevention can become the key foci of a young person's life.*
- *These partnerships can take different forms and can involve a GP/nurse surgery at the Foyer, and/or*

service partnerships with local health promotion, drugs, sexual health or counselling services.
(Foyer Federation, 2001)

Again looking at the mental health needs of young offenders, the risk factors are very similar to young people in and leaving care. Perhaps this is not surprising, especially when one considers the high percentage of young offenders who have previously lived in circumstances that led them to being looked after. This is the conclusion to a review of young offenders with mental health problems:

> *Young people who offend are much more likely to have mental health problems; these problems are likely to be similar to those of the general adolescent population but more severe (conduct disorder, emotional disturbance, hyperactivity and attentional problems). Problems arise in inadequate screening and assessment, lack of staff training, insufficient funding, limited treatment options and a lack of research. Meeting these needs is a multi-agency responsibility requiring shifts of understanding and increased communication between key players.*
(Hagell, 2002)

There is also evidence of similarity in terms of young offenders' high levels of depression, strong mood swings, levels of self-harm, and substance misuse (see, for example, Anthony and Collins, 2003 and Lader et al., 2000).

Direct work with young people

Gilligan's (2001) general work on valuing young people and 'promoting resilience' is also highly relevant here, in highlighting risk and protective factors in child welfare work. This individual approach to problem resolution is one that will be drawn on later in this book in terms of good practice, service models and modes of intervention.

Stein has also identified the serious issue of mental health problems. He has produced a three-fold typology of groups of young people leaving care, the moving-on group, the survivors group and the victims group (Stein, forthcoming) with the challenge to service providers to engage more fully with the second and particularly the third 'damaged' group. According to Stein it is the second group which will rely heavily on leaving care services for assistance (for example for help with their health and well being) and the third 'most damaged' group which are most likely to suffer isolation and mental health problems. The difficult tasks for leaving care

services will be to prioritise contact, monitor, and effectively engage with the second and third groups. In Barn's study (forthcoming) about black care leavers' experiences, health and well being issues are also included as a significant area.

It is also vital to acknowledge that in direct work with care leavers the issue of staff and young people *engaging effectively* is central to any work done (VCC, 2004). As the *Blueprint* report puts it:

> *We have to focus on the child in everything we do – putting their needs and interests ahead of those agencies involved and the adults around them . . . the involvement of children and young people in developing a child-centred ethos is central to success.*
(VCC, 2004: 72)

As we will see in Parts Two and Three of this book research findings are presented from care leavers' perspectives about how staff worked with them, listened to them and acted, or were unable to act on, their views and wishes about improving their health and well being.

In this chapter we have examined the policy and research context about the health and well being needs of care leavers, and outlined recommendations for change, at the organisational and direct work levels. We now move onto examining what the CLCA 2000 states about assessing and meeting the health and well being needs of care leavers. The main mechanism for this is individual Pathway Plans.

The CLCA 2000 and health and well being

The CLCA 2000 attempts to address health and well being through the following guidance about the aims and content of Pathway Plans.

Pathway plans and health

The Guidance to the CLCA 2000 (DoH, 2001a) states the following:

> 1. *A holistic health assessment and the maintenance of detailed health records will provide the platform for pathway plans to promote a healthy lifestyle, ensure appropriate use of primary health care services, plan access to specialist health and therapeutics services where necessary and promote leisure interests.*
> 2. *Pathway planning should also pay attention to the need for young people to have accessible information on healthy living, sexual health and sexuality, and mental health as well as the health, dietary and cultural needs of young people from minority ethnic communities. It*

should also ensure that disabled young people obtain access to mainstream health care services (GP, dentist, optician etc) as well as to any specialist service related to their impairment.
3. The Pathway Plan should note where a young person is entitled to free prescriptions and the action taken to obtain and update the necessary forms. Completion of the form to access the NHS Low Income Scheme, where appropriate, should be considered a routine part of the pathway planning process.
4. Pathway planning for the health needs of care leavers should be based on the guidance arising from the consultation document 'Promoting Health for Looked After Children'.

(Department of Health, 1999b)

The CLCA 2000 guidance sets out a holistic model of health, including the contribution of a number of agencies. In addition to good practice guidelines, new regulations in the Children Act (Miscellaneous Amendment) (England) Regulations 2002 revise the existing legal framework. The essence of this framework is that health assessments have to include physical and mental health and health promotion aspects, i.e. the 'annual medical' based on physical health checks is now officially acknowledged to be inadequate, and to quote the guidance 'impersonal and stigmatising'. In order to deliver the vision of better health and well being for children looked after and leaving care the government has developed a national service framework (NSF) for children, based on new national standards.

The *NHS plan* (2002a) also includes a number of core principles that are pertinent to the provision of care for looked after children and Primary Care Trusts (PCTs) are the lead organisation for assessing need, planning and delivering all health services.

Promoting the Health of Looked After Children Guidance (2002)

This health guidance sets out a framework for the delivery of services from health agencies and social services to more effectively promote the health and well being of children and young people in the care system.

Principles of Good Health Care from the guidance

The core principles in this guidance include the following:

Health assessments and health plans will promote the current and future health of the child or young person who is looked after and not focus solely on the detection of ill-health. Health assessments will cover a range of issues beyond those of physical health which include developmental health and emotional wellbeing.

(DoH, 2002c: 12)

Again Primary Care Trusts (PCTs) are seen as the key agency to plan, manage and monitor the guidance and these should:

- *Ensure that the health and wellbeing of looked after children and young people is an identified local priority.*
- *Ensure that structures are in place to plan, manage and monitor the delivery of health care for all looked after children.*
- *In collaboration with social services, identify an appropriate designated doctor and nurse to provide strategic and clinical leadership to a defined geographical population, and ensure that they are appropriately trained.*

(DoH, 2002c: 19)

The Guidance adds that corporate parenting will provide personal, social and health education complementing that which is provided by schools. Health care and health promotion policies should describe clearly the areas to be covered, how it should be done, and the roles and responsibilities of social workers, carers and other agencies. The topics that should be covered include: emotional health and well being; healthy eating; physical activity; safety and keeping safe; oral and dental health; sexual health; and drugs, alcohol, and tobacco.

According to the Guidance and in terms of mental health, looked after children and their carers are expected to have access to a full range of child and adolescent mental health services (CAMHS). These are to assist in the *prevention* of mental health problems, as well as helping to *reduce the impact* of established mental health disorders on children and young people's lives. In sum then *the key changes outlined in the health guidance include:*

- A health assessment to be undertaken as soon as practicable after a child starts to be looked after, once available health information has been collated.
- The audit of a child's health at the health assessment is expanded and now includes physical and mental health, and health promotion.

- The first health assessment will be undertaken by a suitably qualified medical practitioner, which may include a physical examination.
- A written report of the health assessment and a health plan is to be prepared for each child.
- For children aged over 5 years the review should be at least once a year.
- Such health reviews may now be undertaken by whoever is deemed most appropriate. This might be a registered nurse or midwife under the supervision of a registered medical practitioner.
- Notifications are now required to both the PCT in the area from which the child is leaving and the PCT area to which the child is moving.

The following analysis of the health guidance for care leavers (DoH, 1998b, 2000b) suggests a limited understanding of the problems whereby needs are simply identified and listed but issues of poverty, inequality and resource are largely ignored. In the Guidance the word 'need' is listed 302 times, the words Pathway Plan' are listed 135 times, the word 'health' is listed 87 times, 'resources' 11 times, disability seven times, 'holistic' and 'self-esteem' and 'well being' three times each, 'stress' once, and 'poverty' nil times. It is tempting to conclude from this Guidance that so far as social services are concerned there is lots of need, few resources – so look to the NHS for help. For young people there is lots of need, no acknowledgement of poverty or the direct link with health inequalities – so look to Pathway Plans and social services for help. For health services the Guidance suggests that PCTs will work with social services, possibly after the needs assessment is undertaken by social services, which, in turn, is looking to health to take a lead!

At the time the CLCA 2000 was introduced the *Framework for the Assessment of Children in Need and their Families* was being used for the assessment of all children in need and their families, and this included care leavers and other groups. The *Assessment Framework* and the *Looking After Children* system were brought together to create the *Integrated Children's System* which is to provide a common framework for assessment, intervention, planning and review for all children in need (Department of Health, 2002). *The National Service Framework for Children* and *National Service Framework for Mental Health* are highly relevant for young people leaving care and will be used to develop new national standards and improve services. *The National Service Framework for Children* is concerned with children's overall well being, not just with their health, in medical terms. These changes particularly apply to children looked after. However, it is the CLCA 2000's needs assessments and Pathway Plans mechanisms, (drawing on the *Assessment Framework* anyhow) which are recommended as the ways in which care leavers' health and well being needs are assessed, and, wherever possible, addressed.

Conclusion

This chapter has introduced the term social exclusion and its contribution to understanding how care leavers become socially excluded and therefore how they can stop becoming socially excluded. Following a discussion of the policy relevance of both the terms 'social exclusion' and 'health and well being,' research evidence about both the importance and challenge of addressing health and well being needs was presented. It was argued that a number of commentators have noted the difficulties service providers have experienced in identifying and meeting health and well being needs, especially care leavers' stress related mental health needs. The provisions of the CLCA 2000 and Guidance to promote the health of looked after children were described and reservations expressed about the efficacy of such an approach without other fundamental changes about NHS funding priorities and targets needing to be being made.

Part II

Implementing the Children (Leaving Care) Act 2000

The Leaving Care Projects and the Young People in the National Leaving Care Research Study

Introduction

In the previous two chapters it was argued that care leavers (and indeed other groups such as young offenders) from time to time face all or many of the multi-dimensional disadvantages characteristic of socially exclusion, namely poverty, denial of active citizenship, and inadequate education, health, housing, employment and living standards. A combination of child welfare, housing, education/employment/training, benefit, legislation, and performance indicators have combined to seek to achieve sustained improvements. Individual resilience also needs to be taken into account. Yet, and according to research findings, despite gradual and uneven improvements to care leavers' life chances, it is the area of health and well being, especially mental health and counselling services, which still presents a huge challenge for service providers. It is also the case that improvements to education for those in care, and much better placement stability, also remain key challenges for social services departments (see, for example, Jackson et al., 2003).

Because of the critical importance of each of these life chance areas, and their intricate interconnection, a holistic or 'whole person' approach is often called for in working with care leavers. Child welfare legislation affecting care leavers is then designed to improve their life circumstances by placing additional statutory requirements on local authorities. As we have seen, the leaving care legislation recognises that inter-agency partnerships are necessary to deliver the range of services that are necessary to support care leavers. Therefore in terms of evaluating the CLCA 2000 we need to be concerned about its impact on the health and well being of care leavers beyond simply checking out physical health or mental health service improvements. An evaluation of the impact of the CLCA 2000 on the health and well being of care leavers also demands an examination of changes in the range and appropriateness of a range of other services.

This includes the range and provision of accommodation, education or employment or training services and relevant outcomes (including the numbers entering and remaining in those areas), and of critical importance, the identification of mechanisms designed to improve care leavers' financial circumstances.

As one way of gauging the health and well being of care leavers, a national leaving care research study was undertaken of post-CLCA 2000 developments and this chapter introduces the findings of that study. It explains the origin and scope of the research study, describing the participating leaving care teams and young people's profiles, including their employment, occupation and accommodation circumstances. It is argued that the education/employment/training and financial circumstances of care leavers are essential elements of their health and well being. This will be followed by a discussion of the implementation of local authority leaving care policies and the ways in which ring-fenced funding for services for care leavers was used to improve care leavers' services.

Origin and scope of the national leaving care research study

The study was commissioned by the Action on After Care Consortium and originated from a recognition that it is vital to evaluate the impact of legislation, here the CLCA 2000. This author has undertaken two previous national surveys of the impact of legislation on leaving care teams and young people leaving care. Those studies (about the impact of the Children Act 1989) were based on questionnaires received from 26 and 46 leaving care teams respectively (Broad, 1994, 1998). Those studies, together with the study described here are the only national leaving care surveys that record legislative compliance and post-legislative policy/practice developments at a national level. The 1998 study, which fully acknowledged pockets of good practice, and high levels of individual worker commitment, concluded that at the national policy level:

> Overall the availability and quality of services to young people leaving care remains a lottery in terms of entitlements from the state, and local authority policies and implementation. As was the case in 1994 … leaving care work still remains unsafe in the hands of the Children Act 1989.
>
> (Broad, 1998: 267)

Methodology

The national leaving care study was based on a comprehensive, 40-question questionnaire booklet distributed to 300 local authorities/ leaving care teams/voluntary organisations in England and Wales where the CLCA 2000 applies. Completed replies were received from one in six local authorities, or 52 leaving care teams, representing a 17% return rate, which is within the normal range of responses for postal questionnaires. This number of responses fulfilled the project's aim of producing a national survey of leaving care work post the CLCA 2000. The study was also promoted on various web sites, including that of the national leaving care advisory service in 2002, in newsletters, by voluntary organisations and elsewhere. The sampling frame contained both purposive and cascade samples.

The questionnaire included both pre-coded and open-ended questions. Part 1 contained similar questions to those asked in earlier studies conducted by the author about young people's life chance issues in order that comparisons could be made across the three periods. Part 2 of the questionnaire contained targeted questions about the implementation of the CLCA 2000 so far as local authority and voluntary sector leaving care services are concerned. It included sections on Pathway Plans, personal advisors, financial support, case responsibilities, and health issues. The answers to all the pre-coded questions were entered using SPSS software system to enable some statistical data analysis to be undertaken.

The returns consisted of nominal data (for example about the accommodation, education circumstances of young people attending the teams), ordinal data (here using responses with five point scales) and more open-ended qualitative data, (for example entered by respondents in open-ended 'comments' boxes). All the questionnaires were returned to the University between 12–18 months after the CLCA

2000 was introduced. The study presents a comprehensive overview of achievements, difficulties, trends, and patterns, from the important perspective of leaving care teams following major legislative change being introduced.

Scope of the research study

Since this comprehensive mailing resulted in returns from 52 leaving care teams in England and Wales representing one in six of all local authorities, this study meets and indeed exceeds the necessary requirements to be described both as a national and a representative study. It is in fact the largest survey of leaving care work ever conducted in the United Kingdom. There is also cross-referencing of other post CLCA 2000 research findings, including leaving care teams' case study material (Allard, 2002), foster carers' views (Fostering Network, 2003) the findings of the West Midlands Child Care Consortium survey of leaving care work (2002) and Hai and Williams (2004). By drawing on these other research findings it is possible to check, compare, and triangulate some of the results presented here. The statistical data presented here is predominantly based on information provided by respondents' drawing on local or team databases. The study also draws on other statistical information (for example DoH statistics) and, to make comparisons over time, with similar previous surveys of leaving care work (Broad, 1994, 1998). It is also important to note that since team leaders, rather than practitioners, completed the vast majority of questionnaires, answers will reflect the formers' perspective of the implementation of the CLCA 2000. It can not be known whether team leaders' responses are likely to be more positive, or not, about post CLCA 2000 developments than practitioners, who are more likely to have more day-to-day contact with young people leaving care.

Key research questions raised in the study

- What are the characteristics/life circumstances of young people leaving care who are receiving help from leaving care teams/social services departments?
- How do these compare with the sample population of young people leaving care from the 1994 and 1998 research studies?

Table 1: Staff composition of leaving care teams (n = 50 teams)

Type of staff	Numbers	Expressed as a %
Specialist leaving care social workers	252.10	45.5
Specialist staff who are personal advisors	131.50	24.0
Specialist staff – other	98.80	17.8
Specialist education/employment staff	62.00	11.1
Specialist health staff	11.60	2.1
Total number of specialist staff listed (*note*)	556	100

Note: The slight discrepancy (of 41) between the total number of staff listed earlier (595) and the total number of specialist staff shown here in Table 1 (556) is not significant (7%) and can be explained by simple counting errors and omissions in respondents' returns.

- What has changed since the CLCA 2000 was introduced?
- How is the CLCA 2000 being implemented so far as policies and practice are concerned?
- What post- CLCA 2000 funding, staffing and other resources are in place?
- How do pre and post-CLCA 2000 services compare?
- What more, if anything, needs to be done, and by whom, to further improve practice, services and policies?
- What are the health issues/concerns raised and how are these being addressed?

We begin with a description of the participating leaving care teams and the young people who attend them.

The leaving care teams in the study

The 52 leaving care teams included 39 local authority teams (representing 75% of the sample) seven joint local authority/voluntary organisation teams (14%) five teams run solely by voluntary organisations (14%) and one 'other' (not specified). The profile of this study is significantly different from the 1998 study in that significantly more (45% more) local authorities, fewer (27% less) voluntary organisations, and 19% less joint local authorities/voluntary organisations are included. It is not possible to say whether these responses reflect wider trends about the delivery of services, although it is likely that the responses will even more fully reflect the local authorities' or corporate parent perspective on implementing the CLCA 2000.

The study records the work and views of leaving care teams that were established both before and since the CLCA 2000, with most of them established before the Act was introduced. 13 leaving care teams (or 26% of the sample)

started after 2000, 11 (22%) between 1996-2000, and 26, or just over half (52%), prior to 1995. From previous surveys we know that the biggest growth period for new leaving care teams was after the introduction of the Children Act 1989, between 1990 and 1995, when 21 new teams were started. According to the current survey 26% of responding teams were established in anticipation of or immediately after the introduction of the CLCA 2000. Therefore this research is highly relevant in terms of providing an analysis both of more established and less established teams.

Staffing

The 52 leaving care teams had a total of 595 staff (full time equivalent), the equivalent of a ratio of 12 young people to 1 staff member. This ratio compares favourably with the 1998 average young person to staff ratio of 15:1. Again there were considerable variations between local authorities and voluntary organisations where the former had larger numbers of staff and young people than the latter. This slight improvement to the ratio is confirmed by the frequency with which 'growth in staff numbers' appears later in this book in Chapter 6 as a key 'achievement' area (interestingly, also identified as a 'problem' area) by leaving care services.

Teams were also asked to identify the composition of their team as a way of understanding how resources and plans had taken shape post-CLCA 2000.

Comment

There are an average of 11.9 staff at each team (n = 50). Since previous studies have not provided a breakdown of specialist staff this makes comparisons with those findings impossible to

Table 2: Ethnic origin of young people in study compared with 1994 and 1998

Ethnic origin	1994 Study no. (%)	1998 Study no. (%)	Current study-no. (%)
White	670 (77%)	2579 (78%)	4983 (83%)
Black	153 (18%)	449 (14%)	534 (9%)
Mixed race	N/A	N/A	261 (4%)
Asian	19 (2%)	100 (3%)	105 (2%)
Other	29 (3%)	191 (5%)	91 (2%)
Total no. responses	871 (100%)	3319 (100%)	5974 (100%)

make. Nevertheless, it is significant that after extra funding was made available through grants, the highest number of staff, after leaving care social workers, are personal advisors. What is also very noticeable is the very low number of health staff in leaving care teams. This finding, combined with others in Chapter 4 and Part Three in this book, about health, confirm the serious and continuing difficulties in identifying properly funded good practice examples of health and social care providing specialist health staff or services for young people leaving care. Whilst recognising that in theory there are other 'health agency-based' models of health care for young people leaving care, we were not given any examples, only of three 'developing strategies.' It is most unlikely that the 11.6 health workers in post across 52 leaving care teams working with 6953 young people can be anything more than a token response either to young people's health needs or to meeting the expectations provided in the health Guidance (DoH, 2002c). Nevertheless an increased range of workers that reflects a more corporate approach both to 'parenting' care leavers, and funding regimes is welcomed.

The young people in the study

The leaving care teams reported that the total number of young people with whom they are working, and who are affected by the CLCA 2000 is 6953. As a result of different levels of responses there are some minor discrepancies between this total figure of young people with whom the leaving care teams were working, and other figures provided by respondents in this study. These include, for example, the accommodation figures (total number = 4464) or the occupation figure (total number = 4304), or the ethnic origin of the young people (total number = 5974).

The gender breakdown is 50%: 50%. This finding is within 1% of the gender breakdown

percentages in the 1994 and 1998 studies, exactly the same as Wade et al.'s 1998 sample, and only slightly different for all looked after children (56%: 44%) as at 31 March 2002 (DoH, 2003: 8).

Ethnic origin of the young people

In this study by far the largest percentage (83%) of young people leaving care are white, with the second biggest grouping 'Black' accounting for 9% of all the young people. Young people described as 'mixed race' (a category not included in the two previous surveys by this author) accounted for 4% of the young people. The different ethnic categories used were the standard categories used for the 2001 census and for DoH returns. Table 2 provides the full breakdown.

Comment

It is likely that the significant change in the percentage of Black young people from previous surveys compared with this survey can be explained by definitional changes (such as the inclusion of 'mixed race' as a distinct category in this survey), rather than by any other changes during that period. Young people attending the leaving care teams who are either Black or mixed race accounted for 13% of all the young people in the study and continue to be over-represented in the leaving care population. This 13% figure is virtually the same, as one would expect, as the total percentage (14%) of children looked after who are either Black (7%) or mixed race (7%) (DoH, 2003:8). According to national data and in the UK as a whole 3.2% of the population are Black or mixed race (Social Trends, 2002). This finding suggests an alarmingly high, four-fold over-representation, of black and mixed race young people in the care leaving population compared with the population as a whole.

Teams were further asked to provide numbers of eligible, relevant, former relevant and

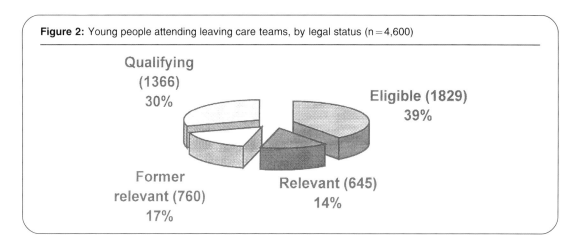

Figure 2: Young people attending leaving care teams, by legal status (n=4,600)

Qualifying (1366) 30%

Eligible (1829) 39%

Former relevant (760) 17%

Relevant (645) 14%

qualifying young people with whom they are working. Figure 2 provides a summary of responses.

Comment

Respondents were only able to give information or knew about 4,600 (or 66%) of all the young people affected by the CLCA 2000 and with whom they work. This indicates inadequate information systems. The number of qualifying young people is reducing as a significant group since those aged 18 to 21 at the time of the implementation of CLCA 2000 in October 2001 will no longer be included. However, there should be an increase in the former relevant children. This would be reflective of the aim to improve outcomes by more flexible needs-based, not age-based, services; for example converting foster care placements to supported lodgings for young people at 18 years of age. All these changes will have implications for reviewing, planning and developing resources.

Young people with a physical disability, learning difficulty, or statemented

Another question (5) asked teams to estimate the numbers of young people attending their team who (a) have a physical disability, (b) a learning difficulty, or (c) are statemented. Whilst recognising categories (b) and (c) are not mutually exclusive the study was keen to establish this information in order to identify need. The 45 teams that responded to this

question indicated there were 165 young people with a physical disability, 410 young people with a learning difficulty and 352 young people who were 'statemented' in order to access special educational needs. These numbers represent 3%, 8% and 7% respectively of the total number of young people attending these teams (n=5196). The combined 11% figure for those with either a physical disability or a learning difficulty compares with previous research findings of 9% (Broad, 1998: 191) and 13% (Biehal et al, 1992: 41) for these two groups.

Policy and practice

The high numbers with physical disabilities, learning difficulties or statemented has important implications for future service development especially in respect of meeting the health and well being needs of those with mild learning difficulties who don't fall into an easily recognised category of need. Those young people with physical disabilities such as sensory needs are likely to have been identified and given specialist services at earlier stages, including specialist education. Thus there is a vital need for specialist knowledge/ training if they increasingly come within the remit of leaving care services. These findings also suggest a strong need for more targeted research, building on Morris' work (1995) as well as post-CLCA 2000 Guidance about working with these groups of care leavers. This is an area still requiring urgent attention especially since there were so few examples of specific anti-discriminatory policies and practice, as we will see in Chapter 5.

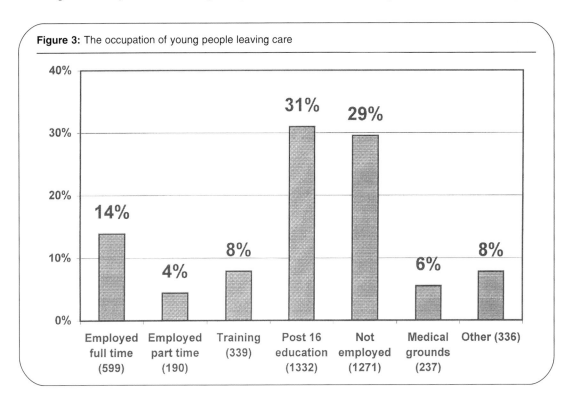

Figure 3: The occupation of young people leaving care

Table 3: Occupation of young people leaving care compared with 1994 and 1998

Occupation type	1994 Study % (No.)	1998 Study % (No.)	Current study % (No.)
Employed full-time	9 (77)	11 (325)	14 (599)
Employed part-time	4 (36)	4 (108)	4 (190)
Training	13 (114)	10 (289)	8 (339)
Post 16 education	19 (162)	17.5 (508)	31 (1332)
Not in employment	49 (418)	51.5 (1497)	29 (1271)
Not working on medical grounds	N/A	N/A	6 (237)
Other	6 (52)	6 (178)	8 (336)
Total	100 (859)	100 (2905)	100 (4304)

The occupation of young people leaving care

Figure 3 summarises the occupation of the young people leaving care described in this study.

Table 3 enables important comparisons to be made between the occupation of the young people in the current study compared with the 1994 and 1998 studies.

Comment

Compared with previous studies the most significant finding here is the much higher proportion of young people in post-16 education,

31%, compared with previous studies' figures of 19% and 17.5%. Linked to this finding is the 22.5% decline, from 51.5% (1998) to 29% (current study) in the proportion of young people leaving care in the 'not in employment' categories.

Apart from those findings, the figures are remarkably similar across the three study periods. Also if one combines the percentages of those 'not in employment' with those in 'post-16 education' the totals are very similar, 68% (1994), 68.5% (1998) and 60% (current). What has changed is the higher proportion of young people leaving care in post 16 education and the lower proportion not working. It should also be noted that the figure in the West Midlands study for

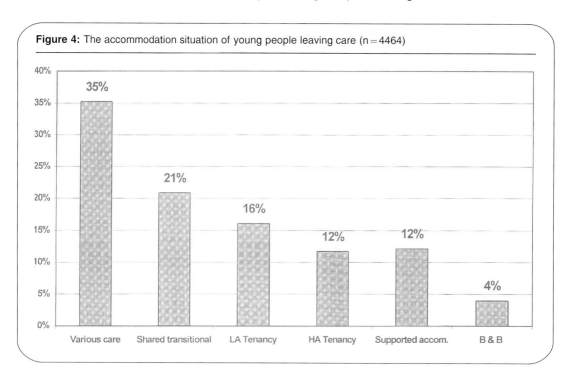

Figure 4: The accommodation situation of young people leaving care (n = 4464)

those young people *not working/in training* is higher, 38%, compared with the 29% figure here (WMCCC, 2002).

Despite these variations there are two key changes in social welfare policy that seem to explain these figures about the higher proportion of young people leaving care in education/employment/training than was hitherto the case. The first concerns the range and availability of government initiatives to maintain 16–17-year-olds in further education and training. The second is the major change in the funding arrangements to support young people leaving care resulting in local authorities receiving incentive funding from *Quality Protects*, up until 2003/4, to support those young people leaving care in post 16 education and training. As we will see later, in Chapter 4, these incentives consist of regular weekly payments, and can be anything between £50–£70, for example, for continued college attendance. These findings suggest strong and direct linkages between the education, employment, and training outcomes for young people leaving care, and government incentives for 16 and 17-year-olds to enter further education and training. Let us now move on to examining the accommodation situation of young people leaving care in the current study.

Young people's accommodation

Figure 4 illustrates the different types of accommodation in which the young people leaving care are living (n = 4464), according to the current study's findings.

Comment

The 'various care' category combines a range of accommodation types listed by respondents including foster care, residential care, bed-sit, living with friends and at young offender institutions. Even if one combines the two 'housing tenancy' percentages (totalling 28%) this is less than the 'various care' category (accounting for 35% of all accommodation), demonstrating the wide variety of accommodation in which young people leaving care reside. Unfortunately, not all respondents provided a detailed breakdown of numbers within each of these 'various care' types. However, it is also possible to examine longer-term patterns for young people leaving care by comparing the accommodation findings with the 1998 study. Table 4 compares the current study's and the 1998 study's findings about the accommodation circumstances of care leavers.

Table 4: Accommodation for young people leaving care: current and 1998 comparisons

Housing type	1998 Study no. (%)	Current study no. (%)
Various (including foster, residential care, friends, other public care)	694 (33)	1572 (35)
Shared/transitional housing	307 (15)	931 (21)
Local authority tenancy	487 (23)	716 (16)
Supported accommodation	215 (10)	543 (12)
Housing association tenancy	294 (14)	523 (12)
Bed and breakfast	99 (5)	179 (4)
Total	2096 (100)	4464 (100)

Comment

There are mixed findings about accommodation here. The key messages to be drawn from this table are first, the similar patterns for the two periods, and second, the significant decline in the percentage of young people with tenancies, from 38% (in 1998) to 28%, in the current study. This finding suggests that there has been a reduction in the availability of targeted accommodation for this group. It is also likely that the impact of the CLCA 2000 has been to extend the provision of supported transitional accommodation. Thus there has been a slight increase, from 10% to 12%, of young people living in supported accommodation. Additionally there is also a noticeable increase, from 15% to 21% in the proportion of young people living in shared/transitional accommodation, and more research would be necessary to examine why this is the case. In the next chapter there is further data about continuing accommodation problems in terms of availability and suitability. Here, and in answer to a further question about accommodation, 84% of respondents indicated that the young people living in these various types of accommodation were living in what the Act describes as 'suitable accommodation' (Regulation 11 (2) of the CLCA 2000). However, the range of answers to this question, from 10% to 100%, points to enormous and unacceptable variations in provision.

Next and having begun to identify the needs of care leavers and their living circumstances, and the services set up to help them, we look at the implementation of post CLCA 2000 leaving care policies produced by local authorities. This will be followed by an examination of how ring-fenced funding for leaving care services is used by local authorities.

Leaving care policies and ring-fenced funding

Leaving care policies

42 or 86% of respondents indicated that they had produced a new policy since the CLCA 2000 and that in 90% of cases this was 'always' or 'mostly' followed (same figures for 1998 survey). However, it was also the case that leaving care policies were 'always' followed in just 10 or 24% of cases, which raises questions about the degree to which services and new policies are actually being implemented. Next is the issue about the provision of ring-fenced funding for implementing policies since the CLCA 2000 was introduced.

Ring-fenced funding

It is vital that ring-fended monies made available via *Quality Protects* to sustain and improve leaving care services go to young people leaving care and leaving care services. Those working in the leaving care field widely welcomed the additional funding for leaving care work provided by *Quality Protects* funding. This followed the identification of leaving care as a grant priority area after the launch of the *Quality Protects Programme* in 1998. It should be emphasised that these monies were designed to support leaving care services, and young people leaving care i.e. post-residential care and post-foster care. This author is unaware of any policy statement indicating that this ring-fenced money was to support residential care or foster care. Thus questions were included in the questionnaire to leaving care teams to establish, as far as is possible, how the leaving care ring-fenced grants were being spent. Table 5 indicates respondents' answers.

Table 5: Use of ring-fenced leaving care monies for residential placements, foster care placements, and out of county/borough placements

Range of responses	Residential no. (%)	Foster care no. (%)	Out of county/borough care no. (%)
'Yes all of the time'	26 (57)	23 (52)	26 (56)
'Yes some of the time'	7 (15)	6 (13)	5 (11)
'No'	3 (6)	6 (13)	5 (11)
'Don't know'	10 (22)	10 (22)	10 (22)
Total	46 (100)	45 (100)	46 (100)

Comment

From Table 5 it can be seen that

- 72% (57% + 15%) of respondents' answers indicated that leaving care ring-fenced monies is 'always' or 'sometimes' used for supporting residential placements.
- 65% (52% + 13%) of respondents' answers indicated that leaving care ring-fenced monies is 'always' or 'sometimes' used for supporting fostering placements.
- 67% (56% + 11%) of respondents' answers indicated that leaving care ring-fenced monies is 'always' or 'sometimes' used for supporting out of borough /county placements.
- Overall between 65% and 72% of leaving care teams stated that ring-fenced funding for leaving care services were being used either 'all the time' or 'some of the time' to fund residential care, foster care and out-of-borough/county placements.

Those ring-fenced monies were to support young people leaving care, rather than prop up over-spent foster, residential, and out-of-borough placements. It is recognised that there is a major policy shift in the CLCA 2000 towards encouraging local authorities to help young people make the transition to independent living not abruptly at 16 but gradually after that time, and in accord with a needs assessment and pathway plan. It is likely that local authorities could argue that this relocation of ring-fenced monies towards sustaining young people in care longer is a 'good thing.' Nevertheless this begs the question about whether leaving care/after care services are being deprived of funding for post-16 work? More specifically it raises the following three questions:

1. Are leaving care budgets being used to relieve over extended fostering budgets or to enable 16 and 17 year olds to have a quality leaving care service within and from foster care?

2. Will specialist staff and resources be lost and reduction again in real terms of leaving care budget or are services embedded in existing and continuing services?
3. Given the high cost of out-of-authority placements can it be assumed that as a reaction to shortages of foster carers and residential placements the knock on effect is to reduce the potential for young people in these placements to be allowed to stay until they are ready?

The evidence presented here indicates that leaving care ring-fenced funding was used more to support fostering, residential and out-of county placements than 'leaving care services' defined as services provided to young people leaving care and moving to independent living.

Discussion

This chapter has presented the staffing and young people's profiles of 52 leaving care teams working with just under 7,000 young people entitled to a service under the CLCA 2000. A slightly higher worker: young person ratio than in 1998 was identified, and this was as a direct result of *Quality Protects* funding which has now ended. The high percentage of care leavers either 'not working' (29%) or 'not working on medical grounds' (6%), combined with the large percentage of care leavers without fixed or settled accommodation (72%) indicates that these care leavers face exactly the types of financial and accommodation difficulties indicative of social exclusion. It will be recalled from the previous chapter that Gordon et al.'s four elements of social exclusion are 'impoverishment or exclusion from adequate income or resources,' labour market exclusion', 'service exclusion' and 'exclusion from social relations.' As we will see in the following chapters, there are also other care leavers who despite being in employment, or holding fixed tenancies, still face social exclusion. Let us now move on to examining how the CLCA 2000 has been implemented, and the consequences for care leavers' health and well being and their social inclusion.

Chapter Four

Developing Education/Employment/Training, Accommodation, Health Services and Financial Supports

Introduction

This chapter describes the pre-CLCA 2000 services provided for young people leaving care and compares them with post-CLCA 2000 services across four key health and well being areas. Let me first explain the basis of the pre- and post-CLCA 2000 assessments made.

The first was a single assessment of the **pre-CLCA 2000 service baseline** across four service areas; *education/employment/training, accommodation, health*, and *financial supports*. The 5-point scale provided was as follows; 1 = 'excellent/consistent'; 2 = 'good'; 3 = 'average'; 4 = 'below average'; and 5 = 'inadequate/inconsistent'. So if a team considered its work and strategy on accommodation was 'excellent/consistent', in terms of appropriateness, flexibility, and relevance, it would answer 'excellent' and so on.

The second more sophisticated assessment required teams to estimate their **post-CLCA 2000 services** across the same four service areas but using different scores for each of five different levels. These levels were 'identification of need,' 'planning,' 'service provision,' 'resources' and, finally, 'outcomes.' In other words there were five different rating levels required on 'health', five on 'accommodation' and so on.

For each of these post-CLCA 2000 service assessments the following five-point scale was provided; 'improved significantly,' 'some improvement', 'remained the same,' 'slightly worsened' and lastly 'considerably worsened.' Let us take 'accommodation' as one example from the four service areas identified. If a leaving care team considered that in terms of 'identification of need' its services concerning accommodation had 'remained the same' since before the CLCA 2000 then respondents would enter a '3' in the appropriate box. If 'outcomes' for accommodation had shown 'some improvement' then a '2' was entered in the appropriate box, and so on.

The analysis draws on respondents' answers to these baseline, and post CLCA 2000 questions, beginning with the service area of 'education/employment/training'. At the beginning of each section the relevant Guidance and Regulations from the CLCA 2000 are presented in order to illustrate powers, duties, and responsibilities for each service area under discussion.

Education/employment/training

Background

There are more powers than duties in respect of the local authority's responsibilities about employment, which essentially centre on local authorities' working with other agencies (as with accommodation) and here, and having a duty to provide assistance as set out in each young person's Pathway Plan.

Context – Education/employment/training

CLCA 2000
Schedule 1 (CLCA 2000) For those who are eligible/relevant or former relevant each Pathway Plan must cover how the responsible authority will assist the child or young person in relation to employment or occupation.

Regulation 11(1) (CLCA 2000) states that the responsible authority must provide assistance, which may be in cash, to meet the relevant child's needs in relation to education, training and employment set out in the Pathway Plan.

Under Section 24A (4) (Children Act 1989) For qualifying care leavers local authorities have a specific power to provide assistance where this is connected with their employment [section 24B (1)], education, or training [section 24B (2)]. It should be noted that any such financial assistance or grant provided under section 24B (2) where this is connected to a course of education or training may be given up to the age of 24 [section 24B (3)].

Table 6: Service baseline levels of education/ employment/training services for care leavers prior to the CLCA 2000

Baseline ratings for education/employment/training	Number and percentage of responses
Excellent	1 (2%)
Good	10 (21%)
Average	20 (42%)
Below average	16 (33%)
Inadequate	1 (2%)
Total number (%) of teams responding	48 (100%)

Service baseline prior to the CLCA 2000

Table 6 indicates the rating leaving care teams gave to their work in this education/ employment/training area.

Comment

Only 23% responses indicated that services were 'good' or 'excellent'. 63% of education/ employment/training services were rated as 'average' or 'good' and 75% as 'average' or 'below average'. It is suggested here that these answers largely reflect the view that education/employment/training is either not recognised by leaving care teams as being their prime responsibility, or that they provided a very average service or both.

We now examine the impact of the CLCA 2000 on education/employment/training by making comparisons between baseline and post-CLCA 2000 services, and by drawing on comments made by respondents in the 'education/ employment/training comments box' provided on the questionnaire.

Service levels after the CLCA 2000

Figure 5 illustrates the responses about how the CLCA 2000 is being implemented in the areas of education/employment/training.

Comment

Respondents reported that as a result of changes introduced since the CLCA 2000, education/employment/training has either 'improved significantly' or there has been 'a little improvement' in 77% of cases, and 'remained the same' in a further 22% of cases. It had only worsened in 1% of cases.

For 25% of leaving care teams it was significantly less likely for there to be any education/employment/training improvements

(i.e., either a little or significant) since the CLCA 2000 without the extra specialist education/employment/training staff being in post (including specialist Connexions/ education/employment staff). For the remaining 75% of teams improvements to education/employment/training since the Act did not appear to be associated with extra specialist staffing.

It was the case however that staff teams which have a higher staff: young people ratio enjoyed consistently better outcomes about education/employment/training since the CLCA 2000 than those with lower staff: young people ratios. This finding suggests that teams having the resources, and the professional investment to work with young people to extend educational aspirations can produce better results.

The existing service baseline seemed to be the most reliable guide to explaining the impact of the CLCA 2000 on education/employment/ training and more reliable than whether there were additional specialist staffing. Those teams that indicated that they already provided either an 'excellent' or 'good' baseline service for education/ employment/ training, were the *only ones* whose services either *remained the same* or *improved* and did not worsen. Thus all but two of the leaving care services whose pre-CLCA 2000 baseline assessment was either 'average' or 'below average' or 'inadequate' had also improved, from a lower start point, to more of a mid-range position, predominantly 'slight improvement' or 'remained the same'. In other words although both higher and lower rated leaving care teams are providing improved services to young people about education/employment/training the lower rated services' improvements remain at the lower end of the scale. The West Midlands survey noted fewer comments from young people and professionals about education/employment/ training, suggesting that they 'felt that education

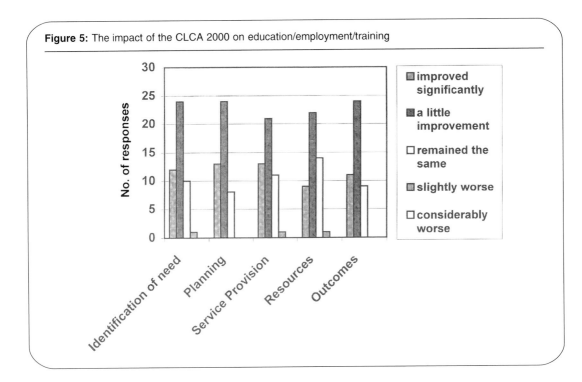

Figure 5: The impact of the CLCA 2000 on education/employment/training

Table 7: Respondents comments about education/training/employment

Education/employment/training	Number of responses
	Positive replies (27)
There are more strategic links with staff	9
More staff/funding for this work	10
Employment schemes set-up	6
More group and individual work	2
	Negative replies (3)
Lack of choice/employment for less able	3
Total	30

and training was not a key aspect of the work of leaving care teams' (WMCCA, 2003: 16). If this is the case, if only partially, this confirms the importance of leaving care teams and young people working closely with Connexions and lifelong learning services.

To complement these findings about post-CLCA 2000 changes about education/ employment/training, Table 7 summarises the comments made by respondents using the education/employment/training 'comments box' provided on the questionnaire. These are grouped separately as either 'positive' or 'negative'.

Comment

Of all the 30 comments made by respondents about education/employment/training the vast majority of the 27 'positive' responses were concerned with *beginning to put in place a strategy* for addressing education/employment/training issues, rather than outcome indicators. This suggests that this is another work area in leaving care beginning to be tackled more strategically than on an individual practice-response basis, with fairly limited and low-level responses, and with unknown outcomes.

Information was also gathered from another question that invited staff to list and prioritise their main 'achievements' and 'problem' areas in response to the CLCA 2000. From those responses we can see that only 7% (13 from 177 responses) considered 'education/employment/training' as an area of progress since the CLCA 2000. These findings indicate that education/employment/ training remains a critical service gap in terms of improving health and well being outcomes.

Accommodation

Background

Accommodation for young people leaving care is or should be about the funding and provision of a range of appropriate, affordable, suitable and supported accommodation and it is not simply a 'bricks and mortar' issue. Garnett (1992) found that leaving care plans were often based on short-term considerations leading to unsatisfactory and temporary accommodation. Biehal et al.'s study (1992: 43) found that young people leaving care experienced 'accommodation problems, including temporary accommodation, drift and homelessness.' There is also evidence (for example, see CHAR, 1995) that young Black people continue to be over-represented in the homelessness figures as a result of racism and a lack of specialist accommodation. Additionally, and according to evidence submitted to the 1996 Inquiry into Preventing Youth Homelessness, two thirds of young people leaving care experienced homelessness (CHAR, 1996: 56). The three main reasons given in that enquiry for that situation were: the (young) age at which most care leavers make the transition to independence, their disadvantaged position relative to other young people, and the lack of adequate support and preparation that they receive (CHAR, 1996: 56). In a general sense these findings, though alarming, are not new. A number of studies have reported on both the unsatisfactory situation in general regarding the availability of housing, and inadequate housing finances for young people leaving care. Since the CLCA 2000 Parsons (2002), Broad and Fry (2002) and Stein et al. (2002) have all emphasised the good practice requirements of suitable accommodation.

Context – Accommodation

CLCA 2000 Guidance [S23], and Regulation 11, the Children Act 1989 [S24], Homelessness Act 2000

Councils have a duty to meet the needs of *relevant children* where the 2000 Act requires the responsible local authority to support them by providing them with or maintaining them in suitable accommodation unless they are satisfied that their welfare does not require it [Section 23B(8)(b)]; and the needs of *former relevant children*, where the local authority is required to assist them to the extent that their welfare requires it [Section 23C (4)].

The 2000 Act also requires a local authority to ensure that any local authority care leaver in *full-time further or higher education* has suitable accommodation if they need it during a vacation (Section 24B(5)).

Regulation 11 (2) defines *suitable accommodation* as accommodation which, so far as reasonably practicable, is suitable for the child in the light of his needs, including his heath needs, in respect of which the responsible authority has satisfied itself as to the character and suitability of the landlord or other provider.

The CLCA 2000 Guidance discourages bed and breakfast accommodation, other than for emergency short-term use.

The Homelessness Act 2000 places a duty on housing and social services departments to co-operate and joint agreements must ensure that care leavers needs are properly assessed, gaps in provision are identified, and most critically, that effective strategic planning takes place to provide and deliver support and services. There are other provisions and exclusions about the duty to accommodate.

It is worth recalling the breakdown of the young people's accommodation types in this survey as discussed earlier. 35% are living in foster/ residential care/YOI/friends, 21% living in shared/transitional housing, 28% in tenancies (both local authority and housing association),

Table 8: Service baseline levels of accommodation services for care leavers prior to the CLCA 2000

Baseline ratings	Number and percentage of responses
Excellent	6 (12%)
Good	12 (25%)
Average	20 (42%)
Below average	5 (10%)
Inadequate	5 (10%)
Total no. (%) of teams	48 (100%)

12% in supported accommodation, and 4% in bed and breakfast. The analysis of accommodation for young people leaving care will begin by an examination of the service baseline for accommodation.

Service baseline prior to the CLCA 2000

Table 8 illustrates the service baseline for accommodation prior to the CLCA 2000 as rated by the leaving care teams.

Comment

79% of responses indicated their accommodation baseline service was 'average' or above, and 62% 'average' or 'below average'.

All the leaving care teams were asked to provide an assessment of their service baseline pre-CLCA 2000 with the scale ranging from 'excellent' to 'good' through 'average' onto 'below average' and finishing with 'inadequate/inconsistent'. Let us now examine in what ways the CLCA 2000 is being implemented in the area of accommodation.

Service levels after the CLCA 2000

Figure 6 summarises answers about the impact of the CLCA 2000 on the accommodation situation of young people leaving care.

Progress since the CLCA 2000

With just one exception all 36 of those leaving care services which already identified their accommodation baseline as either 'excellent',

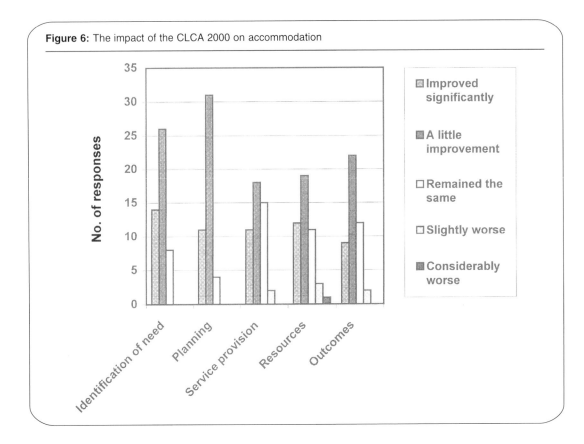

Figure 6: The impact of the CLCA 2000 on accommodation

Table 9: Respondents' comments about accommodation for young people leaving care

Accommodation	Numbers of responses
	Negative (19)
Lack of suitable accommodation	15
Strategic problems in large shire counties	3
Local authorities vary in commitment	1
	Positive (10)
Better strategic links/panels/planning	6
Wider range available/supporting people	3
Significant improvement	1
	Mixed/uncertain (3)
Accommodation strategy still being developed	3
Total number of responses	32

Note: A further 14 respondents did not provide any answers in the accommodation comments box provided.

'good' or 'average' before the CLCA 2000 reported that accommodation had either 'significantly improved', or there had been 'a little improvement' since the Act. Of the 10 leaving care services that identified their accommodation service baseline as either 'below average' or 'inadequate' before the CLCA 2000 only two had made any significant improvement. Four had shown a slight improvement.

Given the critical importance of accommodation for young people leaving care, and that 'accommodation' is one of the four key service areas focused on in this survey, the questionnaire invited respondents to use the open-ended 'comments box' provided in the questionnaire to record their views about accommodation. These are presented in Table 9.

'Lack of suitable accommodation' answers included the following:

- Lack of follow-on accommodation.
- No private landlords.
- No choice of accommodation.
- Problems accessing supported accommodation – 42 beds lost.

There was some evidence of particular problems for some large shire counties of housing and social services working together to deliver a coherent corporate parenting strategy to support young people leaving care. It is too early to know whether or not *Supporting People* has increased the scope for permanent accommodation for care leavers or not.

It is vital that social services have joint working arrangements with housing authorities and it is also relevant to note here Shelter's observations

(2003) about the impact of the Housing Act (2002) on such arrangements. In respect of joint working with social services, 21 out of the 28 authorities said improvements were needed to their joint working arrangements with social services. Authorities suggested necessary changes, including:

- Formalising working arrangements.
- Improving mutual understanding of each agency's work.
- Improving communication.
- Improving engagement with the relevant social services' staff.
- Improving social services' understanding of their role to support homeless people.
- Improving the way social services plan and prioritise.

Accommodation needs to be safe, affordable and appropriate to the young person's needs and circumstances. Sufficient housing stock, funding sources, and joint protocols between housing and social services are necessary for there to be a chance that supply can move towards demand. Accommodation is not simply a 'brick and mortar issue'. According to Parsons 'It is about the timing of the move, the suitability and maturity of the young person wishing to live independently, and the support available' (Parsons, in Wheal, 2002: 105–13). Young people at a leaving care seminar sponsored by the Roberts Trust (2002) expressed their views about accommodation in the following terms. The young people said they needed information and an element of choice about suitable accommodation. This involves making individual assessments (acknowledging each young person is different), an acknowledgement that not everyone suddenly becomes an adult at 18, and flexibility on the part of the local authority about move-on possibilities. The young people also spoke for a 'siblings together' placement policy, help with rent payments, stable accommodation and what they described as 'additional needs' (these included a study desk and lamp).

An earlier national study of leaving care about the implementation of the Children Act 1989 by this author (1998) found that the 'lack of affordable accommodation' was second only to 'local authority planning' as the most important problem facing leaving care teams. It is highly recommended that a range of suitable supported accommodation is made available, for example by local authority housing departments and voluntary organisations, and whose service standards can be set and/or closely monitored by leaving care teams/personal advisors.

Health

Background

The area of 'health', embracing emotional, physical and mental ill heath has been identified as one of the most important yet neglected areas of social policy for young people leaving care. In 1998 the House of Commons Select Committee concluded: 'The failure of local authorities to secure good health outcomes for the children and young people they look after is a failure of corporate parenting' (House of Commons, 1998, para. 265). Next the consultation document *Promoting the Health of Looked after Children* (DoH, 2002), following a consultation document three years earlier (DoH, 1999) was a much delayed policy response to that House of Commons Report. As we will see 'health' does not feature strongly in the CLCA 2000 and where it does, it tends to direct social services departments towards health agencies for service provision. Additionally there is no specific acknowledgement of poverty of young people leaving care or the impact of poverty on health. The inclusion of health as one of the identified children's developmental needs within the *Framework for the Assessment of Children in Need and Their Families* (DoH, 2000) is the clearest acknowledgement that 'health' requires

assessment by social services and other agencies together. There are other ongoing policy initiatives that will be having a positive impact on the health of young people leaving care including local CAMHS (Children and Adolescent Mental Health Services) and a range of national and local teenage pregnancy, sexual health, and substance misuse initiatives.

Context – Health

CLCA 2000

Regulation 7 and Schedule 1 provide the regulations and statutory requirements about assessing and planning through the Pathway Plan (Chapter 5) and then meeting the health needs of young people leaving care. In particular the CLCA 2000 Guidance (p22) states that Pathway planning for the health needs of care leavers should be based on the Guidance contained in *Promoting the Health of Looked after Children* to be published by the DoH in 2001 (published in 2002).

Service baseline prior to the CLCA 2000

In the 1998 survey of leaving care services it was found that leaving care teams did not list 'health', either as an issue with which to deal, or a problem. It was as if that survey's findings were that leaving care services 'do not do health' either in terms of identification of need, assessment or service provision. So it should not be a surprise, though a disappointment, considering the introduction of the CLCA 2000, and the health Guidance, that the lowest service baseline for leaving care services is that concerning health. Table 10 summarises respondents' answers about service baseline levels for health.

Comment

These responses are by far the **poorest** of the four baseline service areas. 59% of responses were rated as 'average' or 'good', and a staggeringly high 82% as either 'average' (42%) or 'below average' (40%). We already saw that 'health' was the lowest rated of the four baseline service areas (accommodation, education/ employment/ training, and financial supports) prior to the introduction of the CLCA 2000.

Table 10: Service baseline levels for health services for care leavers prior to the CLCA 2000

Baseline ratings	Number and percentage of responses
Excellent	1 (2%)
Good	8 (17%)
Average	20 (42%)
Below average	19 (40%)
Inadequate	0 (0%)
Total number (%) of teams responding	48 (100%)

Figure 7: The impact of the CLCA 2000 on health

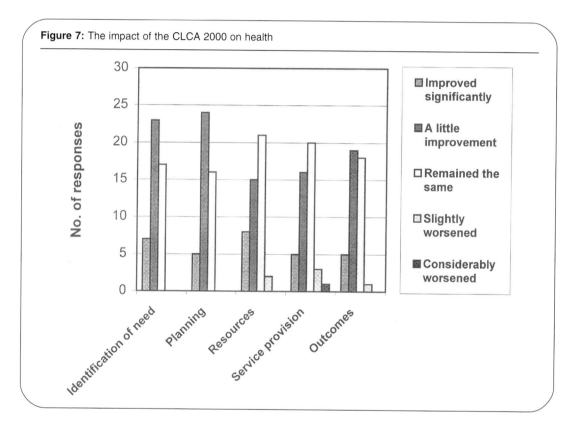

Service levels after the CLCA 2000

Figure 7 illustrates respondents' views of the impact of the CLCA 2000 about the health of young people leaving care.

Key findings

It is highly significant that whatever the position of leaving care teams' initial health baseline assessment there has been very little move towards any improvement in any of the five categories, but especially so in service outcomes and service delivery.

Furthermore 'health' as a service area/issue, did not feature in any of the 351 answers provided by teams asked to identify 'progress' areas, or 'problem' areas, suggesting that health issues are very low on respondents' agendas. Additionally of all the four key topic areas (accommodation, education/employment/ training, finance, health) about which leaving care teams were asked to complete comments boxes, again it was 'health' that both attracted the lowest number of total responses and the lowest number of positive responses. These findings suggest that health issues for young people leaving care, if they are being addressed at all, are

Table 11: Respondents' comments about health services for young people leaving care

Health	Number of responses
	Positive responses (10)
New health workers appointed (e.g. nurse)	7
Better strategic relationship with health	2
New health provision in LAC made a lot of difference	1
	Negative responses (15)
Mental health services/CAMHS – poor/unresponsive/unavailable	12
Lack of any link to teenage pregnancy strategy	2
Shortage of substance misuse services	1
Total number of responses	25

Note: 27 (of the 52) respondents did not provide an answer.

much more likely taking place outside the leaving care services.

The findings indicate slow and uneven progress, and for those with a below average baseline, minimal indication of any significant improvement. There were steady improvements identified in terms of identification of health needs and service planning. However, improvements are both less visible and less common when moving from assessing and planning services to having an impact on resources. This point is illustrated by the finding here that *more health services had worsened or remained the same than improved*, again from a low baseline.

30 of all 47 respondents stated that in terms of identifying needs health had improved either 'slightly' or 'significantly improved'. By combining the categories 'slightly improved' 'significantly improved' and 'remained the same' across all five service categories we can see that there is a gradual decline in the number of responses, from 47, 45, 44, 41, and 42, moving from health 'identification of need' through the 'planning' 'service delivery' and 'outcome' categories. What is also significant and noticeable is that whatever the position of leaving care teams' initial health baseline there has been very little move towards any improvement in any of the five categories, but especially so in service outcomes and service delivery.

This low priority by leaving care teams to health is confirmed by the fact that of all the comments boxes provided those concerning health had the poorest response rate (25 of 52) and the lowest number of positive answers. Table 11 provides a breakdown of those 25 replies.

Individual comments made about health

Positive

- 'All young people leaving care have a health assessment'.
- 'PCT has appointed a worker to focus on care leavers health issues' (54 young people at that team).
- 'We now have a looked after nurse for looked after children'.

Negative

- 'Total lack of appropriate mental health services'.
- 'Health provision is not available to those who do not have a mental illness diagnosis'.
- 'Young people leaving care feel blocked by health services due to waiting times and systems'.
- 'Health services are improving but continues to be a shortage of health related substance misuse services particularly for under 18s'.
- 'Accessing funding for young people with mental health/learning difficulties is a major issue'.
- 'Health needs mainstreaming'.

There is therefore a climate of increasing awareness of the health needs of young people leaving care, but not yet a coherent or consistent vision, strategy, structure and resources for meeting them.

Recommendations

- Health authorities, Primary Care Trusts, and other relevant authorities to review their health information and policies for care leavers, as part of a strategic and coherent response to the CLCA 2000's Guidance.

- The health needs of young people leaving care to be much more fully acknowledged as concerning not just physical health check-ups but acknowledging lifestyle, poverty, self-esteem, resilience issues.
- Specific health targets, fully costed and funded are necessary to ensure that health and well-being issues are prioritised, planned and delivered in young person centred and informed ways.

Financial supports

Background

Since the first seminal research in this field was conducted (Stein and Carey, 1986) research evidence has consistently reported high levels of unemployment among young people leaving care, a lack of automatic entitlement to benefits at 16–17 and high poverty levels amongst this group. More recently strong links between poverty and physical and emotional ill health have been identified by young people in research studies (Broad, 1999; Monaghan and Broad, 2003). Other research studies have reported, at best a lack of clarity, and at worst, deliberate obfuscation, about financial entitlements for young people leaving care. The CLCA 2000 sought to address this major issue in a number of ways. These included transferring the responsibility for making financial payments/grants/allowances, and managing budgets, for payments for all care leavers (including 16–17-year-olds) from the benefits system to the 'responsible authority' i.e. the local social services department. The CLCA 2000 Guidance also indicated that other important sources of financial support, for example incentive or one-off payments, can be accessed by financial assessments and planning via the young person's Pathway Plan.

In this section we examine the responses of leaving care teams to questions about current services and outcomes in respect of financial support. The answers to further questions about financial support, about weekly allowances paid, about offering financial incentives (amount and criteria), leaving care grant (average amounts) and further comments about financial arrangements are also included in this section.

Context – Eligibility

CLCA 2000 Regulations and Guidance (p16).

Financial arrangements for eligible children . . . are not changed by this new legislation.

Former relevant children . . . will also continue to receive their principal support from the same sources as they did before this legislation was enacted. However they will also be able to call on assistance from their responsible authority under the duties at sections 23C and 24B(5).

Relevant children will receive their support from their responsible authority. They will no longer be eligible to claim Income Support, Jobseeker's Allowance or Housing Benefit. Levels of support will be agreed and set out in the Pathway Plan, and should be subject to the minimum standards (set out in Guidance, Chapter 9).

Context – Minimum standards

CLCA 2000 Regulations and Guidance (p64).

The responsible authority should always use its best efforts to ensure that the package of support for any individual young person is the one which will best meet their needs, wants, circumstances and abilities. Since the package will normally include help linked to specific areas, such as education, and since the responsible authority will not be bound by the DWP rules limiting accommodation options for this group of young people, the value of the package should generally be well above the level which would have been supplied through the benefits system. These minimum standards are intended to protect young people against the possibility that they might be offered inadequate assistance. They are not to be seen as the norm. No young person should receive a package for their accommodation and maintenance – whether paid directly to them or handled on their behalf by the responsible authority – which comes to less than they would have received if they had been entitled to claim Income Support or Jobseeker's Allowance,

Table 12: Service baseline levels of financial support for care leavers prior to CLCA 2000

Baseline ratings	Number and % of responses
Excellent	2 (4%)
Good	15 (31%)
Average	24 (50%)
Below average	6 (13%)
Inadequate	1 (2%)
Total number (and %) of teams responding	48 (100%)

> and Housing Benefit (or equivalent successor benefits) at the rates and with any premiums which would have applied to them and their circumstances.

Service baseline prior to the CLCA 2000

Let us start in this area of major importance with a summary of respondents' assessment of their pre-CLCA 2000 service baseline so far as financial supports for young people leaving care attending their teams are concerned.

Comment

81% of replies indicated either 'average' or 'good' for the provision of financial support – the highest percentage for these two ratings across the five areas. 63% reported either 'average' or 'below average' as their financial support baseline.

The analysis of financial supports for young people leaving care drew on a number of questions about weekly payments, financial incentives, leaving care grants, and other financial arrangements, beginning with the amount of weekly allowances paid to young people.

Weekly allowances

Respondents reported that the average weekly allowance paid to eligible, relevant and former relevant young people was £27, £43, and just £18 respectively. The most frequently listed amount paid to all eligible and relevant young people, £42.70 is the same as the weekly state allowance paid to young people seeking work. From these findings and contrary to what is stated in the Guidance (p79) the vast majority of weekly

payments are being made at the minimum 'benefits level.' In addition, and as we saw earlier, there are significantly different levels paid to eligible, relevant and former relevant young people.

Next we look at the provision of leaving care grants to young people by leaving care teams to assist young people making the gradual transition to adulthood.

> **Context – Leaving care grants**
>
> **CLCA 2000 Regulations and Guidance (p64).**
>
> Many authorities operate a system of leaving care grants ... For relevant and former relevant children, the Pathway Plan should cover the help that the responsible authority is to provide when they leave care, such as the resources needed to set up home. Authorities should be clear about what they would expect to provide for this purpose. They will also need to recognise that not all young people will be successful the first time they try to live independently, and that they may need this help more than once. (DoH, Guidance)

Leaving care grants

Respondents reported that in 42 (or 91%) of cases a leaving care grant is offered to young people. This is a higher response than for earlier surveys which found that 83% and 75%, in 1998 and 1994 respectively, indicated that they offered leaving care grants. In the current survey those 4 teams (9%) that indicated they did not offer a leaving care grant gave no explanation.

The average amount of the leaving care grant provided by leaving care teams for each young person, according to responses, is £1,156. The average amounts ranged from £400 to £2,000, and the most frequently listed amount (or mode) was £1,000, listed by fifteen leaving care teams. It is not possible to make direct comparisons with previous studies due to different counting procedures, and problems in trying to compare different amounts over long periods of time. Nevertheless whilst there remains a lack of consistency in payment levels and a wide range of grant provision, from £400 to £2,000, the evidence suggests that there are higher average levels of leaving care grants than in 1998.

Table 13: Activities supported by financial incentive payments (n = 45 respondents)

Financial incentives	*Number of replies*
Support for young people staying in training	19
Support for young people staying in education	9
Support for young people staying in employment	6
Single payments	11

Context – Sanctions and Rewards

CLCA 2000 Regulations and Guidance (p64).

A relevant child has an absolute right that accommodation and maintenance should be provided by his or her responsible authority so long as his or her welfare requires it. This duty on the responsible authority is not qualified by any requirements on the young person. However other support will normally be linked to the Pathway Plan. Councils may wish to set up a system of rewards and incentives linked, for example, to attendance for education. In this way support will be given for specific purposes and the reviews of the Plan will make sure that this is working as intended. If this is not the case, the Plan may need to be revised to reflect the new situation. . . . A good parent uses rewards and incentives to encourage a child in achievement. In more difficult circumstances though a parent would not make children homeless, or cease to feed them, if they behaved badly. However the parent might apply sanctions such as loss of privileges or would withdraw funding if it was being abused.

Financial incentives

The survey found that 43 (90%) of all teams offer financial incentives. The following table, Table 13, shows for what activities leaving care teams (n = 45) pay incentives to young people.

Comment and further findings

Table 13 shows that 75% (34) of *all* financial incentives are paid to encourage, reward, and sustain young people, wherever possible, in education/employment/training. This finding provides an excellent example of the consequence and impact of government policy and funding structures. By this is meant the combination of values (rewards/sanctions for attending education/training, employment) policy, through DoH Guidance backed up by dedicated funding. The availability of financial incentives, via *Quality Protects* funding mechanisms and the switch of monies from the benefits system to social services has enabled leaving care teams to link welfare and financial policies, and provide a much clearer financial payment structure for supporting young people leaving care. These findings do *not* confirm that the young people have sufficient levels of funding, or payments. However a *system* of grants, incentive payments, one-off payments and financial assessments for all young people leaving care has been created by the CLCA 2000.

Examples of financial incentives

- £15 per week to remain in education/training.
- Incentives paid for anything to do with education/employment/training.
- £20 per week living independently on low income.
- £50 vouchers for clothing if in education/employment/training.
- £20 per week education premium for 16/17-year-old (over 18 £10 per week).
- £70.34 (higher rate) is payable to young people in employment/education.

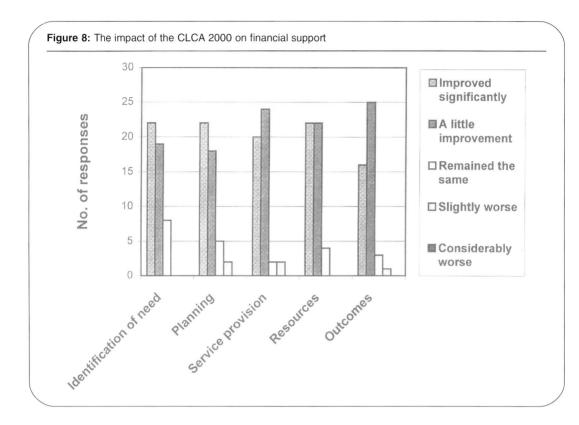

Figure 8: The impact of the CLCA 2000 on financial support

- £10 per week for 80% college/training attendance.
- £10 per week for relevant young people in education/training.
- £30 per week post 18 if still in further education.

Examples of single payments

- £100 bonus for those in E/E/T.
- £30 per week for those in further education/training/employment (except those receiving educational maintenance allowances).
- £72.70 per week guaranteed income.
- £30 per week for college attendance.
- £15 for each new staff interview involving young people.
- £10/£15 for young people participating in consultation events/research.

Service levels after the CLCA 2000

Figure 8 shows the impact of the CLCA 2000 on financial supports for young people leaving care.

Comment

Respondents reported that the CLCA 2000 has had a positive impact on the assessment, planning and delivery of financial supports for young people leaving care. Teams reporting that matters had either 'improved significantly', or 'shown a little improvement' (whether in terms of identification of need, planning, resources, service delivery or outcomes) accounted for between 83% and 92% of all responses.

How to further improve financial matters?

In the West Midlands study (WMCCC, 2003: 18) the young people identified ways in which advice and help on financial matters could be improved, as follows:

- Written information to complement other advice.
- More time with advisors to talk through and clarify issues.
- Continued and follow-up support rather than one-off advice.

Discussion

This chapter has highlighted the results of the national leaving care survey across four key service areas, education/employment/training, accommodation, health and financial resources. There are positive signs that education/ employment/training is improving in terms of outcomes for care leavers. In turn this should both enhance their opportunities for social inclusion and, in many cases, produce a more positive effect on their health and well being. It was also found that those leaving care services which already had established staff numbers, and multi-disciplinary teams and high staff: young person ratios enjoyed better education/ employment/training results than more poorly resourced teams. It was also most noticeable that a majority of positive findings regarding education concerned plans to work more closely or collaboratively, rather than either more resources or better outcomes. In other words the positive health and well being outcomes that can flow from improved education/employment/ training were still being planned to come on stream in a majority of teams, rather than in place and influencing outputs and outcomes.

Research and good practice guidance suggest the following are key factors so far as the education of care leavers is concerned:

- Placement stability and continuity.
- Intensive compensatory inputs (for example from mentors, employers/training organisations).
- The development of a 'valuing and promoting education' culture whilst children are looked after.
- Seeing 'engagement' with education as integral to emotional stability and development of self-esteem.

At the policy level there are problems of funding 19-year-old care leavers, usually late developers as a result of their background and being in the care system, in further education. It is sometimes as if education for care leavers is primarily defined in terms of improvements to formal qualifications, rather than it also being about informal learning, self-esteem, personal and social awareness, and social and vocational skills.

Next and in relation to accommodation it was found again that those teams or services that were already performing well and highly rated or at least rated as above average were by far the more likely to show steady improvements than those which started from a lower baseline level. In the latter cases the momentum for change remained slower and peaked more at the 'slight improvement' or 'remained the same' levels of post CLCA 2000 change. When planning accommodation to meet the needs of young people leaving care, evidence indicates that the involvement of the young person in the assessment and decision making, to be conducted in a planned way, together with 'a support package' are likely to be more effective than other approaches. It is further recommended that if temporary 'supported accommodation' is considered, that full checks are made on service providers, and that they be properly supported, i.e. as well as the young person. For those young people who move away outside their home areas it is especially important that there are agreed protocols about high standard services agreed between authorities. There was little sign of these being in place outside a few areas of England, most notably Northwest England (Parsons, 2002). In the survey it was found there remained a lack of suitable accommodation for care leavers.

The poorest and lowest number of responses were in relation to health, both at the baseline and post CLCA 2000 evaluation points. In the sense that it can be argued that 'health' is not the business of leaving care teams, this is not a surprise. However since the CLCA 2000 this argument does not hold in that leaving care teams are legally responsible for producing Pathway Plans including ways of identifying and addressing health needs. On the other hand they are required to identify needs in partnership with health stakeholders and perhaps it is more to the NHS, especially CAMHS, that we need to look about the inadequacy of resources and priority.

Lastly and in relation to financial supports it was found that the most frequent average weekly payments for all eligible and relevant young people was £42, the weekly rate paid to unemployed young people. There are improvements about the planning and delivery of financial payments to care leavers since the CLCA 2000 but the payment levels still remain low, at state benefit levels. It was also found that a *system* of grants, incentive payments, one-off payments and financial assessments has been created by the CLCA 2000 and this has improved the financial circumstances for care leavers compared with their dire, uneven and poor financial circumstances prior to the CLCA 2000.

Again this will have helped, directly or indirectly their position viz a viz social exclusion.

Having produced the research findings about four key issues at the policy and service impact levels the next chapter records the ways in which the mechanisms introduced by the CLCA 2000 for undertaking needs assessments and planning services were taking shape after that Act's introduction. The next chapter also begins to move beyond the policy issues towards those concerned with practice developments.

In particular there will be an emphasis on the identification and provision of services for specific groups, the role of personal advisors and anti-discriminatory practice developments.

Chapter Five

Responding to the Challenges of Anti-discriminatory Practice and Service Planning

Introduction

The aim of this chapter is to report on the national research study's findings about specific mechanisms introduced in the CLCA 2000 for fulfilling its aims of improving the health and well being of young people leaving care. This chapter will pay particular reference to the introduction of Needs Assessments, Personal Advisors and Pathway Plans. In so doing it will also make reference to other post CLCA 2000 studies, such as those by Hai and Williams (2004) and WMCCC (2002). In order for the health and well being of all care leavers to be assessed and improved it is vital that post-CLCA 2000 leaving care policy and practice developments are properly funded and show signs of improvement. This is especially the case for the specific groups of young people discussed here.

The chapter's focus will be on examining the provision of leaving care services for specific groups of young people entitled to leaving care services under the provisions of the CLCA 2000. These are care leavers remanded to local authority accommodation, those released after having served a custodial sentence, care leavers who either have a physical disability or a learning difficulty, and unaccompanied asylum seekers leaving care. It is especially important to examine issues about service eligibility, entitlements and outcomes for these specific groups of young people who previous research and practice have identified as either missing out on or receiving inadequate services. Young parent care leavers, another group previously identified as having particular, and often unmet needs, are discussed in Part Three of this book in one dedicated chapter. We begin then by summarising service assessment and provision for those named groups as evidenced in our study.

It will be recalled from Chapter 3 that 13% of the young people attending the 52 leaving care projects in the national research study were black or mixed race. In terms of special needs 3% of all the young people were reported as having a physical disability, 8% a learning difficulty, and 7% had been statemented. Information was not collected in this study about the number of asylum seekers leaving care at each project. However, according to the DfES (2003: 14, quoted in Hai and Williams, 90) an estimated 7% of all care leavers in England are asylum seekers with the proportion in London's leaving care teams being much higher, in some cases accounting for anything between 20%-50% of a team's caseload.

Before presenting practitioners' responses to questions about leaving care policies and practice since CLCA 2000 about young people who are disabled, and unaccompanied asylum seekers leaving care, let me present the CLCA 2000's regulations and guidance about those two groups.

Services for specific groups

Context – Disability

CLCA 2000 Regulations and Guidance (p13).

Disabled young people may well face more barriers than other young people who are being cared for or leaving care, and may also have needs specifically related to impairment. It is essential to ensure that these needs are met when preparing these young people for leaving care and subsequently, providing aftercare. At the same time, care must be taken to ensure that these young people do not fail to achieve their full potential as a result of under-expectation on the part of those caring for them.

Context – Unaccompanied asylum-seeking children

CLCA 2000 Regulations and Guidance (p13).

Unaccompanied asylum-seeking children (UASC) are covered by the Children Act 1989 and the new provisions introduced by the CLCA 2000 in exactly the same way as other children in this country. However they will also have an immigration status – applying for asylum, acceptance as a refugee, granted exceptional leave to remain or refused leave to remain – which will need to be taken into account by councils providing services for them. The Home Office has responsibility for immigration issues . . . It aims to resolve all asylum applications within six months; that is, two months for the initial application and four months for any subsequent appeals. Any young person who enters the country, as an unaccompanied minor claiming asylum should therefore normally have their case resolved while they are still a minor. While they are under 18 the local authority will be responsible under the CLCA 2000 for their care and accommodation.

Respondents were asked to record the level of their post CLCA 2000 practice in respect of their work with young people remanded to local authority accommodation, young people post-custody, young disabled people, unaccompanied asylum seeker, and young parents. As described in the previous chapter respondents were provided with a choice of five ratings (ranging from 'significantly improved' to 'significantly worsened').

For all of these four groups of young people and when 'identifying the needs of young people' 'service planning,' or 'service provision' a majority of respondents (55–58%) reported that practice had 'remained the same' since the CLCA 2000. Also for these six groups of young people and when commenting on 'resources' or 'outcomes' a majority of respondents (63–66%) reported that matters had also 'remained the same' since the CLCA 2000.

In other words when one shifted from 'identification of need' and 'planning' (i.e. intentions) to 'service delivery' and 'outcome' functions a significantly higher percentage of respondents reported that there had been **no change** since the CLCA 2000.

The following are the limited answers given from respondents who were asked about who is providing services for young people with a disability, unaccompanied asylum seekers and young people on remand if the leaving care teams

in which they work are not providing a service to those young people. These answers help to illustrate the anti-discriminatory work that is being done and identify who is undertaking it.

Young people with a disability – *examples:*

- 'Referred to or joint work with children with disabilities team' (8 answers).
- 'Young disabled people in the disabled team'.
- 'Decision still to be made on how service for children with disabilities might change. i.e. the fit between transition arrangements and the CLCA 2000.
- 'Transition team to adult services'.
- 'Specialist team- but problems arise over diagnosis and gatekeeping'.
- 'Joint work with special needs team'.

Young people who are unaccompanied asylum seekers – *examples:*

- 'Joint work with asylum seekers team' (4 answers).
- 'No experience of working with asylum seekers' (4 answers).
- 'Leaving care team (if legally entitled to a service)'.
- 'Personal advisor for asylum seekers-we expect improvement'.
- 'Asylum seekers post 16 would be referred to family support services unless they had been looked after'.
- 'Refugee forum'.

Young people on remand – *examples:*

- Referred to joint work with Youth Offending Team (11 answers).
- Duty team look after remands (2).

Next we invited leaving care services to describe 'the ways in which anti-discriminatory issues are systematically operationalised' in their work, whether in work with parents, or lesbian/gay, disabled, black/mixed race young people. The aim of this question was to establish levels of awareness, and activity about this subject and detailed practice answers were not sought.

In the discussion that follows, the term anti-discrimination is used, rather than equal opportunities, for a very important reason which requires explanation. It seems that in terms of its popular usage, rather than its intention perhaps, the term 'equal opportunities' has become an umbrella term, often expressed as somewhat passive written organisational aims covering a range of intentions. In short it has lost the punch it had, or strove to have, in the 1970s and 1980s. By contrast the term anti-discriminatory, meaning against discrimination (like anti-apartheid or anti-war) indicates **actively** working for change, here against all forms of discrimination and oppression. It is its active ingredient and messages that are crucial. The main themes of anti-discriminatory practice (adapted from Thompson, 1994) are:

- A recognition that discrimination occurs, usually systematically and structurally, within organisations, as well as at the practice level, for a range of groups.
- The recognition that social work is a political activity in terms of legislative powers but also in sets of power relations.
- Traditional social work relates primarily to the level of the 'case' and not wider issues, or the three levels of the personal, the structural and cultural.
- A recognition that work with young people needs to take place at the personal, and cultural and structural levels to be fully integrated and anti-discriminatory.
- At the personal level the emphasis will be on personal empowerment and political and social education.
- If they do not already do so, staff require anti-discriminatory training to fully understand what constitutes discrimination and anti-discriminatory practice and policies.
- The actions of staff, project teams and organisations will either challenge or support discrimination.

Ince also argues strongly for a strengths-based approach in working with black and dual heritage young people and points to ways in which resilience can be built up and developed (Ince, 2004).

In drawing up the questionnaire the view was taken that anti-discriminatory work and policies apply to a number of discriminated against groups, which can be listed separately, including women, parents, black people, disabled people, people who are gay or lesbian, or discussed together. Rather than specifying particular groups the view was taken that the two specific questions about anti-discrimination should be expressed in general terms, allowing the

respondents to interpret the question in accord with their understandings and priorities. It was also felt necessary to emphasise the point to all projects, even those with nil or few black young people, (often voluntary organisation projects based in counties), that anti-discrimination also, perhaps especially, applies to their work. It was the aim of obtaining as wide a range of anti-discriminatory practice examples and understandings as possible that underpinned the approach taken. However despite, this aim of encouraging wide ranging responses, different group's answers tended to focus largely on work with black young people. Respondents also often regarded 'Anti-discriminatory work' as synonymous with 'special needs work' with single parents although only six respondents identified work with young parents through the provision of crèche facilities. This modest finding suggests a need to identify and share research, practice and development work about working with young parents. However, this is described in Part Three where 33 young people who are parents or parents-to-be discuss their health and well being experiences and services, rather than here, given the paucity of responses in the national care leavers study about this particular group.

Anti-discriminatory policies and practice

Whilst anti-discriminatory issues are discussed throughout this book as an integral part of good practice which improves health and well-being, the view was taken that distinct elements to this work do exist and can be identified separately. As long ago as 1991 the *Patterns and Outcomes* report concluded, in respect of ethnic minority children in public care:

> *The future challenge for social workers and managers will be to move from rhetoric or lip service to action. Racial and ethnic issues must be raised to their proper place alongside those of culture, class and gender without ignoring, exaggerating or distorting any of these essential elements in each child's individuality and personal history.*
>
> (DoH, 1991: 17)

The Children Act 1989 recognises that Britain is a multi-cultural society and that cultural background and beliefs are important. For each child and young person the importance of culture, language, racial origin and religion must be considered with other factors relating to their welfare (Section 22 (5)). In that this section of the Children Act 1989 represents, to this author's knowledge, the first reference in child care legislation incorporating the recognition that Britain is a multi-cultural society, that legislation represents something of a symbolic milestone. Yet it seems to this author that this section and the guidance in this anti-discrimination area (see the guidance, DoH, para. 7.52 on enabling certain groups to develop their self-esteem) is very weak. Essentially the above section places a duty on local authorities to adopt an approach that is sensitive to different groups' needs. This approach in relation to ethnicity is often described as an 'ethnically sensitive' approach, and is a most important one to emphasise for individual practice.

Yet this approach contrasts with an anti-discriminatory approach, which emphasises the structural and institutional, as well as the individual, nature of staff-client interaction and discrimination. Such an approach then calls for institutional responses, and not simply on case-by-case and individual responses. It requires not simply practice changes by workers to be more sensitive to clients' needs but requires institutional changes as well. Based on experiences from the criminal justice field (see this author, 1991) it is also recognised that such changes are complex and demanding on all institutions, especially those consisting mostly of white staff. The CLCA 2000 regulations did not go any further than those accompanying the Children Act 1989 in respect of issues of culture, race and anti-discrimination, as the following regulations and guidance demonstrates.

Context – Culture, race

CLCA 2000 Regulations and Guidance (p5, para 7).

Key principles of the Children Act include: taking into account the views of young people, consulting with them and keeping them informed; giving due consideration to young people's race, culture, religion and linguistic background; the importance of families and working with parents; safeguarding and promoting the welfare of young people they are looking after; and the recognition of inter-agency responsibility.

At the organisational level the Race Relations (Amendment) Act 2000 requires that public authorities in carrying out their functions shall have *due regard* to the need to eliminate unlawful racial discrimination, promote equality of opportunity, and promote good race relations between people of different racial groups. Specific duties at the organisational level include the following:

- Preparing and publishing a Race Equality Scheme.
- Assessing which functions or policies are relevant.
- Arranging to monitor adverse impact.
- Assessing and consulting on impact, arranging to publish results.
- Providing access to information.
- Arranging for staff training.
- Implementing measures to monitor and reduce race discrimination in employment.

Young people leaving care often face systematic discrimination and face social exclusion in terms of employment opportunities, accommodation, education and participation. Young people who are black, mixed race, or who have physical disabilities or learning difficulties, parents, gay/lesbian young people or unaccompanied asylum-seekers also face discrimination. In this survey respondents were invited to respond to the question 'in what ways are anti-discriminatory issues systematically operationalised in their work? Respondents were encouraged to respond to issues about parents, lesbian/gay, disabled, and black/mixed race young people. Responses were limited and they are summarised in Table 14. Three levels of intervention are identified: local authority policy, team, and case-by-case levels.

Comment

The 1:2 ratio of anti-discriminatory work policies (excluding 'no answers') conducted at *team level*, compared with the total number of answers, illustrates the powerful role that teams and the individuals in them can play in terms of anti-discriminatory practice. Anti-discriminatory work at the *policy level* accounts for just 1 in 5 of all answers. This finding suggests that anti-discriminatory policies have much less impact on practice than team policies and case-by-case decisions, although the two should be directly linked (also see Thompson, 103 on this

Table 14: Anti-discriminatory practice and policies in leaving care work

Anti-discriminatory topic work/policies	Level at which anti-discriminatory work described	No. responses
	Local authority policy level	(12)
Anti-discriminatory work is guided /led by local authority policy		8
Culture/values of organisation (general)		4
	Team level	(30)
Young parents/crèche		6
Staff balance		6
Team discussions		6
Young people involvement/consultation		4
Gay/lesbian initiatives		4
User guide		2
Disability work		2
	Case-by-case	(16)
Work with asylum seekers		7
Work with black/Asian young people		6
Individual needs assessment/supervision		3
No answers		(12)
Total		70

point). These ratios about anti-discriminatory practice, team and local authority policy levels are virtually the same as those from the 1998 survey (Broad, 1998: 180) suggesting that anti-discriminatory levers predominantly operate at team and individual levels, with all the discretionary elements and inconsistencies that can then follow. As Colman warns, about social care organisations in relation to the Race Relations (Amendment) Act 2000, 'They now need to show they have moved from paper compliance to showing evidence of real outcomes' (quoted in *Community Care*, 2003).

Also there were both *more answers* and *more confident answers* when the leaving care teams were working with 10% plus black or mixed race young people than when working with just a few. For an example of the latter in one team (county team based in the North of England) with just two black or mixed race young people from a total of 115 young people attending the team the respondent replied:

All young people who meet the requirements under the CLCA 2000 or Children Act 1989 (S24) receive a statutory service irrespective of ethnicity, sexuality or race.

At six other teams (in London) where 30–50% of the young people attending them were either black or mixed race, answers were both more comprehensive and confident. For example:

- We have a range of translated information for care leavers where the second language is English.
- There is a special form for unaccompanied asylum seekers to highlight needs backed up by good practice guide.
- We make constant efforts to mitigate anti-discriminatory effect of asylum and immigration policy and practice.
- We attempt to recruit team members whose ethnicity/race/culture /religion reflects that of service users.
- A black counsellor is available (spot purchase).
- Anti-discriminatory practice has to be operationalised through Pathway Plans and needs assessment.
- All individuals are responded to on a needs-led basis and Pathway Plans incorporate culture and diversity.
- Black cases panel.

The major difference between the 1998 and the current national study is that unaccompanied asylum seekers did not feature in the former study at all, and the current study shows the considerable impact that unaccompanied asylum seekers are having on some leaving care services. For some leaving care teams (especially in London but also elsewhere) working with unaccompanied asylum seekers has generated important and complicated workload, resource, and planning issues (see Broad and Robbins, forthcoming). For example, one of the responding London borough's social services department's reported working with 121 asylum seekers aged between 16–23. Not all of these are entitled to receiving leaving care services. Nevertheless that same borough's leaving care team's workload included an estimated 30–40% who were asylum seekers. The key care planning issue concerns the legal status of asylum seekers and their entitlements to a service under the CLCA 2000 and how this relates to their legal status post-18 (to be returned to their country of origin) under immigration and asylum legislation (Home Office).

There have been real concerns about entitlements for unaccompanied asylum seekers and the resource and planning implications, the former pointing to 'Potential shortfalls in leaving care costs' (Association of Directors of Social Services, 2004). The 'Hillingdon Judgement' (2003) did not change the law regarding the Children Act 1989 or the CLCA 2000. Therefore the need to assess continues to apply equally to unaccompanied asylum seekers as to any other child/young person. The 'Hillingdon judgement' upheld the policy spelt out in the circular *Guidance on Accommodating Children in Need and their Families* (DoH, 2003b). This means that it will be important to assess each individual on a case-by-case basis, preferably agree it with the young person and record the assessment carefully. Arguably the circumstances of unaccompanied asylum seekers (without an adult to provide them with parental support) mean that the likelihood is that most of them should become accommodated.

The above circular (DoH, 2003b) recognises that young people aged 16 plus can not be compelled to accept accommodation under Section 20. Although young people might decline to be accommodated it will be very important that where this occurs the local authority can demonstrate that the full implications of declining accommodation under Section 20 are explained. One of these is that the young person concerned will not later become former relevant and so be entitled to care leaving services in the future.

In relation to the study and anti-discriminatory work, teams were asked to describe ways in which this work was conducted, and 'young people with a disability or a learning difficulty' was listed as one of four prompt areas. In response, only two out of the 76 answers made any mention of young people with a disability or learning difficulties. Whilst most young people leaving care with a physical disability may not be referred to leaving care teams the overall figure reported here was 3%. In addition 8% of the young people attending the leaving care teams in this national study were reported as having a learning difficulty.

The findings from this part of the research study suggest that anti-discriminatory practice/strategies are mostly initiated at team level, reflect local circumstances and organisational cultures and are predominately seen in terms of direct work with black and minority ethnic children, unaccompanied asylum seekers, and the composition of staff teams. These pragmatic anti-discriminatory responses contrast with the implementation and interpretation of organisational policies.

Next we look at another key area of policy and practice in relation to promoting the health and well-being of young people leaving care, namely the provision of support for young people in placement at sixteen years of age. In this part we examine respondents' answers about post CLCA 2000 developments both about re-accommodating young people in placement after sixteen years of age, and about changes in policy and practice which encourages young people to stay in placement. Again the answers to both these questions adds to our understanding of how the needs of care leavers are being addressed since the CLCA 2000.

Supporting post-16 placements

Re-accommodating young people

Respondents were asked to indicate whether practice towards re-accommodating young people to stay in placement after 16 has changed since the Act. 35% (14) of respondents reported that practice and attitudes practice towards re-accommodating young people to stay in placement post 16 *had* changed since the CLCA 2000.

The comments from respondents about re-accommodating young people included the following:

Positive comments:

● Improved slightly though this area had a good record prior to legislation.

- We have not discharged at 16 in the past and have built up a supported lodgings scheme approved under fostering regulations. That has enabled us to keep young people in the system in home cases into their 20s.
- With case responsibility for 16 plus with leaving care teams there are now more consistent decisions.

Negative comments:

- Still unlikely that young people will be re-accommodated.
- Very little change.
- It is no better – does not provide the financial disincentive which was envisaged.

Encouragement to young people to stay in placement post-16

The answers to questions about whether practice about enabling *young people to stay in placement post-16* had changed since the CLCA 2000 were also disappointing in that only 57% (21) of teams reported that this had happened.

Comments from respondents about young people staying in placement included:

- Needs of young people are now being considered.
- We have about same number of young people staying on.
- This is changing – the problem is getting social work field staff and residential staff to change attitudes to caring for longer.
- We encourage the young people to stay with carers anyway.
- Young people continue to be accommodated in placement post 16 as the favoured option.
- It appears more and more effort is being made to accommodate young people to 18.
- A great awareness has always existed but ring-fenced money has helped to retain specific placements.
- Young people are definitely staying in placement longer.
- New guidelines enabling young people to remain with carers post 16 introduced this year.

In other words in only a minority of cases have the 52 leaving care teams policies and practice encouraging young people to stay in placement changed since the CLCA 2000. On the other hand there have been some positive changes, in 57% of cases concerning young people being

re-accommodated and 35% being encouraged to stay in placement longer. So once again the study points to a range of mixed results about how the CLCA 2000 is being implemented. Linked to policy issues about post 16 arrangements is the matter of who holds case responsibility for children and young people leaving care.

Case responsibility for young people leaving care

The context for this question is about whether a social worker or a member of a leaving care team carries the statutory responsibility for a young person's case. According to the Guidance (DoH, 2001a, para 51):

> *The responsible authority might expect the personal advisor to take charge of setting up the review and to be responsible for recording the outcomes. However this need not always be so. It will be a matter for each local authority how it runs its leaving care service and it might be that someone other than the personal advisor has case responsibility – especially in the case of an eligible child who will still have a social worker. Under such circumstances it might be that the case holder is best placed to run the review. Authorities may have dedicated review staff who perform this function for all looked-after children and care leavers.*

The study sought to establish how case responsibility arrangements had changed as a result of the CLCA 2000. 39% (19) of all teams (n = 49) stated that they 'always' held case responsibility, a further 47% (23) of teams reported that they 'sometimes' held case responsibility, and 12% (6) 'did not hold' case responsibility. Asked whether these current arrangements had changed since the CLCA 2000, 56% (23) of all teams said 'no' and 44% (18) said 'yes.'

Respondents were also asked to complete a 'comments box' about this topic. Table 15, summarises those responses, sub dividing them into 'positive', 'negative', or 'unclear' groupings. As Table 15 shows, the number of negative and positive responses were fairly balanced. Overall, respondents held mixed views about changes about who holds case responsibility.

Comment

The study found that there was variation about who holds case responsibility, and it is not known whether any one way is better in terms of

Table 15: Teams views about case responsibility

Team views	No. replies
Positive changes	(17)
Can plan and better manage decision making/prevents drift	11
Better inter-agency work	1
Better support for 18–21	2
More personal advisors involved/more positive	3
Negative changes	(14)
Less support for 18+	2
More work	4
Not happened due to shortage of social workers	3
Social workers keen to transfer – regardless of need	3
Confusion about who supports who	1
Restructure of services needed	1
Mixed/unclear responses	(11)
Ever more 16+s placed with leaving care team	6
More responsibility	2
Priority for allocation still lies with looked after team	1
Significant that young person is existing only by looked after team and have other input not just social services department	1
Already had case responsibility	1
Total	42

young people's outcomes, than another. What is clear is that there are important workload issues arising from the transfer of case responsibility and that the Guidance seems to assume that sufficient resources are either already available or can be made available. The key factor for those leaving care teams that regarded the holding of case responsibility as a positive matter, is that, alongside the transfer of financial supports to social services from social security, it enables better management planning with young people to be undertaken. Where there are insufficient resources the transfer of case responsibility appears to have become another logistical problem for leaving care teams to juggle. What follows are typical quoted comments made about transfer of case responsibility by those teams holding it:

- Good in theory bad in practice.
- Increased responsibility.
- Quicker decision making.
- More of an interface with foster carers.
- Some conflict between social work and personal advisors.
- Even more crucial that referral /transfer system is effective.
- Pressure on teams to take on even more young people.
- Young people referring by age not by need.

- Change attitude of social services to do Pathway Plan before 16.

Having examined respondents' views about the critical areas of provision and encouragement for young people to remain in placement, or be re-accommodated, and about case responsibility and case management, we now turn to other major new areas introduced in the CLCA 2000. These concern the provision of personal advisors, and the undertaking of needs assessments and Pathway Plans.

Personal advisors, needs assessments, and pathway plans

Context – personal advisors

CLCA 2000 Regulations and Guidance Chapters 1, 3, 5, Schedule 12.

It is the duty of the local authority to appoint a personal advisor for all eligible children, relevant children or former relevant children (S19 (b), 23(b), 23 (c)). This may include specialist leaving care scheme support, support by carers and social workers, and support by youth workers, befrienders, mentors or volunteers. This is underlined by the introduction of personal advisors under the 2000 Act (Aims and objectives, 1.9 (h)).

It is expected that in the majority of cases the young person's advisor as set out in the 2000 Act will also act as the Connexions Service personal advisor for these young people, and a common foundation training course is being developed. Local authorities will need to consider in each case the issue of continuity for looked-after children, first at the age of 16 when the requirement in the 2000 Act comes into effect, and again at 20 when they leave the Connexions Service client group (Chapter 3 paragraph 29).

In relation to the assessment of young people's needs the views of the personal advisor shall be taken into account (Chapter 5 Regulation 7).

Functions – (12)(a) To provide advice (including practical advice) and support. 12 (2)(b) where applicable, to participate in his [the child's or young person's] assessment and the preparation of his Pathway Plan. 12 (2)(c) To participate in reviews of the Pathway Plan. 12 (2)(d) To liaise with the responsible authority in the implementation of the Pathway Plan. 12 (2)(e) To co-ordinate the provision of services and to take reasonable steps to ensure that he [the child or young person] makes use of such services. 12 (2)(f) To keep informed about his [the child's or young person's] progress and well being. 12 (2)(g) To keep written records of contact with him [the child or young person]. (Chapter 6)

Personal advisors

Respondents were invited to answer specific questions about personal advisors. Only 60% of the 3,233 relevant, eligible, and former relevant young people entitled to a personal advisor were reported as having one. In addition only 56% of respondents reported that their personal advisors had been provided with a written job description, suggesting that this important role is not yet sufficiently clear enough to be committed to writing. The survey also found that where there were personal advisors, the majority, 65%, were already leaving care workers, 27% were social

workers, 5% Connexions staff, and 3% 'other'. In the survey none of the respondents indicated that the leaving care personal advisors were also Connexions personal advisors to those same young people, as the Guidance suggests should be the case (Guidance, Chapter 3, paragraph 9).

Where personal advisors were in post in a leaving care team the ratio of young people to advisor was 20:1. To fulfil the complex co-ordinating, support, planning and liaison functions laid out in the Guidance (Schedule 12) such a low staff: young person ratio seems totally inadequate and unrealistic.

Comment

It is disappointing that some eighteen months since the CLCA 2000 was introduced, and with personal advisors being flagged up as a requirement months before the Act's introduction, that only 60% of all young people were described as having an allocated personal advisor. Where there are personal advisors in post the ratio of 20 young people to each one seems a demanding one for the staff member and could provide real frustrations for young people needing help and support and guidance. It seems that the majority of leaving care teams have simply absorbed this extra duty, and this maybe on pragmatic grounds, due to lack of funding/choice or it may be a deliberate policy. 'Who is best suited to be a personal advisor?' was always a difficult question when the CLCA 2000 was drafted and discussed. There is a case for arguing that unless a personal advisor is simply a dedicated person to advise the young person then its commissioning, monitoring and networking roles probably require someone outside the line management or supervision of the young person. The personal advisor also has, or should have, a vital role in relation to needs assessments and Pathway Plans.

Needs assessments and pathway plans

Context – Needs Assessments and Pathway Plans

CLCA 2000 Regulations and Guidance (p41).

All eligible, relevant and former relevant young people are entitled to both a needs assessment and a Pathway Plan (13)

Paragraph 19B(4) of Schedule 2 requires the responsible authority to carry out a needs assessment for each eligible child with a view to determining what advice, assistance and support they should provide both while they are looking after him or her and when they have ceased to look after him or her. The needs assessment will then be the basis for preparing the Pathway Plan. As a looked-after child, an eligible child will already have had a needs assessment in order to formulate a Care Plan, and this should form the basis for the assessment required under the 2000 Act.

Section 23B(3) makes the same provision for a relevant child for whom this has not already been done while he or she was being looked after.

The Pathway Plan should be pivotal to the process whereby young people map out their future, articulating their aspirations and identifying interim goals along the way to realising their ambitions. It will also play a critical part in making the new arrangements contained within the 2000 Act work. Each young person will be central to drawing up their own plan, setting out their own goals and identifying with their personal advisor how the local authority will help them. The authority should work to ensure that the Plan (Regulation 8, paragraph 20), applies.

Respondents were asked to estimate the percentage of eligible, relevant and former relevant young people who had a comprehensive needs assessment and, separately, Pathway Plan. Earlier we saw that the leaving care teams were working with 1829 eligible, 645 relevant, 760 former relevant, and 1366 qualifying young people.

It was reported that on average 61% of all eligible, relevant and former relevant young people have a needs assessment. In addition it was reported that 70% of all eligible, relevant and former relevant have Pathway Plans completed on them. This compares with identical research findings elsewhere, that 61% of eligible, relevant and former relevant young people have a Pathway Plan, with 46% stating that they did not have a copy of their Pathway Plan (WMCCC, 2002:11).

In identifying whose responsibility it is to complete the needs assessment, responses indicated that it was predominantly someone in the specialist leaving care, adolescent or 16 plus team. In identifying whose responsibility it is to complete the Pathway Plan a range of answers were given which generally indicated that whilst the child is looked after, it is the social services looked after team's responsibility, and then the leaving care team's responsibility for after-care. However, in a significant number of cases it was indicated that it was the personal advisor's role to complete the Pathway Plan.

All eligible, relevant, and former relevant young people are entitled to a comprehensive needs assessment and Pathway Plan, and needs assessment and pathway planning are both a legal requirement as well as being pivotal to accessing funding and services. Therefore it is especially disappointing to find that an average of only 61% are receiving this assessment and a higher percentage, 70% having a Pathway Plan. If there is not a sound assessment then this would seem to invalidate the Pathway Plan. Hai and Williams study (2004) found considerable variation between local authorities regarding their completion of Pathway Plans, and emphasised the critical importance of the timing of such plans and the need for flexibility.

Out of borough/county arrangements

For young people moving out of the area to another local authority there have been long-standing concerns that services for them are at best poor and inconsistent, and at worst, not provided at all. Additionally, since a legal judgement in the late 1990s, the originating local authority is now legally required to fund the provision of services for a young person leaving care moving into another local authority's area, and out-of county placements are expensive, compared with local placements.

In the survey respondents were asked to indicate the ways in which their teams/ local authorities responded to young people moving in and out of area. A significant number (24) of leaving care teams studied either had 'in place' (17) or 'were developing' (7) inter-area protocols. A further significant minority of responses (14) indicated that they either operated on 'a case-by-case basis' (11) or had 'reciprocal arrangements' (3).

Comments made about out of county arrangements included:

- This creates more demands for services.
- This is a major issue in our area.
- Good when there is an agreement but it creates problems when there is not.

In North West England, the East Midlands and elsewhere there have been positive moves made to introduce inter-area protocols, and these are supported by the Department on its *Quality Protects* Leaving Care Project web site.

Discussion

For the majority of those young people on remand/young offenders, young disabled people, unaccompanied asylum seekers qualifying for leaving care service, service provision has remained at the same, unsatisfactory level since the CLCA 2000. Anti-discrimination work takes place more on a case-by-case basis than as a result of organisational imperatives and there were many examples of good individual practice.

Extra encouragement since the CLCA 2000 given to young people to remain in placement post 16 was occurring in 57% of cases. However, just 35% had introduced changes to enable young people to be re-accommodated. There was a range of ways in which case responsibility duties were carried out. Yet it is in the key areas of Personal Advisors (only 61% of young people have one allocated) needs assessments (60% have had one) and Pathway Plans (70% of young people have a completed one) where the implementation of the CLCA 2000 is showing very uneven and gradual progress.

What are the implications of these key findings for the well being of young people leaving care in terms of the stability, funding, comprehensiveness and effectiveness of leaving care service provision? They strongly suggest that for an estimated 50% of young people attending the 52 leaving care teams in the study, and according to a variety of indicators discussed here, the structures and arrangements designed to lift and improve the life chances of care leavers are still not in place. Despite modest increases in staffing for leaving care teams and better staff: young person ratios identified earlier, the reasons given for these strategic and operational problems and difficulties are a combination of lack of sufficient funding, funding spent on looked after children rather than leaving care services, and increased caseloads.

In this chapter we have examined in some considerable detail specific post CLCA 2000 changes, implementation problems and achievements. In the following chapter we will draw back from presenting detailed findings to providing a summary overview of the national leaving care research study's findings, especially in so far as they impact on the health and well being of care leavers.

Chapter Six

Progress and Challenges Following the CLCA 2000: A Summary

Introduction

The three aims of this chapter are to:

1. Collate and summarise the national research study's findings about the impact of the CLCA 2000 on services for care leavers.
2. Examine the key progress and problem areas facing leaving care services.
3. Begin to gauge whether changes to leaving care services are likely to have improved the health and well being of care leavers.

Comparing pre- and post-CLCA leaving care services

We saw in the previous chapters in this part of the book about the national leaving care study how leaving care services provided a baseline and post-CLCA 2000 rating across four service areas. Whilst the area of health is a particular focus of this book, the other three service areas are also of critical importance so far as well being is concerned. The wider issue of whether or not care leavers are more or less likely to feature in future social exclusion statistics as a result of the CLCA 2000 will not be discussed here but in the book's final chapter, after further research evidence and findings are presented.

Table 16 illustrates and compares the pre-and post-CLCA 2000 ratings across those four key service areas.

'Education/employment/training' and 'health' can be seen as the poorer performing areas, making nil or minor improvement or in the case of health, getting worse. Much higher levels of service provision and improvements were reported in the remaining areas of 'accommodation' and 'financial support'.

Progress and problems

Finally leaving care teams were asked to list and prioritise the five areas where they considered they had made the most progress since the CLCA 2000 and separately the five areas that presented the greatest problems. This was a more open-ended section of the questionnaire which

teams found useful in airing their views about progress and concerns.

Comment

Let us first examine the area of progress reported by leaving care teams. Figure 9 shows that planning and assessment, and young people's finances are the two areas where there has been the greatest progress since the CLCA 2000, reflecting the Act's aims and priorities.

Typical answers about *planning and assessment* included:

- Encouraging social services to complete and submit Pathway Plan.
- Produced Pathway Plans which are completed with young people.
- Implementation of needs assessment and Pathway Plans which young people's feedback indicates is user friendly.

Typical answers in the *young people's finances* category included:

- Paying weekly allowance for relevant young people.
- Financial protocol fair and clear.
- Not having to claim housing benefit for relevant young people.
- Financial arrangements prevent delay.
- Ensure that young people receive all financial entitlements.

Housing, the third most listed progress area includes issues both about better protocols and about additional stock. Examples included:

- Improved liaison with housing department.
- Increased focus on accommodation for young people.
- Development of a more coherent housing strategy.
- Increased floating support accommodation.
- Increased number of semi-independent placements.

Increases in the number of staff working at leaving care teams was regarded as another important area of progress which made the profile of leaving care higher, and their work more manageable.

Table 16: A comparison of pre and post CLCA 2000 leaving care service ratings

Service area	Baseline ratings – pre CLCA 2000 (% of responses)	Current ratings – post CLCA 2000
Education/employment/ training	'Average' or 'good' (59%) 'Below average' (41%)	'Slight improvement' 'Slight improvement'/'remained the same'
Accommodation	'Average' or 'good' (73%) 'Below average' or 'inadequate' (27%)	'A little improvement'/'significant improvement' 'Slight improvement'/'remained the same'
Financial support for young people	'Average' or 'good' (78%) 'Below average' (22%)	'Significant improvement'/'slight improvement' 'Remained the same'
Health	'Average' or 'good' (55%) 'Below average' (45%)	'Remained the same' 'Remained the same'/'slightly worsened'

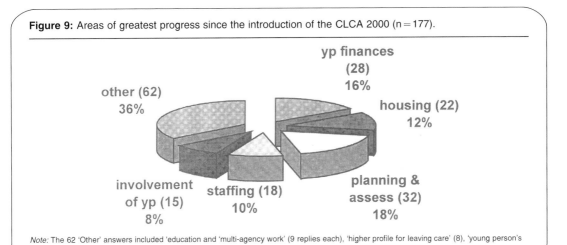

Figure 9: Areas of greatest progress since the introduction of the CLCA 2000 (n = 177).

yp finances (28) 16%

other (62) 36%

housing (22) 12%

involvement of yp (15) 8%

staffing (18) 10%

planning & assess (32) 18%

Note: The 62 'Other' answers included 'education and 'multi-agency work' (9 replies each), 'higher profile for leaving care' (8), 'young person's advisor' (7), and 'contact with young people' (5).

Let us now look at the greatest problem areas reported by leaving care teams.

Comment

'Young people's finances', 'lack of resources' and 'social services culture' and 'housing' were the four most listed problem areas. Significantly, and as we saw earlier, 'housing' and 'young people's finances' were also two of the three most listed single progress areas.

Comments about *young people's finances* (31 replies) as the most listed problem area included the following:

- Lack of funding to manage the implementation of the Act.
- Main problems remain financial pressure to discharge young people too early.

- Not having financial regulations agreed by cabinet and circulated to teams.
- Problems in monitoring financial packages for care leavers in employment.
- Dishing out the money-young people resent it.
- Budget setting-understanding that the ring-fenced money is not new money but a top slice of the standard spending assessment – it is a budget which has got to be accounted for and managed very carefully but not enough infrastructure to do so.
- Lack of funding for supporting young people entitled to services under S24 of the Children Act 1989.
- Improve the practical arrangements for paying maintenance money to relevant young people.

Lack of resources (27 replies) included the following responses:

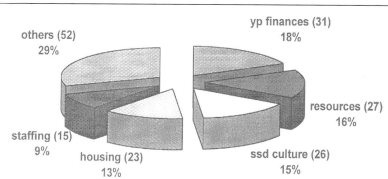

Figure 10: Greatest problems areas since the introduction of the CLCA 2000 (n = 174).

others (52)
29%

yp finances (31)
18%

resources (27)
16%

ssd culture (26)
15%

staffing (15)
9%

housing (23)
13%

Note: 'Other' responses included 'young person's adviser' (10 replies), 'assessment and planning' (11), 'discrimination towards young people leaving care' (4) and 'management structure' (5).

- There are simply not the resources to meet the need.
- Having a massive agenda of work plus deadlines which are too tight.
- Concern about rising numbers of young people coming into team and lack of sufficient staff.
- Pressure to provide service for children who are not care leavers (e.g. homelessness placements for under 16s).
- We do not have the resources to provide a decent service to 18 plus.
- Because our local authority was providing a high level of service before the CLCA 2000 the level of grant was relatively low and left little scope for additional services.

Social services culture (26 replies) respondents replies included the following:

- Helping residential social workers to change their approaches with other teenagers.
- Social workers wanting to relinquish early responsibility of cases.
- Apathy from professionals with and outside agency towards the legislation and young people leaving care.
- Lack of training/understanding of the Act by social workers/other agencies.
- Ignorance by colleagues inside and outside the organisation about the Act.
- Lack of awareness of legislation in terms of basis details despite 8 training days, being sent briefing papers etc.
- Convincing colleagues that 16 really is too young to be discharged.

- Selling the Act to social workers.

Housing problems (23 replies) centred on teams having an insufficient number and type of affordable stock, both for supported and emergency accommodation. Examples given included the following:

- Providing the amount of accommodation that is required.
- Locating suitable accommodation for 16–18-year-olds.
- Crisis arrangements-emergency accommodation.
- Shortage of supervised lodgings.
- Some young people are moving into unsafe accommodation against advice and are being supported by their personal living allowance.
- Problems implementing an accommodation strategy with 11 district boroughs compounded by social services reorganisation.

Staffing (15 replies) respondents' replies centred on shortages and included:

- The team has been without a manager for several months so unable to determine policy, procedure or standards for young people.
- Problems in recruiting staff re socio-economic factors and national recruitment crisis.
- Not enough key posts vacant.

The study also found much better levels of improvement in financial supports for care leavers. However, overall, the two areas of 'finances' and 'housing' were marked out as both key areas of progress and problems, indicating that the improvements need to be further built on post CLCA 2000.

Concluding comments

There have been then a mix of progress and problems since the CLCA 2000 was introduced, and often the same issues that are reported as progress, especially 'housing' and 'young people's finances' 'social services/assessments' and 'staffing' were also presented as problems. 'Education/ employment/training' and 'health' were reported as the poorer performing areas, making nil or minor improvement, or in the case of health, actually *getting worse*. Yet these responses do not tell the whole story because according to this study there have been significant increases in care leavers in education/ employment/training. So what is the explanation for these seemingly contradictory findings? There are two possible explanations. The first is that a majority of leaving care services (59%) reported that baseline services were already 'good' or 'average' and for those services further improvements were slight. Next and after re-examining and cross tabulating the data it was found that leaving care teams which already had a higher staff: young people ratio enjoyed consistently better outcomes about education/employment/training than those with lower staff: young people ratios. For middle and higher performing leaving care teams, education/ employment/training gains were more to do with their existing high service baseline, professional investment in education, government incentive funding, and staffing levels funded by *Quality Protects* funding, than simply improvements resulting directly from services following the Guidance.

Overall, alongside the scope for optimism gleaned from this study's research findings, the research findings are very varied and point to a mix of:

- *Positive changes* – for example in improvements in the areas of assessment and planning, education and training, accommodation, assessing young people's finances, and staffing.
- *Continuing problems* – especially in the areas of resources, health (a very low priority), service strategies for young people with a disability, a social services culture whereby young people are still discharged at 16, lack of suitable accommodation.

- *Mixed responses* – for example, about pathway planning, employment, staffing.

There remains considerable variation across and between local authorities about the extent to which the CLCA 2000 is being implemented and funded. This applies to the key areas of education, employment and training, accommodation, financial support and provision of health services, and health care/health promotion.

Examples of effective funded strategic health and well being services were *not* provided and since poverty is directly associated with poor health and poor self image the areas of *emotional health problems facing care leavers* (especially levels of depression/self-harm) needs addressing as a matter of urgency. In this key service area care leavers, appropriate peers and professional staff need to work together and develop and build up young people's emotional resilience and self-esteem. These matters are explored in depth in the next part, part three of this book. This will focus on the views of care leavers about what is needed and what helped to improve their health and well being.

In many instances the transfer of financial responsibilities for young people leaving care away from the Benefits Agency to local authorities has had a positive overall effect in terms of planning, budgeting and accountability. This funding regime is based on the 'good parent' model and the 'child who does more gets more' model. What is much less clear is the positive effect of the financial changes for those children and young people who do not attend education/ employment/training establishments, and who are struggling to manage their relationships, lifestyle, accommodation and their money. If they do less do they get less?

Finally there are two trends in service delivery post CLCA 2000 that are highlighted by this research study.

The first trend is the wide variation in service provision, service models, resources, and outcomes across the different leaving care teams. Thus in one leaving care team where services are reasonably well resourced (and have been for some time), it continues to attract funding, appears to have good staff relationships, and enjoy good working relationships with other agencies. Yet in another, sometimes an adjacent borough or county, the very opposite is the case, and that particular struggling leaving care team's work often reflects a struggling local authority.

The second trend is that there has been less progress in the 'service delivery', resources' and 'outcomes' (what happens to young people) areas than the 'assessment' and 'planning' functions. However, a significant percentage of respondents, between 20–35%, reported 'a slight improvement' in assessments, services and outcomes for young people leaving care since the CLCA 2000 was introduced. *This is an important positive finding.* However, a majority of respondents, 55–65% overall, reported that 'assessments', 'services' and 'outcomes' for young people leaving care had 'remained the same' since the CLCA 2000 was introduced. These findings have enormous implications for improving the health and well being of young people leaving care because better assessments are simply not enough on their own.

For some care leavers their health and well being will have already improved as a direct result of the CLCA 2000, perhaps in terms of their education/ employment/training, financial circumstances, and improved self-esteem. For others, changes to their current health and well being are more closely linked to their own resilience levels and their background. For yet others, perhaps those that are able to access and use social care services, their health and well being will have improved as a result of improved services. Individual backgrounds and profiles are also critically important. Stein's (forthcoming) three-fold typology of care leavers identified as 'the moving on group' (and making good use of services), 'the survivors group' (high needs for services) and 'the victims group' (services unlikely to help them overcome poor starting points) is helpful here. It should help in identifying different levels of need and resilience in order to target services.

In this part, part two, of the book then we have seen that the CLCA 2000 and Guidance predominantly focuses on the here-and-now and on the language of service improvements, education targets and indicators. The next part of the book, part three, describes the terms in which groups of care leavers defined their health and well being. Based on a larger research study undertaken by the author with Monaghan (Monaghan and Broad, 2003) it focuses on *care leavers perspectives.* As we will see their perspectives, confirmed in other research, call for a much fuller recognition of and engagement with the impact of their background and upbringing on their present health and well being. It then goes on to analyse in what ways these young people who have been in the care system consider their health and well being needs have been /are being met and how they could be better met.

Part III

*Young People's Perspectives on their Health
and Well Being*

Chapter Seven

Introducing the Health and Well Being Research Study and the Young People's Participation

Introduction

This chapter, the first of four in this part of the book, introduces the health and well being research study and describes how the young people and the three research sites were selected as well as the ways in which the young people participated in the study.

Aims of the health and well being research study

The research project set out to identify, record and, hopefully, in the longer term, through involving the young people and staff in the research study, and disseminating the research findings, to improve the health and well being of young people leaving care.

The specific research aims were:

- To identify the health and well being needs of young people leaving care.
- To identify those young people's experiences of services.
- To increase awareness of the key issues, both locally and nationally.
- To raise the awareness of other agencies, both locally and nationally.
- To record care leavers' own perspectives about their background, life styles, health and well being needs, and the links between all of them.
- To record their views about the types of services received and services still needed, the ways in which these services are delivered, and any recommendations for improvements.

The scope of the research

The emphasis of the research study was to gather information, reflections and ideas from care leavers about their health and well being experiences when in care and since that time. It was felt that the research's innovative brief and perhaps most valuable contribution was to establish what young people who have been in care say about their health and well being needs. This brief included questions about their

background, their experiences of health and well being services, why they needed them or did not need them, and inviting them to highlight which services and types of professional responses and engagement were helpful or not. Again through interviews, the research study also gathered the views of staff at the three projects, and to a lesser extent, gathered information from the key agencies themselves.

The study presents research information about a group of 57 young people who have been in care and who were part of a wider cohort of 102 young people attending three social care projects for young people facing social exclusion. Research about the health and well being needs of this wider cohort are summarised in the author's two-year research study about the health and well being of young people facing social exclusion (Monaghan and Broad, 2003).

The first was a project helping young people with accommodation and education/employment/training in Manchester (a Foyer project). The second was a project to support young people in Newcastle (the In-Line Project) and the third was a project for young people leaving care in Manchester (Barnado's Manchester Leaving Care Service [BMLCS]. 24 of the group of 57 care leavers interviewed were attending either the Foyer in Manchester or the Newcastle In-line Project, and the remaining 33 were attending the BMLCS. The research findings presented in this part of the book include discussion and analysis of all those 57 care leavers living circumstances, health and well being issues, and their views of services needed and/or provided.

It is important to note that the 33 care leavers from the BMLCS are all young women who are either mothers or mothers-to-be and research findings about this group are presented both here, alongside the findings about the 57 care leavers as well as in Chapter Ten. This presentational structure is employed because as well as having more general needs, these mothers and mothers-to-be had specific pre-natal, and/or post-natal, parental and child care needs. It is especially important that this group of young women's voices is heard, not least because young women in and leaving care are reported as having relatively high pregnancy rates. For example the Biehal et al. study (1995) found that 50% of their sample of young women coping with earlier motherhood by ages 16–19 compared with 5% in the wider population. It is also important that service providers and planners for this group of young people listen to, understand, and wherever possible, act on their views, concerns and needs about 'what works' and what more is needed to improve their health and well being needs. Here then the specific needs and concerns of these 33 young mothers and mothers-to-be are set out alongside the other, accommodation, finances, supports and relationship, issues which impact on their health and well being.

The young people in the study

First let us consider the advantages and disadvantages of drawing together research findings from different groups of care leavers. In respect of the group of 57 young people who had previously been in care it was always one of the aims of the earlier research study about social exclusion to ensure that the care backgrounds of the 102 young people facing social exclusion would be recorded and disseminated (Monaghan and Broad, 2003). The aim of this approach was to produce a *purposive sample* (Denscombe, 1998: 15; Royce, 1995: 169) of young people leaving care about their health and well being. It also enabled comparisons to be made with the 45 young people (from the cohort of 102 young people) who had *not* previously been in the care of the local authority.

The *main advantages* of this approach are that:

- The experiences of a range of young people who have been in the care of the local authority are included (i.e. not simply those most conveniently available young people from one or two nearby local authorities).
- In a field where there is a paucity of information about the health and well being of care leavers and information that derives from their direct views and experiences, this contribution is very important.
- The focus of the earlier wider study of 102 young people facing social exclusion was on exactly the same topic, improving their health and well being, and thus directly relevant here.

- The young people discussed here includes those who left care several years before they were interviewed, enabling them to have longer-term reflections about their experiences.
- This sample complements the comprehensive strategic survey's findings presented in the previous part of this book.
- It provides qualitative information from the young people themselves about their well being.
- It provides additional quantitative information about the health and well being of young people leaving care, an area much overlooked in leaving care research studies.
- Through already having collected the same information about a similar size of non-care leavers (45) vital comparisons can be made between the two groups.
- In many cases it offers the advantage of understanding the experiences of young people leaving care several years after they have left foster/residential care.
- It provides a sound basis for drawing out good practice indicators.
- Comparisons with other research studies can be made to confirm (or challenge) the research findings and identify common points of interest.

The main disadvantages of this purposive sample are that:

- The experiences of a small selective sample can not claim to be representative of all UK care leavers.
- In drawing statistics from a sub-group of 57 care leavers which contains 33 young parents who are women, there will inevitably be an over-representation of women, and mothers and mothers-to-be in the sub-group.
- Although the same 'core data' was collected on all the 57 young people, there is more information from the 33 mothers and mothers-to-be still attending a leaving care team than the other 24 care leavers who were not attending specialist leaving care services, about their transitions after leaving care. This is as a result of the in-depth interviews that were undertaken with the mothers and mothers-to-be.

Selecting the research sites

The initial health and well being research study set out to interview a total of 100 socially excluded young people attending three projects, most likely but not necessarily, *Children's Society* projects for socially excluded young people. The *Children's Society* guided the research team towards relevant projects working with socially excluded young people and having some focus, even if not an exclusive one, on improving health. It was also necessary for potential participating projects to have some spare capacity to give time to support the research. To be within the funding requirements the research project was also committed to working with young people from a range of different ethnic backgrounds. In some instances the research team contacted *Children's Society* projects that were active in health work but had only one or two young people from different ethnic groups, or in other cases projects that fulfilled the ethnic diversity criteria, but their work did not focus on health issues. In yet other cases *Children's Society* projects fulfilled the health and ethnic diversity criteria but as a result of staff shortages or a project moving its location, or changing its mind about participating, or not being available within the timescale, were unable or unwilling to participate. The result was the research study took place in three research sites where the focus of the work was on improving health and well being.

Young people's participation and research methodologies

A number of research initiatives have attempted to develop approaches based on articulating the perspectives of young people and service users themselves. Others have taken this further and involved young people as researchers or co-researchers (see for example, this author and Saunders, 1998). This research project combines both approaches and for more detailed analysis of the methodological issues around involving young people here see Smith, Monaghan and Broad (2002). Young people were involved in this study in two main ways. At the first project, In-line Newcastle the young people were fully involved as peer researchers, as part of the research team, and in the other two projects, and again given the choice about how to participate, the young people acted more in the role of active participants and interviewees. In all three projects

the young people were supported and given practical and financial assistance.

In terms of research methods there was a range and mix of quantitative and qualitative methods used including semi-structured interview schedules, questionnaires, health diaries and focus groups. At each of the projects the research team obtained a set of 'core data' (about housing, finance, education, etc.) in order to provide data consistency and a sound basis for data comparisons. In addition to this 'core data' there was also 'complementary data' on extra topics raised either by young people or staff, to reflect local needs, and priorities, for example by the young women care leavers who were mothers and mothers-to-be. This statistical data was collected during confidential and anonymised semi-structured interviews and the data was entered and analysed on SPSS for Windows software. It was decided at the outset that the research team would invite the projects to highlight the types of health and well being issues they wanted to explore.

The information that was gathered through interviews with the young people covered a range of issues and areas that the young people felt affected their health, both negatively and positively. These included relationships, accommodation, violence, abuse, bullying, crime, money and being in care, amongst others. The issues that were chosen and selected were as a result of discussions between the researcher, the young people and the projects. There were a total of 37 core questions asked to all the young people with an additional 20 questions asked to the young women working with the BMLCS looking specifically at teenage pregnancy, parenting and young motherhood issues.

There was also an analysis of written documentation made available about policies and action plans of key local health and social care agencies.

The research involved the young people in the following activities:

- Contributing and participating in defining the scope and direction of the research's definitions, development and production (at two research sites).
- Training them to become peer interviewers (at one site).
- Involving the young people to construct and use semi-structured interview schedules for use with other young people (at two research sites).

- Identifying and listing recommendations and good practice (at two sites).

At the leaving care project where the young mothers attended, quite understandably, it was not the wish of the young women to become involved other than as participants and interviewees.

Engaging with the young people and staff

The first research site visited was the In-line project in Newcastle. The three teams that formed this project had already identified health as a major unmet need of the socially excluded young people who used the project. Because of this existing interest in health and well being the teams were welcoming, enthusiastic and committed. There were still several meetings with staff to discuss the research proposal, and related issues such as their involvement, their concerns, and the demands that might be made on them as workers, the practicalities and the time scale. Following these meetings and agreements an invitation/flyer was sent to every young person who used the project.

The letter invited the young people to attend 'a working lunch' with a buffet provided, to explain and discuss the research proposal and answer any questions. The response was staggering. Thirty-three young people attended the meetings at two sites. A further six days were needed to do basic training as a co-researcher/interviewer and to draw up an interview schedule, looking at their health needs, as they saw them, and service provision and delivery. A timetable and plan of action were drawn up, taking account of their other commitments including school holidays, work, childcare responsibilities and availability. It was agreed that no working period would be longer than three days and no day would be longer than six hours. The young people chose a suitable and accessible venue, which was a local resource centre. The young people were given a voucher of their choice and all expenses were met, including travel and childcare costs.

The training programme covered issues such as confidentiality, interviewing techniques, note taking, and active listening skills. Supports, should they be needed, for either the researcher or those interviewed, were also discussed. The young people and the researcher explored definitions and concepts such as power, social

inclusion and exclusion, marginalisation, rights and responsibilities, risky behaviours, emotional well being, lifestyles, relationships and life experiences, as well as issues concerning racism, sexism and other forms of discrimination. The young people discussed health in great detail including physical, mental, sexual, emotional and psychological aspects of health.

The young people and the researcher examined the different type of interviews used in research, open/closed, standardised/non-standardised, structured/unstructured and qualitative and quantitative research methods. Each question was thoroughly discussed as to its relevance, validity and interpretation. Eventually the interview schedule was drawn up. The young people were given the choice to be interviewed by a peer, a member of staff or the researcher. Support was available if needed, as should always be the case, from either the researcher or a project worker.

At the second, a leaving care research site the staff and the research team agreed that the focus of the research would be health issues around teenage pregnancies, pregnancy in care, young motherhood and multiple pregnancies, as well as producing the descriptive 'core data' required from each of the three participating projects. It was decided that the focus of the research would include an exploration into why young women in the care system and leaving care were becoming pregnant at such a young age and why they were going on to have more children at such a young age. This was a particularly pressing issue given all the difficulties that the majority of them were facing.

The service drew up a list of the eligible young women and over a period of several weeks the key workers discussed the research with them and asked permission to give names, addresses and telephone numbers to the researcher. The young women were then invited to any one of three groups, to discuss the research and their participation and they were paid for their time, crèche facilities were provided, transport arranged if necessary and all expenses were met.

At the group meetings the research was discussed, the concepts of health and well being were defined, questions were answered and the young women were asked whether they would like to interview, be interviewed or take part in focus groups. Issues around confidentiality, commitment and the dissemination of information were examined and discussed. The young women wanted either to be interviewed by the researcher or be part of a focus group. None of the young women wanted to train to be a peer researcher. Taking account of their other commitments such as school holidays, work, childcare responsibility and availability, interview dates were arranged for those who wanted to be interviewed and focus groups were arranged for those who preferred to take part in a group setting.

The young women clearly identified physical, mental, emotional and psychological aspects of health. They also understood the wider concepts around the notion of well being. During these discussions it was apparent that the young women felt other issues not automatically considered to be health related did, indeed, have a negative affect on their health and well being such as relationships, lack of support, abuse and violence, accommodation and poverty.

The individual interview schedule and the focus group looked at these aspects of health and emotional well being as well as teenage pregnancy, young motherhood, parenting and children. The researcher carried out 26 in-depth interviews and 14 young women attended one of three focus group meetings. Seven of the young women who attended the focus groups also took part in the in-depth interviews so, in total, the research was based on information about thirty-three young women. The focus groups were transcribed in order to record comprehensive and complicated answers accurately and in full, not withstanding the difficulties of people sometimes talking at the same time.

The third research site was the Manchester Foyer Scheme. A letter of introduction was placed in all the residents' letterboxes, with an invitation to attend one of three meetings where the research would be explained in greater detail. The young people were given a financial incentive to attend this meeting even if they did not wish to continue with the research. At the same time, a development worker at the Foyer promoted the research to the young people, encouraging them to take part and discussing any fears or concerns they had about it. The young people and staff were very enthusiastic about the research and a further three (paid) meetings were planned to discuss it in greater detail and arrange interview times. These meetings were very well attended and the research aims were discussed,

and issues such as confidentiality, support and the dissemination of information were explored and explained at some length.

Apart from the information provided by the Foyer about its aims, numbers of referrals and other administrative details, the bulk of the information presented came from face-to-face individual interviews conducted by the researcher with the young people. In terms of participating in the research the vast majority of the young people welcomed the opportunity to have something to do, to meet other people, and contribute. They saw the value of the research and felt they were helping to identify and improve services for young people, as well as raise the issue of young people and health. Although we could not undertake a follow-up study it is hoped that by taking part in the research the young people gained greater confidence and skills, increased their knowledge of their community and service provision, socialised and made friends and improved their employment opportunities.

Conclusion

This chapter has outlined the aims, scope and focus of the health and well being research project from which the key findings about those 57 young people who had previously been in care, will be drawn. It was argued that the advantages of using this type of sample, and sub-group, not only outweighed the disadvantages, but also make an important and innovative contribution in terms of knowledge, future project and good practice developments in the health and well being fields. This innovative, though by no means unique, contribution, also relates to the ways in which the young people were socially included in the research, either through being a paid peer researcher and member of the research team, formulating the research study's structure and questions, or being active respondents and interviewers.

The research methodologies employed enabled there to be a depth of relevant findings to be collected and shared, especially about the young people's background, and the relationship between their background and their current health and well being, which would otherwise likely have been unavailable and inaccessible.

Chapter Eight

The Young People's Family and Social Circumstances

Introduction

The aims of this chapter are:

- To present personal and social research findings about the 57 young people in the health and well being research project, and who have previously been in the care of the local authority.
- To understand something about their past and their upbringing, as identified by the young people as relevant to their current health and well being.
- To illustrate the clear connections made by the young people between their difficult, and often-abusive and/or violent pasts and their present behaviour and between their past and their current struggles, to survive and maintain levels of self-esteem.
- In order to understand current practice with these young people it is necessary to understand their past and personal histories in so far as this is relevant to understanding both their earlier lives, and social care interventions, and their current life styles, and health and well being.
- To establish that health and well being issues for this group of young people leaving care is about earlier and present emotional, material and psychological matters, and not simply physical and mental health matters, something which research can sometimes overlook (for example as reported to Hai and Williams, 2004).
- To examine what significant differences, if any, there are between the 57 care leavers and the 45 non-care leavers' backgrounds, family relationships and living situation to explore differences, similarities, and levels of health and well being service provision.
- To understand their educational and family background in order to understand and not judge, but act upon in an appropriate way, on their current aspirations, needs and concerns-discussed in the following two chapters.

In this chapter the data, life styles and experiences relate to 57 young people who have previously been in the care of the local authority. Where they are of particular interest and/or significance, statistical comparisons are made between the group of 57 care leavers and the group of 45 non-care leavers, taken from the original cohort of 102 young people.

The young people in the study

Legal status and entitlements

The interviews for the fieldwork were carried out between February and July 2001, after the CLCA 2000 was enacted in October 2000, but just before its introduction in October 2001. The interviewees had all left care before the CLCA 2000 came into force and services with which they were provided at the time were provided within the terms of the Children Act 1989. However, after October 2001 this group of 57 16–21-year-olds (who had previously been in care) became 'qualifying children and young people over 16' under the CLCA 2000. This means they were subject to the CLCA 2000 in that they are afforded the same benefits provided under S24 (Children Act 1989). In addition, the local authority must keep in touch as appropriate, they are entitled to assistance with education and training, and entitled to vacation accommodation (see appendices). Given that most of the services received, and/or due to be received by these 57 young people, fall within the terms of the CLCA 2000 and the Children Act 1989, comments made about the impact of the former can be made with some authority and confidence.

Age

These 57 young people (or 45% of the original cohort of 102 young people) had previously been in the care of the local authority. The age range of this care leavers group was 16–21 and their average age was 18 years of age. 33 of the 57 young people who had previously been in care were taken into care at between 10–16 years of age and the remaining 17 young people (in 7 cases answers were not provided) were taken into care between the ages of 0–9.

Ethnicity, gender and disability

Of the 57 young people leaving care discussed here 44 are female and 13 are male. Of these 44 young women, 33 were selected for the larger research study on the basis of them being mothers or mothers-to-be. Here those 33 young women's experiences of leaving care are also incorporated and presented, together with the other 24 young people and within the discussion of all 57 care leavers. However, in Chapter 10 there is a separate case study of the needs, experiences, and views of this important, and often over-looked group of care leavers. A decision could have been made not to include those young women's experiences here but that decision could then have led to accusations that their needs and concerns solely stemmed from their roles as mothers and mothers-to-be. This author was keen for there to be an integrated approach whereby their backgrounds, needs and concerns could be combined, in this chapter, with other young people leaving care, and then in the later, and separate, case study chapter, as specific to their other specific needs as mothers. What has been done here then, is to include within the statistical data the 33 young women but limit the illustrative quotations by and about care leavers to those from the other two projects. The illustrative quotations from the group of 33 young women are included in Chapter 10 about these young mothers and mothers-to-be.

42 (or 74%) of the care leavers were white, 6 (11%) were black, 6 (11%) were mixed race, 2 (4%) were Asian and the ethnicity of the remaining 1 care leaver was not known. 12 or 21% of the young people (7 males and 5 females) indicated that they had some form of disability. The disabilities included severe asthma (4), other respiratory problems (2), mental health issues (4) and severe dyslexia (2). A few of the young people also reported mental health issues and forms of dyslexia but did not want to describe themselves as disabled, and these are not included in the 21% figure. Therefore the 21% figure **under-records** the full extent and range of disabilities as defined by the young people. This under-recording and lack of clarity or consensus about what is defined as a disability is also highly likely to distort needs assessments and levels of provision.

Table 17: Type of previous care for the care leavers group (n = 57)

Type of previous care	Number of young people who had lived in each type
Foster	20
Residential	9
Boarding school	1
Extended family	1
Different types	19
Answer not available	7
Total	57

Care history and care placements

The vast majority, forty-five, of the young people were between 0–9 years of age when they were taken into care and the remainder, 12, were aged between 10 and 15 when taken into care. Table 17 presents information about their previous care placements.

When comparing the care leavers (57) with the non-care leavers groups (45) a large percentage (61%) of the former were brought up by people other than their parents and/or social services. Indeed 37% of the care leavers stated that they had started to live with people 'other than their parents' by the age of 11 years of age.

What perhaps is more surprising is that 51% of non-care leavers had also been brought up *outside* their immediate nuclear family, i.e. within their extended family and with friends from an early age. Additionally this 'non-care leavers' group often moved between different carers, and as we will see shortly, were also subject to abuse and violence. However *unlike* the care leavers group, their families were not reported as being known to, or receiving services/monitoring from, social services or other social care services. In other words this group was potentially much more at 'risk' of ongoing physical violence and abuse, as a result of moving between different carers, and being more 'hidden' and therefore not being assessed by social services.

Ages at entering care

In four cases young people had entered care at an early age (under 9) and then left care between 12 months and 36 months afterwards. These four were in care for a shorter period than the remainder of the sample. Therefore particular note will be made of any significant differences in the outcomes of this smaller 'short-stay' group, compared with the remaining 53 who had left care at 15 plus *and* were in the care of the local authority for at least three years.

Placements, length of time in care and reasons for being taken into care

The young people in the care leavers group averaged seven previous placements per young person and the number of their previous placements ranged between 1 and 40. Ten of the young people had lived in over 12 different places in their lives with all the disruption this had on their schooling and relationships.

14 of the care leavers had been in care between 1 and 2 years, 22 had been in care for between 3 and 6 years and the remaining 14 young people had been in care between 7 and 18 years. For the care leavers group as a whole their average length of time spent in care was six years (information about duration in care was only available from about 50 care leavers). Next and in terms of reasons for being taken into care twenty-six young people (or 46%) said they had to leave the family home because of physical violence. A further 17 said they had to leave because of sexual abuse and another seven said their mother was 'unable to cope' with them. Others reported desertion, war, abduction, illness (of parent) and alcohol and drug addictions as reasons why they had to leave home.

If we now move to looking beyond their care history to their family background we can begin to further understand their transitions, supports and contacts, as well as the links they made between their backgrounds and their current situation and, in the next chapter, about their health and well being.

Relationships and contact with family and friends

Early family relationships

A significant majority 70% (n = 40) of the young people reported that relationships in their home in their early life had tended to be at best negative and at worst, violent, abusive and negative. They reported that these relationships made them feel depressed, caused them to use drugs and/or drink excessively, fail in education, take risks with their health and make them lack confidence, as well as have low feelings of value, worth or

love. Constant criticism and rejection by their parents further compounded these feelings of inadequacy and worthlessness. This is what three young people told the researcher in interview:

> Since I was 11 there have been big problems. My stepfather moved in and there were difficulties straight away. I got thrown out eventually. I have no support from my parents now.

> I have a very poor relationship with my mother. I always have ever since I can remember. She puts me down all the time and never has a good word to say about me. She has lowered my self-esteem and confidence and upsets me every time I see her. She is always criticising us. My brothers and sisters either left or were thrown out due to my mother's behaviour. My dad misuses alcohol and that adds to the tension and causes arguments.

> I didn't used to get on with anyone in the family but now I've left, things are a bit better. When I was little I was always 'verballing' with my mum and being the youngest I was always picked on and bullied by my older sisters. I felt everyone was against me.

A majority of young people reported much *more positive relationships with partners and friends* than with family members, for example:

> I get on better with my friends than with my family. It has always been like this. They are good to me and help me and listen to me.

> My boyfriend is very loving and laid back, so is the rest of his family. I have a couple of good friends. I don't know what I'd do without them.

> My friends are my family now. They treat me better than any of my family did. They are always there for me and don't hurt me. They are like I think a family should be, we are really close and I can talk to them about anything.

> I have excellent relationships with my friends, unlike my family who I have a shit relationship with. I go out a lot with my mates, doing sports and socialising. They accept me for me and don't criticise me all the time.

The research study also found both significant differences and some similarities between the care leavers group and the non-care leavers group in terms of families and friends. For both groups there were significant research findings about the absence of birth fathers in their past and present lives. As Table 18 shows only 5% (5) of the original cohort of 102 young people have their birth father still living at the family home, compared with 44% (of care leavers) and 66% (of non-care leavers) who still have their birth mother living at the family home.

Table 18: A comparison of the family background of the care leavers and non-care leavers groups

Questions about family situation	Answers from young people who have been in care (n=57)	Answers from young people who had not been in care (n=45)
Were your own parents in care?	Yes – 40%	Yes – 35%
Do you have a step-parent?	Yes – 78%	Yes – 57%
Does your birth mother still live at home?	Yes – 44%	Yes – 66%
Does your birth father still live at home?	Yes – 5%	Yes – 0%
Do you know who is living at home now?	Yes – 21%	Yes – 4%
Do you have a partner?	Yes – 56%	Yes – 19%
Do you live on your own?	Yes – 44%	Yes – 80%
Is your parent/step parent living at home?	Yes – 17%	Yes – 28%

Partner, parents, contact and step parents

A number of questions examined the family backgrounds in order to establish how they came in to care and how they considered their upbringing affected their lives now. Table 18 illustrates some of the family background comparisons that were made.

As a direct result of the different and re-configured families, both groups had a wide range of relatives and the amount of 'regular' contact (daily, weekly, or fortnightly) between the young people and their families did not vary between the 'in care' and 'non-care' groups. There was significant variation about the level and nature of contact between these young people and their families.

This is what three of the young people said about the complex issue of contact:

My dad is great. He does everything for me. I can phone him up and he does the business. He looks after me.

I see my mum every couple of months. We just don't get on. We fight when we are together. She picks on me and criticizes me for everything.

I haven't seen my family in years. During the war we were separated and I was sent over here for safety. It has been so long. It is hard to keep in touch.

It was three times more likely for the young women than the men to be in 'regular' contact with their family, and this closely related to the large proportion of young mothers maintaining contact with their mothers, if not always receiving support and advice from them.

The levels and extent of family support were mixed, unpredictable, and inadequate despite it

being the local authority which is required and expected to act as the child or young person's 'corporate parent' (taken from the *Quality Protects* programme). Jackson defines parenting as 'the performance of all the actions necessary to promote and support the physical, emotional, social and cognitive development of a child from infancy to adulthood' (quoted in Jackson et al., 2003). Proper, active and consistent parenting is essential therefore if children, young people and young adults are to form supportive relationships, fulfil their educational potential and, overall, maintain a healthy life-style.

Education/employment/training: disrupted education – disrupted lives

For some young people education can provide a bedrock of opportunity and friendships and confidence. For others it can either remain out of reach, due to others low aspirations or, perhaps, just as bad, it can provide another arena where issues of stigma, bullying and exclusion are played out yet again. For the care leavers in this study their experiences of the education system were mostly unsatisfactory, and their early good-will in seeking educational achievement had become lost and entangled in their other personal struggles to keep afloat amidst ongoing changes and placement moves not of their making.

The young people interviewed knew they were not fulfilling their educational potential and although their education levels were poor, many wanted to return to education. The reasons for and impact of these young people's educational under-performing are extremely important for education services and social workers to understand. It is also important to recognise that the vast majority of the young people interviewed regretted being excluded, socially excluded, from education, as a result of external factors. First and in terms of basic information, nearly two thirds (61%) of the care leavers had left school before sitting any examinations. 80% (46) of the care leavers had left school by the age of 16, 61% (35) had left at 15 years, and 19% (11) before they had reached 15 years of age.

When asked the question 'Why did you leave school when you did?' seven care leavers said they were expelled, a further 10 gave the reason they left school/college when they did as being because they were removed into care. In terms of the range and proportion of stated reasons for the young people not doing well at school the reasons given by both care leavers and non-care leavers were similar. These included 'being bullied' 'not interested' 'not motivated' ' and getting in with the 'wrong crowd'. The only significant difference between the two groups was 'being moved around' as a reason, given by seven care leavers compared with three non-care leavers. 51% (23) young people who had not been in care reported their education as 'fine' compared with just 12% (7) care leavers.

A key theme from these findings was that of 'disrupted education-disrupted lives'.

The following quotations illustrate how strongly the young people felt about their education:

I hated school. I was so scared all the time. They would find me and take my money off me and hit me. They used to call me names and get the other kids to do the same. If anyone tried to be my friend they would threaten them and stop them.

I didn't do well at school because I wasn't interested. I could only think of what was going to happen at home (physical and sexual abuse). I got chucked out of loads of schools because of my behaviour. The teachers hated me.

Nobody cared if I went to school or not when I was in care. No one encouraged me to go, as long as you weren't a problem they let you stay off and anyway I was moved around so much I could never settle in any school.

He [a teacher] really scared me. He used to call me names and get the other kids to laugh at me. He used to hold his nose when he was near me. He always called me thick and stupid and always asked me the questions because he knew that I couldn't answer them. If I did get it right, he would say I was cheating and really shout at me until I cried and then everyone would laugh at me again and call me names because I'm a boy and I shouldn't cry.

This quote has a resonance with the Scottish comedian Billy Connolly's experiences at school (for his biography, written by his wife, see Stephenson, 2002).

I hated going to school because everyone used to laugh at me because I never had the right uniform and what I did have was always second hand and too big or too small for me. I remember always being sat outside the Head's office because I never went on school trips. I couldn't even play sports because I never had a change of clothes. I always felt an outsider, like I didn't belong. I never took part in anything.

When asked why they wanted to enter/re-enter education (rather than in work or training), most felt that they needed basic education (as received in a school setting) rather than work place training:

They laughed at my writing; one man said his bairn could write better than me.

When I started in the shop I realised I knew nothing . . . nothing about geography, history or anything like that. When they talked about holidays I didn't know where the countries were. I didn't even know where places in England were.

One woman in work told me to use a dictionary but I couldn't because I can't spell.

Despite seeking both positive as well as negative experiences about post-16 education, there were only a few positive experiences volunteered and these included the following:

I didn't want to go to college when I first came here but I'm so glad I did. I have learnt so much.

I can't wait to start my course. I've always wanted to do drama and I never thought I could do it but they have helped me so much here and encouraged me that I got a place. I just wish (name of worker) was still here to see me.

Overall 35 (or 61%) of the 57 care leavers had been bullied, and a significant percentage (77%) of this group were bullied whilst at school and not at home or in care. Just 6 of the group of 57 care leavers were still in any form of education and 39 (68%) stated that they would like to return to education. However, if they were in education they would not be available for work and so would not be entitled to benefits.

Implications for education

There are serious financial disincentives for 19-year-olds leaving care seeking to enter further or higher education and these significant problems are ignored in the CLCA 2000 and related guidance (also see Jackson et al., 2003). Many of the young people interviewed stated that they wanted a 'second chance' or if necessary a 'third chance' to return to education. Although there are also a range of practical and placement support matters to take into account when it comes to education, overall the cost, location, availability, flexibility, and suitability of education for post-16 care leavers and indeed pre-16-year-olds remain largely unresolved issues.

The implications for these young people's education are that there needs to be more support for young people/children to continue their education when moving around in the care system. This is belatedly being recognised as a 'guidance issue' and joint social services/ education guidance for looked after children has been published (DoH/DfEE, 2000). The research evidence indicates that there needs to be specialist support systems in place and incentives to continue in school. Also some 16–17-year-old young people find themselves unable to afford college as this affects any benefits they receive. For example they cannot claim unemployment benefit, as they are not available for work if they go to college and as there are no grants anymore, this means they have no income.

It would also help enormously if more informal, community, and vocational education was recognised, accepted, and provided with longer-term funding. So for example at one of the projects there was a support and training worker who helped the young people with reading, writing, mathematics, history, culture, computer studies, job application forms and curriculum vitae. He worked in a 'young person centred' way, at the young person's pace and was extremely popular. He was on a short-term contract and after the funding was not renewed the work became subsumed in others duties, but without the previous focus or dedicated time available. There needs to be much more acceptance both that formal education is not the only form of education and that it does not suit everyone. According to this research study it is the absence of a real choice either about provision of systematic support for formal education or acknowledgement of informal education's value which hold back a large majority of care leavers from fulfilling their potential and maintaining a less stressful, more balanced life style.

Training and employment

The young people had mixed views about their employment and training to date. This is what some young people told the researcher:

I'm in roofing full-time and I enjoy it most of the time. I have a laugh and like finishing a job and seeing the end result. It makes me feel better, but I don't like getting up in the morning.

I like to be busy and support myself and meet people. I feel I have proved people wrong who said I couldn't do it.

I hate it, it's shit. They treat you like a skivvy. They make me do everything and pay me fuck all, but they know I need the money and I'm not likely to get anything else because I'm too thick.

Next we move onto examining another major area of importance for young people in transition to adulthood, namely their accommodation situation. Again the author will seek to highlight and draw out those aspects of accommodation that the young people considered affected their health and well being.

Accommodation

The young people had a strongly felt need to feel safe and respected where they lived. Table 19 shows the number of young people leaving care with their own or shared accommodation. None of the young people described themselves as homeless.

Twenty-two young people (all women) lived with their child or children, five lived with their partner, six lived with their partner and their child or children, another five lived at home with parents, one each lived with a friend, a sibling or a carer and child. 42% of the young people's accommodation was listed as 'waiting for repairs' in or on their properties, half of these being classed as 'urgent'. These included broken door and window locks; smashed doors and windows; broken fires, central heating units and other forms of heating; exposed electrical points; no hot water and, in some cases, no water at all. Other examples given were of outer communal security doors regularly vandalised and damaged so they did not lock and allowed anyone to wander around the flats. Many of the young people reported feeling depressed, stressed, scared and unable to sleep over the lack of urgency that they

Table 19: The accommodation situation of young people leaving care (n = 57)

Accommodation types	Flat	Hostel	Bedsit	House	Shared	Mother and baby hostel	Total
	15	17	0	19	2	4	57

felt the local council attached to their requests for repairs. Two young people said in interview:

One of my windows has been broken since I moved in, six months ago, and it is still broken. They say it isn't urgent so I have to put a board in it . . . It doesn't make me feel safe . . . and I don't sleep well at night.

The security doors to the building never lock, people just kick them in to get in. They do get repaired but then they just get booted in again. It is scary when people just wander round outside your door all night.

While most young people considered that living on their own was 'good' for their health, a third felt it made them 'depressed' or prone to depression, and feeling vulnerable and isolated. These findings strongly indicate that not only does living on one's own not suit everyone, but that there should be an individual needs assessment made, as well as more of an element of choice about suitable accommodation. Some of the accommodation was not in suitable areas either.

Notions of feeling safe and secure were very important to these young people. Unfortunately, however, when asked how they felt about the area they live in, nearly half of the young people with their own tenancies reported 'not feeling safe' or 'secure' in their homes. The reasons for this included living in a 'bad area', 'communal security doors broken', 'drugs and drug dealers in the area', 'vandalised', 'dirty and untidy areas', 'violent and threatening neighbours', 'racism', 'repairs not carried out' and 'robberies, burglaries and muggings'. This is what five young people said from two of the projects:

My neighbours come in and take my things and my money. I'm so scared of them. I feel like killing myself.

I feel unsafe and vulnerable. It's a very rough area; people are on drugs and drink a lot. At night it's very noisy with people shouting and fighting and throwing things off the top of the flats. I sometimes think, 'what's the point' (of going on). I tried to move but the woman at the housing said 'we can't all pick and choose where we live.' I bet she doesn't live in a place like this.

I'm in a ground floor flat even though I begged them for a higher flat. I don't feel safe or secure. The area is a shithole, a craphole and full of drug dealers. They've taken over the estate. I just stay in on my own. It makes me so depressed.

There's loads of weirdoes around here, we're so close to the centre and the universities, all the nutters hang out and the muggers.

We're too close to . . . and . . . with all the drugs and the dealers. You get a load of hassle when you go out. I hear gunshots every night. It scares me.

These rather damming comments about accommodation issues from some of the young people suggest an urgent need for good standard practice pointers about accommodation and support to be established and rigorously followed.

Practice pointers: planning for better accommodation and support

- It is essential to plan and fund a personal support package for young people leaving care based on a comprehensive needs assessment, and stock of suitable accommodation.
- Preparation for independent living should be addressed in reviews.
- It is vital to have a choice of accommodation available that is needs and not finance led.
- Wherever possible do not rush a young person on to move-emphasise planning.
- Set out an alternative plan in case the proposed accommodation breaks down.
- Plan ahead and establish the policies and procedures concerning subsequent accommodation that may be needed.
- Check on the financial requirements of supported accommodation and the possible grants or benefits available.
- The young person must be fully involved and consulted, preferably underpinned by procedures about how this should be done.
- Living on one's own does not suit everyone and it helps to make some vulnerable young people depressed and unwell. If possible there needs to be more of an assessment element, choice about accommodation, and more floating support offered.

Table 20: Sources of financial support for care leavers (n = 57)

Categories	Frequency	Valid per cent	Cumulative per cent
No money	2	3.5	3.5
Income support	27	47.4	50.9
Child benefit	1	1.8	52.6
Job seekers allowance	9	15.8	68.4
Sickness benefit	2	3.5	71.9
In employment	6	10.5	82.5
Various	6	10.5	93.0
Social services	4	7.0	100.0
Total	57	100.0	

● A high degree of planning and co-operation between the housing, social services department, and benefit agency is essential for a properly planned supported accommodation package upon leaving care.

Financial circumstances

In contrast with the research findings presented in Part Two of this book about the higher numbers in education/employment/training than before, there are a very high proportion of this group of 57 care leavers in receipt of state support of one sort or another. As Table 20 illustrates just six or 10% of all the care leavers were in employment. This finding is largely though not totally explained by the higher proportion of young mothers who told the researcher that they were not available either for work or post 16 education because of their parenting responsibilities and lack of child care facilities. Whatever the source of the financial support all the young people received it was regarded as 'totally insufficient' to meet their basic material needs.

The average amount of money per week received per care leaver was £78 compared with £46 per week for the group of 45 non-care leavers. This minimal level of financial support makes an almost inevitable impact on the young people's health and well being. Although once again we sought to stretch out information by asking balanced and open-ended questions about life style, well being and finance issues, again and again the answers from many of the young people pulled the researchers back to focusing on the young people's agenda. This was clearly about the frustrating impact of lack of money, and the accompanying lack of opportunities to participate and maintain a real sense of well

being. Indeed if we go back to the earlier cycle of social exclusion (Figure 1) we can see how lower expectations and reduced opportunities to participate reinforce each other in a downward deteriorating spiral of further exclusion. What is needed is a way to break that cycle, and this book's last chapter emphasises the contribution of risk assessments, and resilience strategies as a means of breaking what is not an unbreakable cycle. What follows are typical quotations by the young people about their financial circumstances and the limits these place on their lifestyles:

It kills me to live like this. My head is done in. I don't know how much longer I can cope. I feel so depressed and stressed.

I'm so fed up. I can't see my life improving. I can't buy the things I need and that makes me worry even more.

I'm so angry and depressed. I get so bored and lonely because I can't go out.

How do they expect us to live? I only get £32 a week because I'm paying back a loan I had to take out for basic living things like pots, pans, bedding and clothes.

I just can't manage to pay back what I owe so I get deeper into debt.

I don't have enough money for food and toiletries most weeks. I live on bread and pasta. I can't remember the last time I had fruit or vegetables.

I don't live, I just exist. I can't afford to go out or do anything. I worry about what's going to happen in the future. I can't afford to save a penny up for when I move out of here.

In many ways it is a surprise that a much higher percentage were not in debt, given the poverty-level benefits they received. 56% of the care leavers were in debt, compared with 40% of the non-care leavers and the average level of debt for care leavers was £505 and for those young people who had not been in care, the average amount was £200. Whilst it is imaginable that these debt figures compare favourably with typical student debt levels this would be misleading because the size of some of the debts reported were significant. Not only were some of them of a significant level, they were also far higher than the non-care leavers group. So for care leavers, debts ranged between '£0–£8,000' compared with the non-care leavers whose debt levels ranged between '£0–£1,000'. The main difference between the two groups was that over a quarter of the care leavers had multiple debts including rent, catalogues, bills, fines and loans. Also it was the backlog of unpaid rents that accounted for the main difference between the two groups of young people, as well as the fact that a higher proportion of the non-care leavers group was in employment.

Conclusion

A significant proportion of care leavers (and indeed non-care leavers) are brought up and are living away from their birth home, with relatives and friends, from an early age – it is as if placement instability has an early origin. The average of seven previous placements per care leaver with a range of between 1 and 40 placements, and with ten having lived in over 12 different places in their lives is an indicator of high disruption on schooling and relationships. The average length of time spent in care was 6 years and the main reason for being taken into care (for 46%) was physical violence. Sexual abuse was the reason given in a further 30% of cases. Abuse, exclusion and moving around between different family members, and in and out of care, were key early experiences for the young people. Current family structures varied considerably with very high proportions of absent fathers (95%) and mothers (45%) reported. Many young people (79%) did not know who lived in their current family home. Whilst there was significant variation about the level and nature of contact between the young people and their families, contact by young women with their mothers was three times more likely than by men. For a majority of the young people who already had experienced a highly unsatisfactory upbringing, attending school, potentially a place where compensatory and positive experiences could be possible, became another very unsatisfactory and unsettling life experience. Many, not all, of the young people interviewed expressed a desire for a second or third chance to return to education, depending on course types, and the sorts of practical and placement supports available. It would also help enormously if more informal, community and vocational education was recognised, accepted, and provided with longer-term funding. As we saw earlier notions of feeling safe and secure are very important to these young people, yet unfortunately the young people's experiences of accommodation was very mixed.

Chapter Nine

The Young People's Health and Well Being

Introduction

The aim of this chapter is to describe the young people's current physical and emotional health and well being and explore the direct links they made between this and negative harmful behaviours in their background. The specific issues of earlier violence, bullying and abuse towards these young people have some prominence here, again because of the direct links made with their current health and well being. The details about the health and well being of the care leavers who were parents or parents-to-be are discussed in detail in the next chapter although some general information is also included here. Let us first summarise the research methods used in relation to the health and well being information that is presented here.

Methodology

At the initial research set-up meetings between the young people and the research team the concept of health and well being were discussed. The topics raised by the young people in those meetings were the ones which they considered affected their health, either positively or negatively and which are discussed here. At first glance it may seem that some of these topics fall outside more traditional definitions of health, as physical health. Nevertheless upon closer examination what the young people discuss are exactly the same sort of wider health and well being experiences and influences on their health found in earlier studies into the health needs of care leavers. These include, about the health of care leavers, those by West (1995), Saunders and Broad (1998); and about health and inequality, McLeod and Bywaters (2000). These topics include relationships, accommodation, violence, abuse, family relationships, bullying, crime, financial circumstances and care history.

The young people discussed what is meant by the term 'health' in great detail and their framework included physical, mental, sexual, emotional and psychological aspects. Eventually there were a total of 37 structured and semi-structured core questions asked with an additional 20 questions asked to the young

parents and parents-to-be, examining teenage pregnancy, parenting, and young motherhood issues. The young people were given the choice about whether health issues were discussed individually or in focus groups and personal detailed health questions were only asked in individual interviews and with the young person's consent.

This is a research study about the health and well being of young people leaving care and not a research study about bullying, violence and abuse in childhood. However, since the young people insisted that the research team needed to understand some things from their past, in so far as they considered these relate to their current health and well being, questions about these three areas were included in the questionnaire schedule. Nevertheless, it seemed reasonable that there should be some criteria on which to base questions about these important areas. Thus there was a three-fold criterion used based on the following three questions:

- (Knowledge and practice) Does this question contribute to an understanding of care leavers' current health and well being?
- (Relevance) In what ways does the question relate to care leavers' current health and well being?
- (Empowerment) Who decides what health and well being definitions are used and what information is provided? (Answer: the young person).

After discussions these criteria were agreed, and in practice this meant that minimal and only relevant information was provided about the highly sensitive areas of violence, bullying and abuse. In only a very small number of cases did the young person not wish to provide information about their background. Let us first examine the relatively straightforward findings about physical health.

Findings about the young people's health and well being

Physical exercise

70% (40) of the young people reported that they exercised every day. The most popular forms of exercise were 'walking' – no cost involved – and in 10 cases, 'swimming'. Other forms of exercise included 'sex', 'running', 'sit-ups' (all three are no/low cost activities) and 'going to the gym'. Only twelve of the young people said they could afford, on a regular basis, to take part in a leisure activity. These activities included swimming, playing in a band, martial arts/boxing and going to a gym. This is what two young people told us in interview:

I sit in bed all day, there's nothing to get up for, I can't be bothered because I know I can't afford it so what's the point. I feel so angry sometimes.

I feel great when I do go swimming or something so it's even worse when I can't afford to do it. I feel really lazy and unfit and unmotivated but it's not my fault that I can't afford to go regular.

When asked more specifically if they had an illness that prevented them from doing exercise 13 (26%) said that they had an illness, the most common being asthma, other respiratory infections, eczema, and other skin conditions, which prevented them from doing exercise. Other reasons mentioned much less frequently for not doing exercise included 'being lazy,' being overweight,' 'being a mother' and 'being too busy.' According to the young people a 'lack of money' and a lack of a complementary or reduced rate leisure card (from the council) prevented them from attending local gyms/swimming pools as often as they wished. Nearly half of the young people reported not feeling healthy 'regularly' and most of the young people knew about healthy eating but felt they could not afford it.

Many of the young people found that the high cost of travel also prevented them from going out to meet friends and family and so increasing their feelings of isolation, loneliness and depression. Nearly 20% said that expensive travel costs had a major negative impact on their lives. It caused feelings of stress, anger, depression and isolation. Again a free travel card provided by local councils would go some way to reducing this sense of isolation due to the high cost of public transport for the majority who were non-earners.

Let us now look at the physical health and well being indicators around substance use.

Substance use

Smoking

48 (84%) of the care leavers stated they smoked and 75% of these smoked every day, with 41

indicating that they smoked between 10 and 20 cigarettes per day. This 84% figure compares with the average for young people aged 16–21 as a whole, of 29% for males and 25% for females (TSA, 1997: 39). Four of the 57 care leavers started smoking under the age of 10 and the majority between the ages of 10 and 16 years of age. These quotations by young people illustrate both explanations and rationalisations for smoking:

I need to smoke. It keeps my weight down.

It helps to calm me down when I get stressed.

The young people were very aware of the health issues attached to smoking but felt that, at the present time, the positives outweighed the negatives for them in that smoking calmed them down, helped with suppressing appetites and made them feel they belonged. Some could detect negative effects on their physical health and fitness. However, many described smoking as their only pleasure in life, or their only means of dealing with stress and depression. For many of the young people interviewed the perceived advantage of smoking-such as enabling them to relax and lose weight-seemed to outweigh the health disadvantages.

Alcohol use

40 (80%) of the care leavers (n = 50) drank alcohol, with six drinking 'every day', nine 'every weekend', five 'two or three times a week', 20 'occasionally' and two 'fortnightly'. It is perhaps worth recalling the official position about alcohol units before reporting on the findings. One unit is the equivalent of a half-pint of beer/lager, or one glass or wine or one single shot of spirits. According to the research study then when the young people drank, six young people drank less than four units in a session, nine drank between four and eight units, four drank between nine and twelve units, and six between thirteen and twenty units. Nearly a third of the care leavers' (16) drank more than twenty units in a session. Nine (18%) said they did not drink alcohol, and most starting drinking between the ages of 12 and 15 years of age. There was reported evidence of high alcohol consumption, especially amongst the young men. It is a significant finding here that 70% of the young people who reported high drinking levels (between 9–20 units 'per session') reported started drinking before the age of 13. The drinking patterns of a fifth of the group, drinking in excess of 20 units per session, i.e. the

equivalent of either 10 plus pints or 20 plus glasses of wine or 20 single [25 mil.] shots of spirit, suggests heavy 'binge drinking' patterns.

Substance misuse

30 (60%) of the care leavers said they used illegal drugs, with 23 (47%) stating that they were taking drugs every day and 21 (42%) stating that they either no longer take drugs or have never taken them. 18 started taking drugs under the age of 14 and a further 10 by the age of 15. The most popular drug used by 21 of the 30 care leavers who used drugs, was cannabis. Other drugs used occasionally were ecstasy, cocaine, heroin and amphetamines. When asked if their drug use affected their health most young people said it did affect their health, usually in a positive way. The reasons they gave included making them feel good, cheering them up, helping them to forget things, helping them to cope with their lives and getting a 'buzz'. However, a few young people said it affected their health in a negative way, in that it made them feel 'paranoid', 'forgetful' and 'moody'.

Let us now look at the research findings about matters of considerable importance in the care leavers' lives, namely violence, bullying and abuse, beginning with the issue of violence.

Violence, bullying and abuse

Violence

In 50 or 87% of cases someone had been physically violent towards them and 80% of the young people reported violence as having been significant in their lives, including 66% saying they had been regularly beaten, when younger. Home was the most violent place to be with 49% reporting violence having taken place in their home, followed by 18% reporting violence towards them on the streets. In relation to physical violence at home one young person said:

My dad used to hit me really, really hard when I was little and as I got older it got worse. He would batter me, get me up against a wall and really lay into me. He would throttle me until I would pass out. He would always aim for my head, slapping, hitting and punching. Then I got a step dad and he started to do the same.

Bullying

66% of the young people reported that they had being bullied earlier in their lives. School bullying tended to start in late junior/early senior years

(years 6–8) and included verbal, physical and racist bullying as well as theft and intimidation. The term 'bullying' includes both physical and emotional threatening behaviour including being browbeaten, persecuted, intimidated, using physical violence, and more psychologically based threats. This is what two young people said in interview:

She would tell everyone at school that she was going to beat me up, they would tell me and then I would be shitting it, waiting for her to get me. She always found out where I was and would beat me up. It got so that I stopped going out of the house. I didn't leave the house for six months once.

They called me names all the time. If I told the teachers, they would tell me to grow up or call them names back, but they didn't understand how scared I was of the group. It made me feel suicidal and very depressed. I just wanted to die.

Abuse

When asked if they had been abused, 37 (65%) of the care leavers, including three care leavers who had been racially abused, said that they had been abused. During interviews, it also became apparent that many of the young people had been abused in more than the one way they had initially reported. Three quarters of those abused were young women and all of those who were sexually abused were young women and both young men and young women had been physically abused. It is a matter of considerable significance and concern that all the 20 who said they had been sexually abused were young women, as well as 15 of the 18 who had suffered multiple abuses. In the majority of abuse cases the young people were abused under ten years of age, and at home.

In 20 or 54% of cases where the information was provided, abuse started at a young age, and by a male member of the family or in two cases by a male member of the extended family. As two young people said in interview:

I suffered physical, sexual and emotional abuse by my stepfather from the age of 6–14 years. It happened at home, in the car, on day trips, on visits, everywhere. In public he would verbally and racially abuse me and also hit me but no one would get involved.

I was sexually abused for years by a family member and I was physically abused by my ma's ex partner. I was emotionally damaged by my ma. She never stopped shouting at me. She made me feel like nothing.

When asked how it made them feel at the time the young people said they felt many emotions and feelings. These ranged from hate, fear, disgust and confusion to feeling worthless, unwanted, lonely, scared and distraught. For example:

> *I used to think, 'why does he hate me so much?' I felt so lonely and confused. I only did what the others did and I would get battered and he would laugh at them. I never knew where I stood. I was very frightened of him and he knew it.*

When asked how they felt now, a fifth felt 'anger' and others reported feeling 'stronger', or 'scared', or 'stressed', 'not able to trust any man again', or 'depressed', or 'OK' or 'having lost all confidence'. Here are typical comments that also illustrate the links between their past and current emotional well being:

> *I get so angry now. I frighten myself. It still has a massive effect on my life. I can't get over it. I think I would stab him if I saw him now. I'm scared of turning into him.*

> *I can't trust any men. I never get drunk around men or in a situation that I can't control. My relationships don't last very long. Lads think I'm funny (weird). I feel I'm being suffocated.*

> *I feel I have to fight everyone to prove myself. I am very violent and aggressive towards everyone. I am angry that nothing happened to him. He got off with it.*

> *When he got sent down that's when I started to feel better. I still get very depressed and will not forget it but I try to live with it. I think it has made me a stronger person.*

Overall then, the majority of these care leavers reported some form of bullying, abuse and violence over long periods of their lives. Most felt, very strongly, that these personal abuses had a greater or lesser affect on their health, especially on their emotional well being and relationships. Yet past abuses were not given as the main causes of their day-to-day stress levels and the research set out to ask the young people to identify the factors they considered affected their current well being.

Factors affecting health and well being

Introduction

The next part of the research study sought to establish what the care leavers considered to be the key factors which impacted on their health and well being. This was done both though structured questions, and entering the answers with the use of SPSS software, and by answering other complimentary semi-structured questions, in one-to-one interviews or in focus groups, or both. Particular attention is given to the relationship between stress and well being, given the prominence the young people gave to describing stress in their lives, its links with their past, and its impact on their present health and well being.

Table 21 shows that the responses attracting the highest proportion of answers were' lack of money' (especially from the non-care leavers group), 'smoking,' 'stress' and 'accommodation' (especially from the care leavers). The answers also indicate awareness and ignoring of the health dangers of smoking. Almost 75% of the young people smoked every day and it was predominantly those smokers who listed it as a key influence on their health. In another question additional factors were sought which affected young people's well being and 68% (34) considered that being in care had affected their health negatively, either physically, mentally or 'in every way'.

When asked if they felt that 'care' had affected their health and well being in any way, just over one third (36%) of the young people felt that care (either local authority care or other care) had affected their health in a negative way. 22% of the young people who said that their mental health had suffered as a result of being in care were young women and 14% of the young people felt that care had affected every aspect of their health, physical, sexual and mental in a negative way, as well as their emotional well being.

A greater proportion of young women than young men felt that care had affected their health in a negative way, and this was likely to be because they were much more likely to have been sexually abused or assaulted in care:

> *I get very depressed when I think about it (foster care) . . . I was always very frightened in residential care. I let myself go . . . I wouldn't go back at night. I got onto drugs there. I got involved in prostitution too. I didn't care about myself because no one else did.*

> *Care definitely affected my health in all ways . . . I had to deal with 18-year-olds . . . it made you get hard and put up barriers . . . like boys would try to break into your bedroom and try to rape you . . . no one would help you. It makes me ill to think of it. I get very angry, an uncontrollable anger.*

Table 21: Factors affecting young people's well being: comparing care leavers and non-care leavers views

Answers	Number of responses in care leavers group	Number of responses in non care leavers group	Total
Lack of money	6	12	18
Drink	1	1	2
Drugs	4	2	6
Asthma	5	0	5
Stress	8	7	15
No support	2	3	5
Accommodation	5	3	8
Poor diet/lifestyle	2	3	5
Smoking	13	10	23
Homelessness	0	1	1
Being pregnant	3	0	3
Being overweight	0	2	2
Answer n/a	7	0	7
Nothing	1	1	2
Totals	57	45	102

Nearly two thirds (64%) of all the young people interviewed felt that care had not affected their health in any way. And more positively:

> Any negative aspects that might have affected my health, my last foster carers more than made up for. I got loads of support, help and love. They made me feel like I was one of the family . . . I still see them now and call them mam and dad.

> I was so grateful to my social worker for removing me from that abusive situation (home). Care was great. I had a lovely foster mam who was really understanding. She would listen to me and help me. She made me better.

Let us now move onto another major area of concern amongst the young people namely the nature and effect of life stresses on the young people. In the research study terms such as 'emotional well being', and 'stress' featured strongly and may serve to describe or include many of the issues found elsewhere under mental health headings.

Stress and poor health

Does stress cause poor health or does poor health cause stress? Or are both propositions true, at least potentially? Table 22 illustrates what young people saw as the main causes of stress. The young people described 'stress' in terms of a severe negative pressure or tension in their lives, usually over which, they felt, they had little or no control. As can be seen from Table 22, the three main reasons for stress were 'lack of money,'

'family relationships' and 'partner's behaviour.' Although not shown in Table 22, when compared with the non-care leavers group, the care leavers were four times as likely to cite 'partner's behaviour' as a significant cause of their stress. Upon further analysis of the data it was also found firstly that it was the young women who cited their partner's behaviour as a source of stress, and, secondly, all but two of the women had a child (or children). It is likely to be of particular significant interest that none that cited 'partner's behaviour' as the main source of stress actually lived with their partner, suggesting a real tension and ambivalence in the relationships young women had with non live-in partners.

Overall then, as Table 22 shows, the three main sources of stress highlighted by the young people were, again, 'lack of money,' and 'family relationships' and 'partner's behaviour.'

What three young people said about stress in their lives:

> I get so worked up and stressed out by never having any money. It affects my whole life, my health, my social life, and my family life. I get so jealous and resentful when I see other people with money. I feel like doing myself in.

> My step dad stresses me out so much. He hates me and tries to turn my mam against me. He thinks he's my real dad but he's not and never will be.

> My friends are always at mine because I'm the only one with a decent flat. But then they cause problems with the neighbours and I get in trouble. I spend most of my money on stuff for them but then when I've got no

Table 22: Causes of stress: care leavers responses (n = 57)

Answers	Valid percent	Cumulative percent
Lack of money	35.6	35.6
Children's behaviour	4.0	39.6
Partner's behaviour/relationship	14.9	54.5
Appointment breakers	1.0	55.4
Child in care	1.0	56.4
Family relationships	21.8	78.2
Health	1.0	79.2
Friends	4.0	83.2
Boredom	1.0	84.2
Accommodation	6.9	91.1
College workload	4.0	95.0
Social worker/staff	4.0	99.0
Everything in my life	1.0	100.0
Total	100.0	

money they never come round or nothing. But they're my mates.

Young people's use of and views of health and social care services

Use of services

Most of the young people (73%) were registered with a doctor, although young men (45%) were much less likely to be registered than young women (just under 100%). 40 or 80% of the care leavers (n = 50) had regular contact with medical or health staff, and only 10 indicated that they never went to them. 38% stated that they only visited the doctor 'as necessary' and 36% went rarely. The young people went to the doctors for a range of issues, but mostly (66%), for general health issues (coughs, colds, asthma, respiratory track infections, ear infections, aches and pains). Although we do not have comparative figures for other young people, this seemed a high figure. A substantial minority visited health services for maternity and family planning services (see the following chapters). There were regular sessions to collect various prescriptions. A small minority, four, saw a doctor for mental health issues and one young person saw a counsellor.

Views of services

Social care

As one might expect, there were mixed views about whether social workers (and indeed other care workers) were helpful or not, and many young people had strong feelings either way. For example:

He was very canny. He used to take us away and get us to do things we thought we couldn't do. He made us feel good and important. He always called when he said he would and never let us down.

She took us away from a horrible situation and put us in care but came to see us a lot and made us realise that it wasn't our fault. She counselled us and stayed with us for years. Any problem I've got she'll help me with, she listens and helped me get my life in order. I don't know what I'd do without her.

On the other hand one young person said:

I had two social workers and both were not very good. They would take me out for the day and talk at me, like it was all my fault, and then drop me off at home and not do anything about it (abuse and violence). They didn't even come in to talk to them (parents). It was only after I started to run away that they put me in care, away from the violence.

Health services

As with their views about social workers, there were very mixed responses by young people about the attitude of medical staff. Half of the young people considered that that doctors have the 'right attitude' and half of the young people thought the opposite i.e. that they did not have the 'right attitude' indicating a wide variation of views. The young people who were happy with their doctors spoke of being listened to, being treated with respect, having things explained to them in an appropriate manner, being given time to talk and of not being judged, for example:

He's always got loads of time for me. He tells me to always book a double appointment when I'm coming to see him. He really listens and takes time to find things for me. He doesn't just give me pills; he discusses what we should do.

She has got so many things for me like counselling and a social worker and helped me get the little one in a nursery. I've never had such a good doctor. It's like she really cares and I can tell she listens to me because she remembers what I've said to her in the past.

Conversely, the young people who were *not* happy with their doctor's attitude spoke of the opposites of the above, i.e., not being listened to, not given time to talk or treated with respect, not being consulted or involved in any discussions about their health and a feeling of being judged and not valued. Several young people spoke of a feeling of not being believed when telling a doctor of their symptoms or of being made to feel a 'difficult' or 'time-wasting' patient.

There were also concerns about doctors being judgemental, moralist and not approving of a young person's life style and making that view or opinion quite explicit. Doctors were also accused of being rude, high handed, arrogant and ignorant of issues as they affect young people in today's society:

He had no idea what it is like to be in my predicament. I could tell that by the stupid questions he was asking. If he had bothered to read my notes he wouldn't have asked the questions. When I had to tell him what had happened to me he looked at me like I was a piece of shit.

Because I'm young he treats me like I don't know anything. He won't discuss anything with me and makes me feel stupid. I think he thinks I'm making it all up. When I walk in the room I can tell by his face he thinks 'oh no, not her again' and he can't get rid of me quick enough.

Of those who had been to their doctor, 60% felt that while doctors offered the right or appropriate services, as we will see later, some considered it was more the way in which services were delivered that made some young people unhappy. 40% of young people felt that doctors did not offer the services they needed, some mentioning 'counselling', 'more support', 'methadone treatment' or 'being given time' and 'being listened to'.

Wide variations in GP services
At one of the projects there was a GP surgery. One GP was reported as very responsive and empathetic to patients, a good listener and offered a range of services, and since that doctor was so popular, there were long waiting times, quite often weeks. According to the care leavers interviewed the medical services varied, depending on which GP was available. One GP interviewed estimated that 'over 50%' of the young people seen presented what were described as 'psycho-social problems', including anxiety, depression, emotional damage, inability to function socially and the legacy of their damaged childhood. This GP used the word 'damaged' a lot when describing the young people's mental health and well being and also said that a lot of young people were very anxious about their level of debts.

In interview the GP considered that the biggest issue that affected the young people's health was their chaotic, risky and transient lifestyle. This put pressures on them, particularly in training and employment projects to conform and change their lifestyle without necessarily having the skills to do this, leading to further stress and depression. Levels of reported sickness to this GP in terms of requests for 'sick notes' for college, work or training were also reported to be high. This is a similar finding to the earlier findings here from the national leaving care study about those care leavers unable to work on medical grounds, another indicator of poor health and well being. The GP also recognised that without a medical certificate young people's training allowances could be withheld.

Implications for service improvements

These young people's perspectives present challenges to the ways in which health and social care services are structured and delivered to meet their needs. From previous research (Broad, 1999) we know that because of their abusive and disruptive past, and sense of isolation and vulnerability, they may invest heavily in the supportive relationships they have with various professionals.

However, generally, social and health workers may need to be more fully trained to work with young people, to respect them (despite the inevitable frustrations involved in working with young people) and work with them in an age-appropriate way. In particular, it is important for them to seek to understand the problem from the young person's perspective, and discuss

Table 23: Recommendations for improving well being: care leavers and non-care leavers views

Headings	Care leavers group	Non care leavers group	Total number of responses
More money	15	19	34
Free access to leisure activities	4	3	7
Better accommodation	9	3	12
Control asthma	2	0	2
More support	7	9	16
Stopping smoking	6	2	8
Improving life style	2	4	6
Having the baby	2	1	3
Nothing – my life is ruined	2	0	2
Answer not available	7	0	7
Nothing, I am fine	1	4	5
Totals	57	45	102

issues with them. This is particularly so when the young person disagrees with a professional assessment or outcome or has not been fully involved in the assessment process. For example, the young people stated that they want to be treated 'properly' and not differently. They spoke of 'wanting respect' and for people 'to be reliable', and they did not want to be 'labelled' as a 'problem'. When one young person was five minutes late for an appointment which had taken four weeks to obtain (!) the appointment was bluntly cancelled by the receptionist and the young person sent on their way. Young people have sensitivities about how they are dealt with by professionals, as is the case for adults. However, by virtue of their age and background the care leavers are perhaps less likely to be as informed and supported as adults, or in the case of young mothers, as older mothers and mothers-to-be, who also often live with partners. As we saw with the GP surgery on the premises, even when having a structure in place which offers health advice and treatment the standard, relevance and utility of that project will vary, depending on staff attitudes and training.

Table 23 illustrates the answers to another question put to the young people about what would improve their well being, this time looking to go beyond recording their perspective to providing positive practical suggestions wherever possible.

Given what we have already established about the young people's minimal financial supports and their accommodation it is perhaps no surprise to see in Table 23 that the three prime means of improving their well being and reducing stress levels were 'more money,' 'better

accommodation' and 'more support.' It is not unusual for care leavers to regard the need for more support as being of high importance in this well being area (see, for example, Saunders and Broad, 1997). This then is the wider agenda for reducing stress and improving well being, namely 'more money' 'better accommodation' and 'more support' – probably not that different a set of priorities from other, more privileged young people 16-19, still living in their own family home with a supportive family.

When asked '*What actually makes you feel healthier?*', many young people reported exercises like swimming, football, going to the gym, basketball and 'working out'. Others reported 'having money', having a 'good time', 'having good friends to turn to' or 'having decent accommodation'. Some of the young people also considered that smoking or taking cannabis made them feel better and, for a minority of others, heavy drinking binges (especially amongst young men) seemed yet another way to feel better, at least in the short term. So there are mixed findings here, both what one might regard as vital common sense messages, about the importance of supportive relationships, but amongst a minority, other less appropriate messages (about the value of binge drinking) and there are health promotion implications here for that small sub-group.

It does seem that many, though not all, young people would value more advice and guidance on safer drinking and drug taking, if presented in a more 'young person centred' way. When their drinking and drug use was discussed, in the research interviews, it was apparent that few had any idea of the long-term implications that large amounts of alcohol and drugs had on their health. Indeed, most thought that the positives outweighed the negatives. However, upon further discussion, many were able to make the connection between, say, their parents' inability to parent them appropriately, earlier drinking and current alcohol and/or drug use. Similarly many could articulate how alcohol and/or drug use had got them in situations they regretted later such as getting pregnant, being violent or causing damage.

Discussion

Stress

Stress had *the* major impact on the lives and health of the majority of young people. This stress was due to a range of factors from both their earlier and current lives including, from the former, violent and abusive family relationships, long-term separation and/or estrangement from family, bullying, particularly in school, severe poverty, inadequate and inappropriate accommodation, loneliness and isolation. Current adverse living circumstances added to these earlier experiences.

As a result of these issues, and because of the feelings of low self-esteem, and of not being valued, wanted or loved, it is likely that many of the young people tended to engage in 'risky behaviours' concerning smoking, drinking, drug use and unprotected sex. Feelings of depression and anxiety, suicidal thoughts, acts of self-harm and low self-esteem and confidence were prominent amongst the group.

In terms of current living circumstances, loneliness, poverty and isolation also affected their health and their capacity to take part in regular exercise or even go out at all. It is worrying that many of the young people reported turning to alcohol or drugs, but not to health or social care agencies, to counter the loneliness and isolation. Living away from home, separated and/or estranged and not always in the looked after system, had contributed to feelings of anxiety and instability with many young people reporting feeling unable to form and maintain healthy positive relationships. The isolation led to many of the young people reporting feelings of depression, irritability, mood swings and powerlessness.

Feeling isolated and feeling different from other young people emphasises the considerable and understandable need for these young people to feel more socially included, accepted and be in receipt of non–stigmatised services and support and/or be part of supportive and appropriate kith and kin networks.

Earlier interventions

Young people felt that they had been let down by many people or agencies in their earlier lives. Many felt that if their parents had been given more support from social services and/or other agencies, the parents would not have been so violent toward them, and that they would not have so many health and well being problems. Many young people spoke about their mother's inability or failure to protect them from male violence in the family home. Again, the young people felt that early recognition of the problem by relevant agencies and early intervention would have helped their mothers to protect and care for them better. Similarly, young people spoke about abuse and violence as a result of drug and alcohol misuse by their parents and, again, felt it should have been picked up sooner by the child protection agencies. Several young people spoke about social workers being 'scared' of a parent or not wanting to appear 'racist' and so failing to act in the young person's best interest or removing them from the abusive and violent situation.

Valued support

When asked what would make them feel better now, over two thirds said 'more money' and 'support' and 'better accommodation'. Most young people mentioned the services of the *Children's Society Inline* as being appropriate, helpful and very supportive. Similarly, several young people mentioned the services of *Pitt Street Project* Newcastle as being accessible, necessary and relevant. Most young people rated voluntary organisations better than the statutory organisations although there were exceptions. Several young people named a social worker, a doctor, a psychiatrist or other professional who had worked with them in a manner which made the young person feel special, listened to, respected and worthwhile.

Ways of working with young people

The implications for the health of the young people and social care agencies are evident from the voices of the young people. According to the young people social workers should be trained to work with young people, to work with them in an age appropriate way, to listen to young people, to look at life from the young person's perspective, to discuss issues with them, even if the young person disagrees with the outcome, and to like and respect young people.

Services needed

The young people we interviewed often spoke of wanting to have had a refuge available for themselves, or mediation services for their parents and family when younger and being subject to abusive behaviour. The need for refuges for children and young people who need a place away from their abusive home is something the *Children's Society* and other voluntary organisations continue to press for at a national level.

For many of the care leavers who were 18–20 years of age, and although the move to independence clock has been wound forward a couple of years after they left care/home to become more independent, and as with other non-care leavers in that age group, they still needed and were largely dependent on accommodation, education/employment/training support whilst in extended transition. Their education was also delayed and as a result of leaving school at an early age, the number now attending either college or wanting to do so was both striking and significant.

We also found that many of the young people also needed ongoing health and social care support of one sort or another. For those care leavers living in the Foyer project there was very little debt. Whether this was because the Foyer is a social landlord, and/or undertakes effective debt management work we do not know. What we did find was that they greatly valued the stability provided by living in the Foyer, even if they also baulked at some of the restrictions placed on them.

Once again we can see not only how the links between the four social exclusion indicators (poverty, exclusion from services, exclusion from social relations, labour market exclusion) get played out to devastating effect on the lives of many care leavers, but the multifaceted, comprehensive responses demanded of social inclusion.

Chapter Ten

Case Study: Young Mothers and Mothers-to-be

Introducing the research study

This chapter, the last in this part of the book, presents a detailed case study of young mothers and mothers-to-be who are leaving care, and attending a leaving care team for services, about their health and well being, life experiences, needs and concerns. The group of 33 young women leaving care discussed here were all attending a leaving care service in North West England at the time the research was conducted and they form a distinct sub-set of the 57 care leavers whose views form the basis of this part of the book.

The purpose of this case study is to present research, and practice findings about a specific group of care leavers, mothers and mothers-to-be, and present their understanding of the term health and well being, their needs, their views about services and ways to further improve them.

The main advantages of this case study are that:

- It further complements the more statistical and practitioner generated data in the earlier part of the book about the implementation of the CLCA 2000.
- It focuses on the needs of a distinct group of 33 care leavers, all young mothers and mothers-to-be who have often been overlooked in leaving care research studies.
- Wider comparisons can be made with the remaining 24 care leavers described in this part of the book since the core data collected on both groups was identical.
- Further comparisons about life chances, health and well being and access to services by this group can be made with the original cohort group of 102 young people.

The main disadvantages of this case study are that:

- Since it does not discuss the health and well being needs and concerns of fathers, (an emerging area for research and practice) other than through the 'stories' told by the young mothers, it presents a partial view of being a parent and a care leaver.

- It carries the usual limits of a case study approach, namely being more illustrative, short-term and experiential than longitudinal.

The legal leaving care status of the young women

As with the care leavers described in the previous three chapters, here the research interviews for this part of the fieldwork were carried out in 2001, after the CLCA 2000 was enacted in October 2000, but before its introduction in October 2001. In other words they had all left care before the CLCA 2000 came into force and services with which they were provided at the time were provided within the framework of the Children Act 1989. However, after October 2001, this group of 33 young women care leavers aged 16 to 21-year-olds who had previously been in care became 'qualifying children and young people over 16' within the terms of the CLCA 2000. This means they were subject to the same benefits provided under S24 (Children Act 1989) and that the local authority must keep in touch as appropriate, that they are entitled to assistance with education and training, and entitled to vacation accommodation. Since most of the services due to be received by these young women from October 2001 come within the terms of the Children Act 1989 this presents the opportunity for informed comments to be made about the impact of the CLCA 2000.

Establishing the research project

At the time the research study was undertaken there were 463 young people eligible for the BMLCS service, with 347 allocated to staff, 44 pending to the team leader and 72 inactive cases. Manchester Social Services refers around 90% of the cases, with other local authorities referring the rest when a young person moves from their area into the Manchester area. Of the 151 young women from the 347 figure, 68 (or 45%) of the 151 young women leaving care and attending the project were either pregnant, or mothers.

The BMLCS and the research team met up and agreed that the focus of the research would be health and well being issues around teenage pregnancies, pregnancy in care, young motherhood and multiple pregnancies. It was clear from the outset that since the BMLCS was actively working with these young women as care leavers, they were keen to gain a fuller understanding of these young women's needs, concerns, and how service provision met and perhaps could more fully meet expressed needs. The BMLCS drew up a list of all the young women who were either mothers or pregnant (68 of the 151 young women) and over a period of several weeks the key workers discussed the research with them. Permission was also obtained for the researcher to seek consent from the young people to contact and interview them. The young women were then invited to one of three groups in different health and social care projects/settings in Manchester to discuss the research and their participation in it.

At the group meetings the research study was discussed, questions were answered and the young women were asked whether they would like to be interviewed or take part in focus groups. As with the other research sites, here key issues such as confidentiality, commitment and the dissemination of information were examined and explained. The young women wanted either to be interviewed by the researcher or be part of a focus group. The young women were paid for their time, crèche facilities were provided, transport arranged as necessary and all expenses were met. None of the young women wished to train to become a peer researcher (the research team's preferred option early on).

The young women were shown copies of a draft interview schedule used in one of the interviews with non-care leavers and further areas and topics of interest were discussed and the young women added issues that they considered to be of importance to their health and well being. These included issues about how they understood their health and well being, being a young mother, parenting and health service provision. The discussions proved to be very lively, with most young women demonstrating a good understanding of the issues as they affect them.

The young women clearly identified physical, mental, emotional and psychological aspects of health. They also understood the wider concepts around the notion of well being. During the discussions it was apparent that the young women felt other issues not normally considered to be health related did, indeed, have a negative effect on their health and well being such as relationships, lack of support, abuse and violence, accommodation and poverty.

Both the interview schedule and the focus group questions looked at all aspects of health and emotional well being as well as teenage pregnancy, young motherhood, parenting and children.

Taking account of their other commitments such as school holidays, work, childcare responsibility and availability, interview dates were arranged. The researcher carried out 26 in-depth interviews and three taped and transcribed focus groups with 14 women. This case study of young mothers and mothers-to-be is based on information about a total of 33 young women since seven of the young women who attended the focus groups also took part in the in-depth interviews.

The young women's family and social circumstances

Background

The 33 young women were aged between 16 and 22 and two-thirds (22) described themselves as white and one-third (11) described themselves as 'mixed race or black'. Half of the 26 young women interviewed had a regular partner, but only six lived with their partner and children. This seems to point to a trend of the vast majority of young women in not living with their partner. Nevertheless, it should be noted here, because of the Unit's rules, that five of the male partners of the seven young women staying at the mother and baby unit were not allowed to stay overnight. Four young women lived on their own, just one lived with a partner (without a child) fourteen lived on their own with their children, one lived with a friend and one lived with a foster carer.

Care history

The earliest age one of the young women was taken into care was at birth and the oldest aged 15 years. 22 entered care after the age of eleven and half of the 33 young women were taken into care between the ages of 11 and 13 years. The biggest grouping, of 16 young women, left care at age sixteen, after an average time of four years spent in care. Four young women left care before the age of 16, one left care at the age of 17 and five left care at the age of 18.

Ten of the young women (30%) said that one or both of their parents/step parents had been in care, 14 (or 26%) said that their child's father had been in care, and five (20%) of the parents of those 14 fathers had also previously been in care.

The ages of their partners or ex-partners ranged from 16 to 40 years (compared with their age range of 16–22) and fourteen of the partners were much older than the young women, and aged between 25 and 40 years of age.

The young women reported that a majority (54%) of their children's fathers had been in care when they were younger and 58% had been in prison. Most of their own fathers had left home at an early age (under 16) and reported being homeless or having to stay at the homes of various friends, family members and neighbours due to violence, abuse or a breakdown in family relationships at home.

A third of the young women spoke of the inability of their mothers to look after them 'probably' due to alcohol and/or drug related issues and/or mental health issues. Most of the young women said that there had been problems with their mums' partner regarding violence or abuse. The following quotes present varying reasons why three of the young women were taken into care:

I was taken into care because my mum couldn't cope with me; she was always off her face. I wanted to do my thing and wanted more freedom. I wanted to go out and stay out late. I broke all her rules. So she put me in care. I could do what I wanted in care. I went a bit wild.

My mum had really bad mental health problems. She used to lock us up.

I was put in care because of the abuse at home. I loved it in care. I had lovely foster carers. They saved my life.

Care placements

25% of the young women had lived in 'various types' of care, including foster care, residential care, family centres, secure accommodation and out-of-area placements and 24% had experienced foster care only. 12% had experienced residential care, and 19% had been placed at home or with family members. The 26 young women interviewed reported that the number of placements they had lived in ranged from 1 to 40. The average number of placements per young woman, with all the accompanying relationship, educational and personal complexities arising from multiple moves, was nine. Seven had experienced between 10 and 20 placements whilst in care.

15 or just under 50% of the young women felt that being in the care system had *not* affected their health and well being at all, but overall, the young women's experiences of care were mixed. These are examples of these mixed experiences:

It was great in care. It made me grow up and made me mature. People say I'm very mature for my age and I have a different outlook on life than other kids my age.

It did my head in. There was no privacy; there were always lots of people around. The staff were dead nosey, always asking questions and watching you. There was a lot of violence from the other kids and stealing. I never felt safe in care.

It has completely ruined my life. It has freaked me out. I hated it. They never listened to what I said. They didn't believe me when I told them what my foster dad was doing to me. They left me there for years until I started running away and got into drugs and prostitution.

In addition to being in the foster and residential care system, almost 58% of the young women had experienced care from others, including family members, especially grand parents and aunts, family friends, neighbours and partner's parents. The most commonly cited relative to stay with was their grandmother, followed by an aunt and then friends (on kinship care and placements with grandparents also see Broad, Hayes and Rushforth (2001), Jenkins (2001) and Richards (2001) and about family and friends who are carers, see Wheal (2001b). The young women tended not to stay there for good, but a pattern of coming and going followed, returning to the family home when things calmed down a little and then leaving again when things 'got bad' again. For example:

I started staying over at my aunt's house because my mum couldn't look after me because of the state of her mental health. I also stayed at my friend's house a lot.

When things got bad I would go and stay at my nan's house. I stayed with her on and off for years until I got too much for her.

I went to live at my boyfriend's mum's house when I was 14 because my dad threw me out. We didn't get on so I stayed at different friends' houses and then a neighbour's house.

When asked why they were taken into care, nine thought it was because of sexual abuse, seven thought it was because of physical abuse, and five said that their mums had been unable to cope with them and that they were beyond control. One had gone into care because her mother had died, another as her mother was ill, another because her mother was an alcoholic and two went into care because they 'wanted to'.

Having looked at the young people's care history let us now turn to examining their education background.

Education

A third of the young women (11) stopped attending school before the age of 14 due to 'going into care', moving around, being excluded, having family problems or a combination of these. The remainder left school between 15 and 16-years-old, with most leaving before taking any exams. Only one young woman had gone on to further education, gained a qualification and was now working in full time employment. Nearly three quarters (19) of the young women intended to return to college as soon as possible, but five felt that the time was not right due to childcare responsibilities. This is what three of the young women said in interview:

I get really embarrassed when I have to fill in forms and the like because I can hardly read and write. I know now that I will have to go to college to learn things.

I am going back to college as soon as my kids are old enough. I want to get a good job with good money.

I didn't like school at the time but now I have realised what I have missed. I am going to go back when the baby is born.

15 young women had left school before they had taken any examinations, two had failed all examinations, five had passed some examinations and one had passed all her examinations. She left junior school at 11 years and never went to her senior school. Two other young women left school at 12, two left at 13, another at 14, seven at 15 and eleven at 16. One young women left college at 22, after being in higher education.

When asked why they felt they had not done well at school, ten young women said that being in care and moving around had had a negative impact on their education. Five said that being pregnant had made them leave school without taking exams, at a young age.

This is what three of the young women said about their earlier education:

Nobody cared if I went to school or not when I was in care. No one encouraged me to go, as long as you weren't a problem they let you stay off and anyway I was moved around so much I could never settle in any school.

I stopped going when I became pregnant because people were looking at me and calling me names. They thought I was shit because I was in foster care and pregnant.

I was in a gang and we thought we were dead hard. We started wagging it and stopped going to school. My mum couldn't make me go so she put me in care and they didn't make me go either.

Financial circumstances

31 (94%) of the young women were not in paid employment and lived on Income Support or a combination of Income Support and Child Benefit (80%), Job Seekers Allowance or Sickness Benefit to support them/their child. The Income Support rate at the time was £41.35 for 16 and 17-year-olds. If the young person had been in the care of the local authority for 12 months prior to leaving care then s/he would receive a top-up of £10 per week or £20 per week if doing 'something useful' such as training, education or work experience. However, after October 2001 (when the CLCA was introduced) the £10 top-up was stopped if the young person was not considered to be doing anything productive but the £20 was increased to £30 if the opposite was the case. This is what three of the young women said about a lack of money:

I can't afford to buy my kids anything. I get so depressed trying to manage everything. I don't have enough money to live on.

I can never get anything new for the kids, its always second hand stuff or things that people give me.

I can't afford to furnish the house; I just don't have the money.

Half of the young women were in debt, with debts ranging from £60 to £4000. The average debt was several hundred pounds and covered household bills, loans, catalogues and drug debts. For example:

It all just mounted up . . . the bills just kept piling up. I don't have the money to pay for them. I owe the catalogue hundreds because that's the only way I can get new clothes without paying for them up front.

Only two of the seven young women in the mother and baby units had any debts, and they were both young women who had lived independently first and then came into the units as they clearly needed additional support. There were also problems about transport for young mothers with buggies.

Transport and isolation

The other young women with babies/children spoke about the need for the buses to be 'low loaders' which enables them to get the buggies/prams on the bus without having to take the baby out and close the buggy. Half thought the transport system was 'OK' but two thirds thought it was 'too expensive.' The expense did have a significant impact on the young women as ten felt isolated because they could not afford to visit friends and family, six felt it limited their travel, seven felt it affected their life and another one felt depressed because she could not see family and friends. As two young women said in interview:

All the buses should be low-loaders so I can get the buggy on. Sometimes I have to wait for ages for a low-loader to come and then when it comes someone is sat on the seat where the buggy should go.

It is so expensive on the bus. I can't visit my family and friends as much as I want to so I get depressed and lonely because I'm stuck in the house all day with the kids.

Accommodation

None of the 33 young women lived with their parents but lived in a range of accommodation, two-thirds in their own tenancy (house or flat), two young women shared a tenancy (house) and the remainder in a hostel or a mother and baby unit.

Just under a half reported needing repairs to be carried out as a matter of urgency including insecure doors and windows and dangerous gas and electrical equipment. There were then frustrations about the poor accommodation, as can be demonstrated by the following typical quotations:

The bathroom window doesn't shut at all, the wood has rotted away, so I'm scared the kids will climb on the bath and fall out the window.

The back door was kicked in by my ex boyfriend and they won't fix it because he has done it before. They want me to pay for it but why should I? I didn't do it and anyway I can't afford to pay for it.

Young women at the mother and baby unit were particularly critical about the building in that it was completely inappropriate for its use. It was a large, old, four-storey house with no lifts or ramps for the prams and buggies and even had a flight of stairs at the entrance to the building. It

caused a lot of stress to the young women as the following quotations illustrate:

I live in a flat on the top floor with my baby. I have to climb three flights of stairs with the baby, the buggy and the shopping. I used to take the baby up first, put him in his cot, then go back down for the shopping and then go for the buggy but I realised that they (the other residents) were nicking my shopping while it was down there so now I take my shopping up first.

I hate it here; the building is so badly designed. Fancy having a mother and baby unit in a building like this, with all the stairs.

Hygiene issues did not appear to be a problem with all of the young women reporting being able to wash, bathe, clean teeth daily, buy toiletries and wash clothes satisfactorily.

Contact with family and friends

22 of the 33 young women reported having problems with their families and/or difficult family relationships. Eleven young women still had daily contact with their family, 8 had contact once or twice a week, 7 at least once a month and a further 7 rarely or never had any contact with their families. The following responses illustrate the range of views expressed about contact:

I haven't seen anyone from my family for years. I don't even know where they live anymore. I don't want to see them to be honest but I often wonder where they are, what they're doing.

I see my mum every couple of months. We just don't get on. We fight when we are together. She picks on me and criticises me for everything.

I see my mum and nan every day. They help me with the kids. If it hadn't have been for my mum and nan I don't know how I would have coped.

Becoming a parent

28 of the 33 young women had a child or children, and two of these were also pregnant. The remaining five of the cohort of 33 young women who did not have a child were pregnant. Of the 28 young women who were already parents 22 had one child, four had two children, two had three children.

The research study was asked to look at the background to the young women becoming pregnant and when asked specifically why they had become pregnant, eleven young women said quite simply because they 'wanted a child'. They did follow this up with reasons such as:

I felt ready for a baby. I really wanted a baby. I was old enough.

I never had any love. No one ever gave me any love or said that they loved me. I never felt wanted so I decided to have a baby to give me that love and whom I could really love.

My boyfriend said he wanted one and would stay with me. We would be a family. He didn't and we aren't.

A further twelve said they had become pregnant accidentally, again for a variety of reasons:

The condom split.

I was breast feeding at the time and thought I couldn't get pregnant. By the time I realised I was pregnant it was too late.

Because I had unsafe and unprotected sex so many times and not got caught I thought there was something wrong with me and I couldn't get pregnant.

Two young women became pregnant as the result of 'drinking too much' alcohol and having unprotected sex. Both young women said they had a dependency on alcohol and regularly became intoxicated to such an extent that they did not care or remember what they did. Three young women said they had had more than one child because they wanted to, that it had been a deliberate and conscious choice and three young women said they had accidentally become pregnant a second or third time.

In interview when asked if they were going to have any more children, sixteen young women said 'no', seven said 'yes' and three said that they would 'consider having more' in a few years, when they were more able to cope. This is what three of the young women said in interview in answer to this question about having more children:

No way. I didn't realise how hard it really is. I never have any rest and I'm so tired all the time. When she goes to school I want to go back to college and do something so I can get a decent job.

I would like another sooner rather than later. I would hate (my child) to be an only child.

When I am older and more experienced I would like another, not now. When I have a nice house, a good job and a partner. I don't want to be on my own all the time like I was this time. It is so lonely and depressing. Maybe in about ten years or so when I've got a career going.

Most of the young women mentioned the need for more money, better accommodation, a good job and a car as being necessary before they would consider having another baby.

Some information was provided by the young women about their sexual health, contraception, and personal relationships. Most of the young women with a child or children stated they did not want any more children. Yet a significant number of that group indicated that they did not always take contraception and were not in regular relationships. However, it was also estimated, based on what the young women replied in answer to other health questions, that approximately half of the young women were having unprotected sex on a fairly regular basis, indicating a need for (further) sexual health promotion and relationship work with many of these women.

Half of the young women felt that having their child had been 'good' for them in that it had stopped them doing 'bad' things and that had they not had their child they would be far worse off now. Many said having their child had changed their lives for the better, in that they had 'calmed down', 'grown up' and 'matured'. They also felt that the responsibility of looking after a child had changed their outlook and perspectives on life, in that they were no longer so self centred or selfish. They felt having children gave them 'warmth, love, attention and a family life' something they had not had before.

When the researcher asked if they could 'turn back time' and, regardless of the obvious love the young women had for their child or children, would they have waited until they were older to have a child? Two thirds of the young women said knowing now what they know they would have waited to have their children. They all said they loved their children very much, but for both their sakes they should have waited until they were older to have the child or children. For example:

I want to give them so much more. I can't afford decent stuff, I only buy crap. I didn't want them to grow up like me; I wanted them to have more than I got. The only thing they will never do without is the love I never got.

I didn't want them to grow up with a single parent. I wanted them to have a mum and a dad but we were far too young to make it work.

My life is ruined now, it's on hold. I've got to look after her for at least sixteen years. I can't believe I was that stupid. I thought it would be so easy.

When asked if anything or anyone might have stopped them from becoming pregnant, nine of the young women said that someone like them, in their position, talking to them, telling them what it is really like might have dissuaded them from having a child. A further nine said that 'nothing' would have changed their minds, that it was a deliberate and conscious decision to have a child. A few had said either they were drunk or that if they had better information on contraception, or felt happy and loved, they might not have become pregnant. Another two young women had no choice as they had been raped.

The young women were specifically asked what advice they would have liked to be given to other young woman about becoming a parent. Nine said to be told 'how tough it would be on their own', five said to be made to 'understand the implications of what they were doing', and three to be told that 'their life was not their own anymore'. However, nine said 'nothing' would have affected them, as they do not listen to anyone and they wanted to have a child.

The researcher asked a follow-up question about what advice these young women would give to other young women about being a young mum and 54% (eighteen) said 'not to have a child so young'. Three young women said the following about this important issue:

They give these crying babies out now in schools, why didn't we have that. It's all changed now.

There's loads of girls who might want to have kids, but they don't realise the responsibility and like me they always think they'll be good all the time, but they've got to realise its at night time, the feeds, the health, you've got to check your baby out like constantly, it's like if the baby's coughing.

They're only in love with the idea, but realistically, I didn't believe it, because at first it's glamorous. Getting this money at first, then your money goes, you have the kid and it's all great, but as time goes on. It's like I can't afford that, but when it first comes along it's like dead easy and then reality hits you in the face.

Three young women said you should only have a child for the right reasons and not as the result of a mistake. Two other young women said you should make sure you have a lot of support, especially from your family and your partner.

I love him so much but I wish I waited until I was older to have hir. That's what I want to say when I see these young girls messing around with lads. It just changes

your whole life and no one realises that until it's too late.

It's dead hard being a mum. No one tells you that. It's dead lonely too and if you are young everyone thinks you can't do it.

However, sixteen (or 48%) of the young women said *it was great being a mum, most of the time.* There were, of course, some problems being a young mum including loneliness, isolation, poverty and poor accommodation but there were good points to it as well. These include the children learning and growing everyday, freedom, independence and a form of respect and status. Four young women felt very tired all the time, three were very scared at the demands made on them and three felt they had no life of their own any more.

Sixteen (62%) of the young women still saw the fathers of their children but less than half (11) of them were involved with their children on a regular day-to-day parenting basis. Fourteen (54%) of the fathers did not provide any parenting for their children and one did 'when he feels like it'. Twelve men supported their children financially.

Physical and emotional health

Health and physical exercise

All the young women were registered with a doctor and most were registered with a dentist. Over two thirds of the young women did some form of exercise and the most popular being walking. The remainder did a mixture of sit-ups; yoga, cycling, dancing, swimming and a small number went to the gym. 62% of the young women did some form of exercise every day. When asked if anything stopped them doing their exercises, there were a range of answers. These included their pregnancy 'making it difficult', 'being too busy', 'couldn't be bothered', 'being overweight', 'the children stopping them' and 'lack of money'. The majority stated that they wanted to exercise more or go to the gym but couldn't afford it. There were then a range of personal, motivational, practical and financial reasons contributing to the young women not taking up more regular exercise, and the young women welcomed attending group sessions which could provide more peer support. Let us now move onto the related health areas of tobacco and alcohol usage.

Smoking, alcohol and substance use

There was a very similar pattern of smoking, alcohol and drug use for these 33 young women care leavers as for the total sample in the previous chapter. Here 27 (82%) of the young women smoked every day, averaging 10 cigarettes a day. They started smoking between the ages of 7–16 years, the average age being 12 years old. Seventeen of the young women drank, with the majority only drinking 'occasionally' or 'less than once a week' although most used to drink excessively before they had children. When asked to explain this, the young women were very conscious about not being drunk when responsible for children. Many spoke about their own parents not being able to care for them when under the influence of alcohol.

Ten young women said they still used drugs on a regular basis but a larger number, sixteen young women, no longer used drugs on a regular basis due to having children. However, when asked further about what drugs they take or have taken, it was clear to the researcher that most still used cannabis on a very regular basis. It was not classed or seen as a drug by the young women, but more akin to a relaxing cigarette. The average age to start to use drugs was 12 years old and most of the young women had tried a range of drugs including amphetamines, cocaine, heroin, prescribed drugs, ecstasy and other recreational drugs. When asked if drug taking had affected their health and well being in any way four of the young women felt that long-term use of cannabis had affected them mentally, reporting lack of concentration and tiredness.

Abuse and bullying

Two thirds of the young women (22) reported being abused prior to being looked after, 2 reporting physical abuse, three reporting mental abuse, seven reporting sexual abuse and 10 reporting a combination of these abuses. Of the 22 young women who reported abuse, 20 were carried out by a man or men who were related to them (father, stepfather, partner, uncle, family friend, granddad and foster father).

Just over half (17) of the young women reported having being bullied, mostly at school by other pupils or their peers but with a few reporting the bullying to be from residents in care (2), neighbour (2), mother (1) or father (1). Just under half (13) of the young women reported

being bullied both at home and at school. Bullying at home tended to start at a very early age, from the earliest memory, at around three years old. School bullying tended to start in late junior or early senior years (years 6–8) and included verbal, physical and racist bullying as well as theft and intimidation. As two women said:

> My mum started on me when I was really little. She never left me alone. She picked on me all the time. She made me feel worthless.

> I was about five or six when some boys in school started calling me racist names. They followed me round all day shouting bad things at me. The teachers did nothing so I stopped going to school. My mum couldn't do anything with me so I got put into care.

Nearly two-thirds (17) of the young women reported being abused in the family home. One young women said she had been physically abused, two reported being mentally abused, six reported being sexually abused, one said she had been verbally abused constantly throughout her childhood and seven young women reported multiple abuses (all of the above):

> My step dad sexually abused me from when I was very little. When I got older (14) I told my mum. She didn't believe me but I got the police involved. He got three years but my mum still doesn't believe me. He's out now and back at home with her. I've got two little sisters. I worry about them.

> My granddad, dad and uncle all abused me. I've tried to kill myself loads of times. I've slit my wrists, took overdoses and I'm very emotional. I lose it really easily. Little things set me off and I go mad.

From the in-depth interviews it is clear that sexual abuse or multiple abuses started at an earlier age than other abuses. Of the thirteen young women who reported sexual or multiple abuses, twelve say it is their earliest memory. All the young women who reported abuse expressed a range of feelings . . . from it making them a stronger person to it ruining their lives . . . from them fearing they may harm their own children to them being certain no one would ever hurt their children.

Physical violence

Just under 90% (29) of the young women reported having experienced severe violence in their lives. This violence came from a range of people including parents, peers, carers, relatives, partners, neighbours and strangers. The earliest recorded violence was a few days after birth to late teens and included hitting, beating, slapping, biting, stabbing, punching, hung over balconies, poisoned, knocked unconscious, and kicking. 20 young women had experienced this violence in the family home; the others at school, in care, on the streets or in their own home. Again, the young women reported this violence as being one of their earliest memories, as being a daily part of their lives:

> *My dad used to batter us for the least thing. He would punch us senseless. His used to strangle us up against a wall. We got taken away and put in care.*

> *The other residents used to hit me or kick me. The workers didn't do anything. They used to tell me to stay out of their way, as if it was my fault.*

> *He used to hang me over the balcony to get at my mum.*

Half of the young women report that violence is still on going in their lives and that it is usually from partners or ex-partners. There were then links between many of the young women who had experienced violence and/or abuse in the past, and their current experiences. Domestic violence was particularly prevalent with many of the young women with partners reporting regular abuse, some on a daily basis. Eight young women said they are currently involved in domestic violence, whereby their male partner is violent to them. These young women also spoke about isolation, loneliness and dependency on the partner in that 'he was better than nothing' and provided company. This is what two women said:

> *He thought I was talking to another guy so he battered me in front of everyone in the pub. No one would help me 'cos he is well known. He fractured my skull with his mobile phone then he drove me around for hours threatening to kill me. I was dead scared. I had to be nice to him. After hours he let me go to the hospital. I was pregnant at the time with his baby.*

> *When we row he just hits me to make me shut up. We row most days.*

Over two-thirds of the young women reported showing physical violence towards others, usually siblings, or someone at school or their partner. The violence included hitting, fighting, beating, punching, stabbing and slapping. The majority of these young women reported that they started to become violent in their early teens.

Four young women reported having a 'nervous breakdown' with one being sectioned and detained under a Mental Health Act. All four young women attributed their breakdown to 'life experience', usually abuse or violence. For example:

> *My ex-boyfriend won't leave me alone. He is violent and has wrecked my house loads of times. I get so stressed. I don't know what to do. I end up taking it out on the kids. I tried to kill myself several times.*

> *I get so stressed when I can't afford something . . . like when my son comes home from school, asking for money for a trip or something and I can't give him the money.*

> *The kids really stress me out, they're so naughty. I can't control them. I know now how my mother must have felt.*

> *My worker is so nosey. She is always asking questions and checking up on me. She watches everything I do. She pretends to be my friend and then tells the others. She does my head in.*

Stress

The vast majority of the young women reported feeling very stressed 'regularly' or on 'a day-to-day' basis. Many young women felt that stress to be a major factor in their lives. The stress came from many areas such as partners, relationships, poverty and children. One-third (11) attributed this stress to their partners' or ex-partners' behaviour. Two thirds reported, fairly evenly in terms of the number of responses, 'children's behaviour', 'inappropriate and inadequate accommodation', 'lack of money', 'unsupportive relationships with family' and 'staff' as causes of stress, affecting their health and well being.

What would help the young women to deal with their stress?

All the young women in the focus groups said that coming together as a group had helped them enormously. They realised they weren't alone, they shared ideas and 'tactics' on how to cope with and deal with stress and they supported each other. They also said they had learnt a lot from each other. They said they would like the opportunity to get together in a group on a regular basis and discuss 'important issues' like the health and well being ones raised in the research. They also welcomed the idea of inviting 'someone' in to talk to them about relevant issues that affect their lives. These included topics such as parenting skills, surviving abuse and violence, increasing self confidence and esteem, communication skills (such as complaining appropriately) and dealing with professionals (like their children's teachers and social workers). They felt that this type of 'open learning' would be beneficial to them and their families.

Most of the young mothers felt that *proper nursery provision* would help them better cope with the stress they felt. If there was at the very least a crèche where they could drop the child off for a few hours per day so they could go shopping or swimming, catch up on sleep or chores, spend time with other children or just have time for themselves to recharge their batteries. The research team also wanted to establish what, from their point of view, actually helps them maintain their health, using a user focused 'what works?' approach. We also wanted to find out what factors they considered affected their health and well being.

What factors affected the young women's health and well being?

The young women gave various reasons as to what affected their health. Eight young women said stress affected their health to varying degrees. Three young women felt their pregnancy was affecting their health in negative way. Five felt smoking was affecting their health, while two young women felt not having enough money to live on had a negative effect on their health. A further two felt that asthma affected their health. Four felt that living in a hostel for homeless young people made them ill and one felt that her poor diet contributed to her continuing ill health. One young woman felt the total lack of support after leaving care had made her ill. Many of the young women spoke about wanting to give up smoking, the effect it has on their health and not wanting their children to copy them and smoke. They explained and rationalised their smoking, stating it helped them to cope with the stress they felt under, it helped them to relax, it suppressed their appetite, helped them to lose weight and, for many, it was the one pleasure in life they had. At the moment the perceived short-term advantages seemed to outweigh the disadvantages.

What helps the young women to maintain their health?

The young women talked here about *feeling valued, having responsibilities and feeling loved through having a child or children*. Many young women said that *becoming a mum had made them healthier*, in that they had stopped using drugs or drinking alcohol, were no longer involved in prostitution and/or had become more settled and now had permanent, safe accommodation. They also tended to eat better than they had before, as they now had to cook for their children so they tended to eat more regularly. Some of the young women who were mothers said they felt better emotionally as they now felt they had *a purpose in life, they felt loved and wanted and they had a role to play and had status in the community*. Again one can see that it is the two 'service inclusion' and 'inclusion in social relations' aspects of social inclusion, alongside 'receipt of adequate income', which are highly valued by these young mothers and mothers-to-be, as being indicative of feeling socially accepted and socially included.

The young women were also more likely to use primary health services such as those provided by a doctor and dentist because their children used these services. So what would make them feel healthier?

What would make the young women feel healthier?

The young women had various responses when asked what, if anything, would make them feel better or healthier. Just under one third (8) of the young women said that more money would help to make them feel better and healthier, four felt that better accommodation would improve their health, three thought that having their baby would make them feel healthier. This is how one young woman described the relationship between shortage of money and health:

> If I had more money I would feel so much better. I wouldn't have to worry about money all the time for a start. I could buy things for the house and my daughter and take her out more and do things with her. I could buy decent food and maybe lose a bit of weight.

A further five felt that having more support would make them feel better. Sadly, two young women felt that nothing could ever improve their health or make them feel better. Several young women spoke about the importance of religion in their lives, in that it helped them come to cope with what had happened to them, as one said in interview:

> *I pray a lot. It calms me down. It has helped to forgive him. It helps me focus on the future and cope with my life.*

What extra supports are needed?

The young women could identify what support they needed now. Two thirds of the young women feel they need support with multiple issues, including housing, repairs, finance, budgeting, social and life skills as well as parenting skills. The young women also identified support in attending college and more support from families and partners. The young women saw a need for a mutual support group (like the research focus groups) to discuss issues and support each other. If it had a budget they could invite people to talk about relevant issues identified by the young women. They would also like local mentors from the community, to be available for advice, help and friendship.

What would help in dealing with violence when younger?

The young women talked of wanting to be listened to and believed, needing face-to-face meetings and taking appropriate action. Several spoke of trying to tell teachers what was going on in their lives, but commented that the teachers tended to over react or under react or not believe them. Few were referred on to the appropriate services. Similarly, many young women were unhappy with the response of social workers, in that decisions were made without discussion, their views and wishes were not taken into account, social workers failed to act, they tended to believe the parent or abuser or they did not support the young person. Several young women spoke about using *Childline* when they were younger. The majority thought it had been helpful but that it was often hard to get through due to it being constantly engaged. Also young women spoke about wanting to have face-to-face interaction when discussing the violence and needing to have a safe place to go. Young women spoke about wanting to have all the options available explained to them in a young person centred way. For example it was important to have information about whether to press charges, what the possible outcomes could be, where to seek help, advice and guidance, information

(especially around sexually transmitted diseases), support and a safe place to live.

What sort of sexual education would help?

The majority of the 33 young women stated that they wished they had not had a baby so young, and wanted to have had better sex education in school, and better PSE (personal and social education) in school. They also wanted more projects and drop-ins, both in and out of school, as well as peer educators rather than adults telling them about these issues. However, since many of the young women did not attend school regularly or up to the age of 16 this raises the question about why school did not sufficiently retain their interest, and what other organisations and people need to be involved in sex education? To help others in the future the young women also recommended slightly 'older' young women like themselves (i.e. about 18–20 years of age) coming to the children's home, foster placement or school to tell them as it is, what its really like as a young mum, both good and bad. Most of the young women who took part in this research would be happy to do this now for younger women. They feel they would have listened to them, would have taken more notice of them and maybe not have had a child so young.

The following case study of 'Alice' (not her real name) illustrates some of these key issues discussed here, about health, emotional well being and violence.

Case study – 'Alice'

Alice is a 20-year-old young woman with two children. The father of her children is in prison, due to be released in two years. He was very violent to her and continues to threaten her from prison. She has now started a relationship with one of his friends.

Alice was taken into care at the age of three due to multiple abuses from her mother's partner. She had about 15 placements in her experience of care, some she said were good, some were worse than home. She has very little contact or support from her family and has few friends outside the care system. She first became pregnant at 14 when she had a termination. She then became pregnant again at 15 and had the child. She had another at 17. Both children are on the Child Protection Register and living with her.

She lives in a council house that needs major repairs to it. It has insecure windows and doors and damp. She has been robbed several times. She has accumulated large debts due to failing to pay household bills and taking out loans. Alice has many health issues including depression, stress, obesity, asthma, sexual health issues and failing to take her medication as prescribed. Her aftercare worker is currently trying to work on raising her self-esteem and confidence and making her aware of her responsibilities to her children. They have discussed her health issues as she sees them and looked at nutrition and dieting.

This case study illustrates the ongoing priorities and pressures facing these young women, indicating that the pursuance of health and well being work which needs to be done simultaneously working with more pressing and wide-ranging financial, emotional and practical social inclusion and resilience building agendas. Having recorded in some detail the background and life style circumstances of these young women and their views about their health and well being, the research team was keen to find out what these young women reported as the responses by health and social care agencies to their needs. Although it was beyond the scope and remit of the research project to conduct structured interviews with, and visits to, health and social care agencies, a number of attempts were made to seek out their views and ideas. Where these were obtained they are included in this chapter.

Views about and use of health and social care agencies

In this section we look at the young people's use of and views about services provided by health and social care agencies, with particular reference to specialist services for black young people, maternity services and teenage pregnancy issues. There is also a further individual case study.

Health and social care agencies

Most of the young women (25) said they would visit a doctor or other health professional when

necessary, with only one saying that she does not see any health care professional. Seventeen young women go for general health issues, such as coughs, respiratory track infections, asthma and the like. All the young women see health professionals for maternity care and three see professionals for drug related issues. One each sees a doctor for family planning and mental health issues. All the young women said they would always take their baby or child to see a doctor as and when necessary.

The majority of the young women (18) say they only visit the doctor as necessary; five go rarely, with one going monthly, one going fortnightly and one going weekly for regular sessions or prescriptions.

Interestingly enough, while most of the young women (20) feel that the health professionals offer the appropriate services and treatments, ten do not feel that the health professionals have the 'right attitude' toward them or do enough to help them.

He doesn't listen to me. He doesn't even look at me. He just writes out a prescription. I know he wants me out of there as soon as possible.

When I walked in he rolled his eyes as if to say 'not you again'.

She thinks I am an over anxious mother. She makes me feel stupid, but this is my first baby and I am scared sometimes.

In the focus groups the young women talked a lot about what it was like visiting the doctor. The following are quotations from the young women about three important practical health and well being issues, seeing the GP, contraception, and child care.

About seeing the GP – this is what five young women said in a focus group:

The doctor told me he had a rash on his face, but it wasn't, it was eczema, I had to go to different doctors and they told me it was eczema.

It took a year for the doctor to find out my daughter had asthma.

It depends which doctor you go and see, like some doctors will diagnose it straight away, but others don't. So what we do is, we'll go to the doctors and if they're not helpful we'll go to a different doctor, whereas they'll give us the information straight away, whereas Dr X is useless.

I got a questionnaire form . . . that's the first time I've been to a doctor where someone has said do you want to fill in this questionnaire about the surgery. I had nothing bad to say about it really at the time.

I read recently, that a doctor has to train for five years to become a qualified doctor, full time training, and they are only taught for about five hours how to relate to people, half a day. Everything else is about how to diagnose people, medicine, but to actually speak to people five hours.

Another key issue which came up in the focus groups was the issue of the 'morning after' pill and contraception.

About the 'morning after' pill/contraception – this is what five young women said about this issue:

I think that the morning after pill is a good idea, when you can get it from the chemist.

I thought they were extending it.

They are selling it to young children, under 16.

If they ask if you're under 16, they just say no, they're not asking for ID.

They should keep selling it in chemists though because someone could go out and you know, and then have to wait for two days for somewhere to open to get it and by then it's too late.

Having a baby or toddler to bring up, it was almost inevitable that they raised childcare issues. This was raised both in relation to their child, and the mother benefiting from the child being cared for during some part of the day, and in terms of making it possible for the young women to have some time to themselves (day time or evening), or of finding employment.

About child care and going out – this is what six young women said in a focus group:

You know when you are with two children constantly 24/7 you just feel that you're going to crack up, I used to work before I had two kids.

I found that because it's private they tend to take in too many children, they overcrowd them because its cash basically and they tend to overcrowd them, I wouldn't say that they don't get better care but they overcrowd them.

If you like going out, suddenly you've got this baby, you've got to get a babysitter, it's like my partners not with me, hopefully mum or dad, you know the family, how can I go out. You get some women who haven't been out for months on end.

I know some people who leave the kids in the house while they go out clubbing, I know one girl like that.

My daughter, she's seven months, I've been out once and everyone offers to baby-sit, people I can trust, but I don't want to, because I love being a mum, I love

being with her. At the end of the day what have you got, when you go clubbing you're just meeting guys that are not worth looking at twice.

I go clubbing after a long hard week looking after my daughter. The weekends are like luxury to me where I can go out and relax by myself with no kids, but it's not every week, I think 'have a good time', I get pampered, go out, but I don't go out to chat up a man or anything.

Specialist services for black care leavers

Several black young women valued the services provided by a specialist project called *Bibini*. This is a registered charity (supported by the DoH) working specifically with black young people in Manchester, providing family support services, play therapy, counselling, case work support and befriending. *Bibini* also runs a children's home (for black children), has an Asian support worker, a disability project worker, volunteers, befrienders and six supported flats for young black people leaving care. *Bibini* works closely with many other agencies to provide a 'joined up' service for black young people in the Manchester area. Staff at the *Bibini* Centre considered that stress affects young people more than is recognised by those normally working with young people (a point echoed by many others, including in respect of black and dual heritage young people, Ince, 2004). The view was also expressed that there are insufficiently targeted services and not enough emotional support, counselling or befriending services for all young people. Mental health services were given as a specific example of a service not readily accessible or relevant to young people, especially black young people.

Maternity services and mother and baby units

Maternity services

All the young women had their children at one of three maternity hospitals in the Manchester area. The significant finding was about the variations in treatments offered and the attitude towards the young women from the maternity staff and health visitors. The young women had mixed views about health and maternity services and wanted to be treated 'properly' and as adults and not differently and as children. For example:

They never talked down to me like some of my friends said they did. They really listened to me, took time to explain what was going to happen and never made me feel stupid. It was always the same one so I got used to her and she understood me. She always made sure I got my appointment when she was on and she was there when I delivered. I really missed her when I left.

She always came round when she said she would and I always had her. I could talk to her about anything and she would help me and not laugh at me. She must have wanted to laugh at some of the things I asked her. I felt I could ask her and she wouldn't go running off telling people just because I was from care. She made me realise I could cope, that I was a good mum.

They were terrible, I mean it was my first baby, I was in terrible pain but it was obvious they didn't believe me until I had the haemorrhage and ended up in intensive care. They sat around gossiping all day, they never helped me and when I got it wrong one actually shouted at me in front of everyone and called me stupid. I didn't know you shouldn't put the baby on the bed when you're changing the nappy.

Somehow they lost my notes and I never got called for my antenatal appointments. When I finally went after going to my doctors to see what's what, they tried to blame me as if I was deliberately trying to avoid my checkups. They got my social worker involved like I was harming the baby or something. I felt they were watching everything I did and making notes.

The young women wanted respect from the professionals and for people to be reliable and keep appointments (a recurrent theme for all care leavers) and they did not want to be labelled or stigmatised. They were very sensitive about this issue. They did not feel as supported, for example, as an older woman living with a partner might expect to be.

Mother and baby units

None of the young women who were interviewed in the two mother and baby units wanted to be there. The following case study, 'Angeline' (not her real name) illustrates that, although not ideal, the unit is a place where Angeline, and others, feel safe.

Case Study – 'Angeline'

Angeline is a 19-year-old young woman with two very young children. She is currently living in a mother and baby unit, which she hates. She has been in care since she was seven, due to physical abuse from her mother and sexual abuse from her mother's partner. When she was in care she

---

was coerced into prostitution by her violent boyfriend/pimp. When she was 16 she became pregnant to him and was placed in a mother and baby unit to prepare her for the birth. With a lot of support from her social worker, key worker and after care worker she stopped seeing the father of her child. After one year, Angeline was doing so well she was given her own accommodation by the local authority. Sadly, however, the relationship with the father of her child resumed. He continued to be very violent toward her, beating her regularly and smashing up the house. She became pregnant again and moved back into the mother and baby unit. The relationship has now finished again and Angeline is working with her support workers on building her self-esteem and confidence, caring for her children, looking at going to college and getting another tenancy from a housing association away from the area.

Although Angeline does not like the rules and regulations of the unit and feels there is little privacy, she does feel safe there and supported by workers.

One group of young women said the building was completely inappropriate and inaccessible for its purpose. It was an old house converted into a mother and baby unit. It had numerous flights of stairs, no lifts, so buggies and prams had to be left downstairs. However, all the young women loved the area it was in. It was in a leafy, middle class area in a nice part of Manchester. They reported feeling safe in the area. The other mother and baby unit was purpose built, very accessible and was in the style of self contained, well-furnished flats. However, it was in a very rough area, notorious for 'drugs, gangs and guns' as one young woman said. The young women there were frightened to go out on their own, did not feel safe and did not want their children to grow up in that area, for example:

Why can't we have a nice building in a nice area rather than a nice building in a horrible area or a horrible building in a nice area?

Furthermore, they complained that partners were not allowed to stay over 'so how could they be a family?' In addition, every young woman reported theft (money, food, clothes, equipment and toys) and intimidation from other residents. They said staff did little or nothing to stop this.

Half the young women reported that the mother and baby unit felt like a prison and that staff were 'too nosey'. They asked too many or unnecessary questions of the young women, their visitors and their children. There was little privacy with staff having keys to the young women's flats and just walking in unannounced. However, most of them did like at least one member of staff and felt they could talk to them about their problems.

Discussions with the young women revealed that they did not feel consulted about the managing and running of the unit. Decisions were imposed on them. Even when they voiced their opinions they felt they were not listened to. However, the housing association which ran the mother and baby unit in the inaccessible building in the nice area was considering demolishing the unit and building a purpose built one in its place. The young women were consulted on this and helping to design a better unit. As they said 'who knows better than us what we need'. The young women were enjoying this work.

Similarly, whilst the young women enjoyed the safety and security of the buildings and the presence of the staff, further work was needed to improve the obvious communication difficulties and relationships between the staff and the young people. The majority of the staff were clearly dedicated to their work but the young women value what services were available as much as whether staff were committed to their work. Residents' meetings, focus groups or discussion groups could, perhaps, help the young women and the members of the staff team to better understand each others perspectives and clarify 'house rules' (for example why were men not allowed to stay over?).

Whilst there seemed to be many positives about living in the mother and baby unit few of the young women spoke about these, including having little or no debt, (budgeting skills taught), excellent access to health care, especially ante natal care, and move-on accommodation support from staff.

Teenage pregnancy services

A specialist named midwife attended all the young women at the mother and baby units and it was evident that the young women liked and trusted her. She spent as much time as they needed, explaining things to them, offering them reassurance and advice, encouraging them and showing them around the hospital. After a child is born she continues to look after both the young mother and the baby. She talks about appropriate parenting skills, how to nurture effectively, as well as basic caring for a baby. The young women liked this continuity. The young women said she treats them with respect, she really listens to them, she goes out of her way to get appropriate services or resources for the young women and she works with a high degree of confidentiality. The young women know they can talk to her about issues that may be causing concern without it being repeated to others without the young women's consent. She also supplied videos and other resources for the young women and ran the baby clinic.

In this part of the book research findings were presented about the health and well being of 33 mothers and mothers-to-be. In the next and last part of the book we examine wider practice and policy developments. First in relation to mental health services then in respect of case leavers who are disabled, and finally, ways froward.

Chapter Eleven

Meeting the Mental Health Needs of Young People Leaving Care: Strategies and Challenges

Panos Vostanis

Introduction

This chapter aims to link the broader social issues discussed in this book to the mental health needs of young people leaving care, and to promote the strategic development of inter-agency services to promote young people's mental health. Some of these issues, e.g. the nature of mental health problems, apply to most other young client groups, whilst others are specific to young care leavers, e.g. vulnerability factors whilst in care and at the time of transition. These are being discussed in parallel, followed by a discussion of the implications for different agencies. The chapter includes two characteristic case vignettes and ends with a discussion about ways forward in terms of the policy framework, agency roles, and the importance of engagement.

Nature and severity of mental health needs

Mental health is a broad concept used differently by agencies in contact with young people and their carers. This includes a range of functions in a young person's life, which enable them to develop physically, emotionally, and socially, sustain mutually satisfying relationships, learn from experience and overcome difficulties and adversities and thus achieve their potential at each stage of their development. Mental health *problems* are conceptualised as emotions or behaviours outside the normal range for age and gender, linked with an impairment of some of the previous areas of development and functioning, with the young person suffering as a result. Examples include persistent low mood (depression), self-harm thoughts and acts, anxiety and avoidance of social situations, pre-occupation with weight and severe weight loss (eating disorders), and oppositional or aggressive behaviours which impact on the young person's life or on their carers. Mental health problems rarely present in isolation, but rather as a combination of difficulties developing over a period of time. A young person with low mood may also present with poor sleep and appetite, negative cognitions about the future, low self-esteem, and ideas of death.

In this chapter, the term mental health *problems* will be used intermittently with mental health *needs*, which indicate what is required for a young person to achieve a healthy life. This distinction is essential, particularly for young people leaving care, as their mental health needs should be met by all agencies, albeit in the context of their own role and perspective. This contrasts with the narrow term of mental health problems (or the more severe mental health *disorders*) which implies a specialist mental health intervention.

In the general population, about 10 per cent of children and young people present with mental health disorders at any one time (Meltzer et al., 2000) and 20–25 per cent with broadly defined mental health problems (Mental Health Foundation, 1999). These rates are higher among older adolescents and young adults, because of the more common onset of severe disorders during this life stage. They also increase in vulnerable groups of children exposed to adverse life events and circumstances (see below) including children and young people looked after by local authorities. Several studies have established high rates of mental health problems among this group (Roy et al., 2000; Richardson and Joughin, 2000). For example, McCann et al. (1996) found that up to two thirds of children looked after in a UK district presented with mental health problems that justified a clinical assessment, predominantly those in residential care. Dimigen et al. (1999) detected that half of their sample of 123 young people in foster and residential care had significant behavioural and emotional problems, often multiple difficulties. Older children were more likely to be affected, particularly those in residential care. Minnis and Devine (2001) found similarly high rates of 60 per cent children in foster care within the clinical range of behavioural and emotional problems.

Part IV

Reflections and Recommendations:
Lessons from Research and Practice

Impact of social and other vulnerability factors on young people's mental health

Mental health problems in young life are usually caused by a number of inter-related factors. Although there is evidence of genetic and individual predisposition, particularly in the development of severe disorders such as psychosis, and developmental conditions such as autism, young people's experiences and life circumstances have also been found to predispose to emotional and behavioural difficulties. This does not mean that exposure to a particular event, even of severe nature, will necessarily lead to mental health problems, but rather that, the more adversities a young person experiences, the more likely s/he is to suffer from mental health problems and for these problems to continue. Many such experiences can be secondary effects of previous adversities.

Adverse life events are acute or (usually) longstanding. Examples of acute stressors are, accidents, severe physical illness (although this may also have long lasting effect), or exposure to violence. Young people may subsequently develop nightmares, fears, severe anxiety or low mood. These can be mediated by their previous experiences, their understanding and cognitive ability, and by adults' reactions to the event. Chronic adversities impact on children's development over a period of years, and have been repeatedly found to be associated with mental health problems. Chronic familial adversities include parental rejection and lack of affection, physical and sexual abuse, family breakdown, parental criminality, parental drug and alcohol abuse, and witnessing violence.

Many of these factors, unfortunately, apply to looked after children and young people, and therefore make them more vulnerable to mental health problems (rather than being in care per se), and explain the previous findings of high levels of mental health needs in this group. In addition, looked after children and young people are exposed to secondary adversities and life events such as frequent moves, further rejection from carers, disruption of relationships with carers and peers, school exclusion, and experience of community violence (Quinton and Rutter, 1984; Minty, 1999). These are inter-related with social, educational and relationships difficulties. Vice versa, children with mental health problems are less likely to achieve placement stability, thus often entering a sequence that is difficult to break (Barber et al., 2001). Young people who leave care can be even more disadvantaged and vulnerable through poverty, becoming homeless, social isolation, and higher likelihood of exposure to drugs and offending (Buchanan, 1999). Many studies with at risk young adults have found over-representation of those who had left the care system, such as homeless, drug users and young offenders (Wrate et al., 1999; Nicol et al., 2000).

The consideration of developmental issues is important in understanding the extent of these young people's needs, in order to plan effective services. Children and young people develop differently in various areas of their functioning, i.e. emotional, social, communication, physical and life skills. Each aspect of their development should be interpreted in relation to what is broadly expected for their chronological age (developmental milestones). Because of the adversity factors discussed earlier, particularly following abuse and neglect, young people in care have a higher chance of both deviance and discrepancy between aspects of their development. This can be misleading in raising expectations to carers and professionals on the young person's *real* level of functioning. For example, a 19-year-old may have the physical and intellectual capacity expected for this age, but may function at a much lower emotional and social level (such as of a 14-year-old). They will thus be unlikely to cope as well with social pressures as a 19-year-old with more balanced developmental functions, even if provided with the same housing and educational opportunities. This is not an uncommon reason for the exacerbation of mental health problems during periods of transition.

Protective factors and resilience

So far, the factors placing care leavers at risk of mental health problems have been discussed. A very positive research finding is that, contrary to earlier theories, none of these vulnerability factors have a critical or irreversible effect on children and young people (Rutter, 1985). Even in the face of severe adversity, young people can develop resiliency and protective strategies, which will help them make a successful transition to adult life. Many young people will never suffer from mental health problems, while even those who do at some point, will break this cycle and achieve their potential.

Established protective factors for young people's mental health and well-being include theirs as well as their parents'/carers' coping strategies (self-efficacy, ability to self-reflect, self-reliance, maintaining a positive outlook, and problem-solving), positive experiences of secure relationships, social and educational attainment, qualities which engender a positive response from others, and friendships. This is a crucial message for all agencies involved in the care of these young people, as they can all help enhance these protective mechanisms and make a difference to young people's current and future life. The implications for each agency are discussed in detail towards the end of this chapter.

Service gaps and barriers for care leavers

Despite the evidence on the extensive mental health needs and vulnerability of looked after young people and those who leave care, these remain largely unmet (Harman et al., 2000; Payne, 2000). There are a number of underlying reasons for this; some are related to the generic provision of mental health services to old adolescents and young people, while others are specific to care leavers and agencies working with them.

Few statutory mental health services work specifically with older adolescents/young adults. In recent years, several reports in the UK have identified deficiencies in the range, quality and distribution of services (Health Advisory Service, 1995; Mental Health Foundation, 1999). This age group usually falls between the upper end of Child and Adolescent Mental Health Services (CAMHS) and the lower end of adult mental health services (Select Committee on Health, 2000). Adult mental health services are usually ill equipped or unfamiliar with young people's needs, while CAMHS may be inappropriate to deal with older adolescents with severe mental illness. The inconsistent service provision can be exacerbated by lack of formal transition arrangements for those who are to be transferred from child to adult mental health services (DoH, 2003), and by lack of consistency in procedures across the education, social services and non-statutory sectors. Smith and Leon (2001) examined the experiences of young people aged

between 16–25 years, and found substantial service user dissatisfaction. In a subsequent study with managers and practitioners working with this age group (Richards and Vostanis, 2004), we identified a number of themes on reasons for service gaps, which are discussed below, particularly in relation to young people who leave care. These themes will be revisited in a later section in relation to recommendations about ways of improving mental health care and service provision.

Developmental issues

Many young people come from backgrounds of family discord or breakdown, or have suffered various forms of abuse or neglect. Previous adverse experiences can impact upon self-esteem and attachments and relationships. When such young people attend an adult service, they can be perceived as less robust, more sensitive, inexperienced and easily distressed, therefore less engaging than other adult clients. Factors such as drug use (as experimentation, form of leisure or coping with stress), low sense of risk, and sexual health often interact with their mental health state (e.g. low mood). Even if the latter responds to specialist treatment it is likely to relapse unless the accompanying risks are also addressed. If services are fragmented, these difficulties are not targeted as part of an integrated care plan.

Difficulties in accessing and engaging with services

Young people leaving care are often difficult to engage, as they have to initiate and maintain contact with services of their own volition, and may not recognise experiencing mental health problems. The stigma and labels attached to mental health are considerable engagement barriers, as well as fears that their peers or family might find out. Young people sometimes have to generate crises to access services, such as self-harm, substance misuse, or entering dangerous situations, some of which may divert them to the youth justice system. Keeping appointments with mental health services is a major difficulty, often resulting in a young person being lost to the service until the next crisis. In contrast, many non-statutory services adopt a more user-friendly and engaging approach combining mentoring activities and therapeutic interventions.

Accessibility to many specialist services can be hindered by requiring referrals from general practitioners and lengthy waiting times, due to limited resources. By the time of the appointment, a lot may have changed in a young person's life, making it difficult for them to re-engage with the service. Out-of-hours support, drop-in clinics, assertive outreach, mentoring, and group work are particularly deficient for this age range.

Issues related to looked after young people and CAMHS

The provision of child and adolescent mental health services (CAMHS) for looked after children varies in the interventions offered and the disciplines or agencies involved. Problems in accessing CAMHS include narrow referral criteria, non-detection of mental health problems, referrers' reluctance to pathologise children's behaviour, and young people's mobility and engagement (Callaghan et al., 2003a). For example, Phillips (1997) found that many social workers might have recognised that a particular young person needed mental health intervention, but did not refer. This could be a result of placement instability, dissatisfaction with CAMHS, and lack of local authority resources. Looked after children have similar difficulties in accessing other health services (Broad, 1999; Ward et al., 2002).

Other problems with current mental health services

Services are often not adapted to young people's needs. Some existing child and adult therapies are more relevant to the respective age range. It can be particularly difficult to engage less verbally confident young men in psychotherapeutic or group modalities. Inappropriate service environments can be off-putting. CAMHS can often be too child-centred (e.g. play materials), while the physical surroundings of adult services (e.g. day centres) may be too adult-oriented. The absence of age-specific in-patient mental health facilities is particularly problematic. Older adolescents in crisis are already frightened and confused, which may be exacerbated by feeling isolated from their friends and family. Maladaptive behaviours learned from older people on acute in-patient wards can encourage dependence upon

hospitalisation instead of developing their own adaptive coping skills.

For young people with behavioural and relationships difficulties (sometimes falling under the diagnostic and understandably confusing concept of personality disorders), there is often no agreement on who is primarily responsible for this group, with social services considering it a health issue, and mental health services as a predominantly social problem. The lack of adequate service provision can result in costly and sometimes inappropriate out-of-county placements, further disrupting the young person's integration in the community.

Some children's services staff are not necessarily well trained to deal with older adolescents' needs and sensitivities. Similarly, adult service professionals are not often experienced and equipped to deal with older adolescents. Although there has been increasing user involvement in service planning in the last few years, and several studies with young people have influenced services (e.g. Saunders and Broad, 1997; Smith and Leon, 2001), services (particularly in mental health) are often set up or evolve without much evidence of young people's views and experiences.

Transfer arrangements from children's to adult services

The obvious dysfunction is the lack of coterminous age transitional points across and within agencies (mental health, physical health, social care, and education). There is little consistency in the upper age cut-off of CAMHS, which varies between 16–18, with some services adopting the 'education' rule, i.e. accepting referrals up to 16 years or up to 18 years if in full-time education. The latter is confusing and discriminatory for young care leavers, who thus lose out even more on sources of help when they need them most.

Difficulties in transfer arrangements between CAMHS and adult mental health services are particularly relevant to young people leaving care, i.e. between 16–21 years. These are due to the different nature of the two services, role duplication, information exchange, coterminous transitional age cut-offs, and lack of designated staff. Young people are generally not well informed about what to expect from the next service. A specific difficulty in transferring young people with emotional, behavioural and relationships problems, is that they may fall outside the remit of the operational criteria of adult services, which are more geared towards severe mental illness (psychosis, depression, eating disorders), therefore resulting in multiple referrals to other agencies. Many young people are discharged from one service and often placed on a waiting list, or have to wait for a first appointment letter with the new service, which could take weeks or months. Most will find it difficult to engage easily with a new mental health professional, while a smaller proportion will act out their distress and end up being admitted to an adult in-patient ward in crisis. This will affect negatively their therapeutic relationship with the adult community mental health team (also see case vignette X at the end of this section). When other agencies are involved, this may not be towards joint transitional planning. For example, there could be one planning process for housing/social care, another for education, and a third parallel or sequential process for mental health.

Communication between services/agencies

Communication difficulties at policy and operational level, across and within-agencies, are particularly important for young people leaving care. Recent policies such as Quality Protects (DoH, 1998) and resulting funding streams have resulted in a number of inter-agency partnerships and wider community links (Callaghan et al., 2004). However, care plans are often fragmented or adopt a 'tick list', either because of limited local agency links or because of unlikely response from some agencies. This can result in multiple referrals to other agencies (e.g. the local mental health service) even in the knowledge that the young person will not be accepted or, more often, be offered an appointment but will drop out before not too long.

Agency involvement often breaks down when young people move out of foster care, which at least previously offered some degree of advocacy and security. The non-statutory sector is again more accessible and better at networking and sharing information. However, communication often depends upon personalities and individual attitudes. Non-statutory agencies can find it difficult to liaise with statutory organisations at a strategic level, such as involvement with steering groups and working parties. Statutory services

can thus be perceived by voluntary agencies as 'removed', 'inaccessible' or not sharing information, with the young person falling between the two (e.g. with repeated referrals between agencies, rather than a seamless service). The different IT and client records systems do not facilitate this process.

Practical needs

Young people's practical and social problems and their impact on their mental health can not be stressed enough. There is limited housing for older adolescents, with care leavers often placed in hostels and bed and breakfast accommodation, with little support or preparation for independent living. Young people may not have the confidence to access benefits agencies, or even afford the bus fare to city-centre based services. Access to leisure and recreational facilities can also be problematic due to financial constraints or disability.

Case vignettes

The complex needs of young people leaving care and the role of different agencies are highlighted by the following two case vignettes. These have been modified in order to present service issues without identifying the young person. Neither vignette is representative of the average young person leaving care, but rather selected to demonstrate difficult to manage mental health problems.

Case vignette X

X was admitted into care at 15 years, because of longstanding arguments with her mother. At the time, X's main difficulties were excessive cannabis and alcohol use, not attending school and making or sustaining friendships. These gradually deteriorated over the subsequent two years. X initially settled in a foster placement and related well with her foster carers. However, she began to self-harm (usually cutting forearms and taking overdoses) and had increasing aggressive outbursts. She had contact with CAMHS and was offered individual psychodynamic psychotherapy, but never really engaged or benefited from it, as her behaviour and distress between sessions could not be contained. She was also vulnerable, as she went missing for long periods. During one crisis, when X smashed her room, the placement broke down and she moved to a children's home. The behaviours, particularly her sexual vulnerability to older men, increased, so did her self-harm attempts. X had some depressive symptoms and was prescribed one course of antidepressants, but did not respond and probably did not take it regularly or long enough as she was frequently absent. As X approached her 18th birthday, she fell between four services (CAMHS, adult mental health, care leaving team, adult social services), with different operational and funding criteria. X had a very good relationship with her social worker, throughout her moves and crises. She also maintained a supportive (rather than actively therapeutic) contact with CAMHS. The two agencies tried to obtain a therapeutic residential placement for X, where she could develop social relationships and self-living skills, receive education (she had been out of school for several years), and intensive therapeutic work. This never materialised because of her age and costs involved. X achieved some stability at a semi-independent placement, but was terrified of living on her own, and gradually re-established contact with her family, where she eventually moved back to. Her transition to adult mental health services was not planned, as she was admitted several times to an in-patient unit following suicidal attempts, but never engaged with therapy.

Case vignette Y

Y was placed on a care order for child protection reasons (sexual and emotional abuse) at the age of 13 years. She moved between many foster and residential placements. These usually started well, but deteriorated and broke down after a few months. Y self-harmed (cutting and overdoses) and was finding it increasingly difficult to function under any structure, with resulting attacks on staff or carers. She had intermittent contact with CAMHS, mainly in response to crises and brief admissions following suicidal attempts. Like the previous young person, Y could not relate to individual therapy during periods of acute distress, and in any case was running away from her placements. Mental health practitioners mainly worked with her social worker, residential staff and foster carers on setting up behavioural strategies. When her absconding, oppositional behaviours and self-harm became too difficult to contain within any available placement, Y was admitted to a local authority secure unit. She settled very quickly and expressed her wish to move to independent living, with some initial support. This appeared a gamble at the time, but with no alternative option. Contrary to some predictions, Y coped admirably well on her own. She remained vulnerable and did not feel confident to face further education or employment for a while. During this period, she retained some supportive therapeutic contact with the mental health service. After two years, Y took up an opportunity through Connexions to resume her training.

The way forward: young people's mental health is everybody's responsibility

Policy framework

The successful outcomes of young people leaving care depend on the effective and co-ordinated input of different agencies. This particularly applies to their mental health needs. In that respect, their mental health is everybody's responsibility, with each agency having both a generic and specific role to play in improving young people's life chances and well being. Policies such as *Every Child Matters* (DfES, 2003) the *National Service Framework* (DoH, 2003) and *Health Promotion Guidelines for Looked After Children* (DoH, 1999) are essential prerequisites in facilitating inter-agency partnerships and bridging service gaps. Also, funding streams to enable joint working at frontline level. Implications for agencies in improving the mental health needs of young people leaving care are discussed below.

Agency roles

Non-statutory youth services often fulfil a range of important functions such as informal support, mentorship, reintegration to social activities, building the young person's strengths, alternatives through recreational opportunities, and sometimes the only realistic opportunity to engage with therapeutic work, even if they do not initially perceive it as such. There are increasing examples of such multifaceted practical, social, educational and therapeutic models within the voluntary sector, often initiated by or involving young people who have been in care. What needs to improve though is their integration with statutory mental health and social services, so that young people are not lost in the system, and limited resources are used effectively.

Care leaving teams can be frustrated and constrained by lack of suitable placements but, overall, they are the key agency to oversee and ensure a smooth transition. The young person's social worker may be their only trusting adult during this period, thus taking on the young person's anxieties and distress. This can be overwhelming, particularly in the presence of severe behaviours such as self-harm. Irrespective of the involvement of specialist mental health services, a hierarchy of needs is important in improving young people's mental health as much as in the rest of their lives. The young person must primarily feel safe. If this is not entirely possible (e.g. the young person absconding or engaging in substance misuse), therapeutic contact with agencies (in broad terms, to even include mentors and peers) should aim at enhancing the young person's self-control and capacity to remain safe, as a parent would normally do. The next step would be to introduce as many positive strategies and activities as the young person can cope with. In some cases, ambitious targets may overwhelm them, and small steps of normalising adverse behaviours have a better chance of breaking the cycle. The young person's emotional state should be at the centre of all decisions and care plans, taking into account both their developmental abilities and wishes.

Education can have a huge impact on young people's sense of achievement and belonging, which will enable them to integrate in society. The social implications are at least as important as the employment and financial gains. Young people who have been in care may be more likely to have learning needs, as they may have missed out on education for varying periods. This requires flexible educational opportunities and entry points to the education system. More importantly, they may not have been used to the structure of a school or college setting, dealing with peer or exam pressures, preparing homework or planning revisions, and particularly not feel as confident as some of their peers. This can not be stressed enough for tutors and other educationalists, who may occasionally have to step back from the rest of the group, to enable a young person to achieve success in relation to their own experience and phase in life. *Connexions* and educational initiatives for

vulnerable and socially excluded young people have been driven by this philosophy. The same applies to *housing* opportunities. Prioritisation according to needs is accepted as a way of compensating for a constantly receding housing stock. Allocation of housing should also take into consideration the young person's holistic needs. A nicely decorated flat is obviously important but, on balance, it may not be the best option if the area is not safe or in the countryside and away from shops and leisure facilities.

Specialist mental health services need to address a number of deficits. Child and adolescent mental health services (CAMHS) need to work more closely with local authorities in planning integrated assessment and treatment to vulnerable groups such as looked after children and young people, including consultation and training to care staff (Callaghan et al., 2004). There is little point in having service filters (such as GP referrals) and lengthy waiting responses for mobile young people and families. As this is a resource issue, the only option is to designate CAMHS staff to work directly with looked after young people and their carers. The upper age limit should be consistent (18 years), as recommended by the National Service Framework (DoH, 2003), which will also necessitate additional resources. Services should adopt a flexible approach, quick response and capacity to try to engage the young person at different times.

The **transition to adult mental health services** should be planned, as much as possible, to prevent crises and acute in-patient admissions. Joint assessments (between the social worker, child mental health and adult mental health professional), involvement of the young person, and introduction to a new mental health professional, are examples of good practice. This, however, can only be achieved by relative consistency on the operational/referral criteria between CAMHS and adult mental health services. These services need to adapt to both the 'child' and 'adult' part of a young person in care, which differentiate them from other clients. Also they need to take into account their identity formation, youth culture, and search for sexual and cultural identity which may not be fully formed for a few years.

The **role of different therapeutic modalities** merits some attention. The term 'therapy' is used in different ways, with varying degree of expectations on its indications and effectiveness.

This stems from the historical identification of therapy with a specific therapeutic framework, i.e. psychoanalytic psychotherapy, which has evolved in the last 20 years. In broad terms, the aim of psychotherapy is to help the young person make links between their experience (e.g. abuse/trauma), feelings and behaviours, which they can hopefully apply in their everyday life. Different schools have emerged and led to the provision of several therapy levels, such as counselling, client-centred therapy, supportive psychotherapy, psychodynamic and psychoanalytic psychotherapy. The setting (individual or group), techniques, professional training and skills, duration, indication (for what type of problem), therapeutic objectives (what the therapist seeks to achieve), and evidence of their effectiveness, vary accordingly.

One needs to add other types of therapy, such as cognitive-behavioural (aiming at restructuring maladaptive cognitions and behaviours, with little reference to underlying causes) and family/systemic therapy (which tries to change relationships and communication patterns in family or wider systems). Also, sub-branches of the previous modalities (e.g. solution-focused therapy). Not all young people will engage or respond to all these interventions, which are rarely all available. The particular challenge for the use of different therapies with difficult-to-engage young people (or, for that matter, children and adults) is that they should be applied, adapted and integrated within a community care plan, rather than be expected to be automatically transferable from therapy courses or tertiary (specialised) centres. Therapeutic objectives should be clearly defined, shared with the young person and agencies, and regularly monitored. If an intervention has not worked, other aspects of the care plan should be reviewed, rather than asking for 'more of the same'.

Young people, particularly those who leave local authority care may come in contact with the **youth justice** system or **drug and alcohol** services. As offending behaviours and drug and alcohol abuse are associated with mental health problems (as cause, effect, or because of mediating factors), these agencies should consider mental health issues and work closely with mental health services. This has partly been facilitated by the establishment of the inter-agency Youth Offending Teams, and emerging models of CAMHS provision

(Callaghan et al., 2003b). Drug and alcohol services for young people remain problematic, mainly because of limited designated resources and expertise for this age group, and fragmented operation from mental health services.

Need for engaging and developmentally appropriate mental health services

The importance of *engagement* can not be overstated for all agencies, in particular for specialist mental health services. Contact with mental health services needs to be adapted to the young person's needs, as much as resources allow. Outreach work and joint assessments with key professionals (not only social workers, but also mentors, drug workers, tutors and youth workers) are good ways of developing relationships with young people who may have a poor experience of services or are fearful of stigma. However, it is useful to remember that a young person may also prefer a hospital appointment, as a neutral environment where they can share their distress in confidence. In those cases, both the referrer and the assessor should explore and alleviate any worries or fears of mental illness and treatment (Anderson et al., 2004).

The young person may or may not wish to be accompanied to the first appointment by a trusting adult, who should also monitor with the young person their future attendance (e.g. whether related to transport problems or ambivalence about therapy). At the same time, professional boundaries are important. For example it is vital to be direct with the young person about the potential risks of being on medication. It is preferable to establish a mechanism of providing prescriptions for short periods and regular reviews of medication, the reasons for sharing information with other agencies, or breaking confidentiality (if the young person or somebody else is considered to be at risk). This can help establish a trusting therapeutic relationship over a long period, i.e. the young person may disengage at some point, but still keep faith in the service to seek help at a later stage.

In conclusion, young people leaving local authority care have inter-related mental health, social and educational needs, which can only be met by a combination of approaches from statutory and non-statutory agencies. They are particularly vulnerable to developing mental health problems, which are often not met by specialist mental health services. Ways forward include inter-agency policy frameworks and local implementation, direct access to child and adolescent mental health services, more engaging services, applied therapeutic interventions, and a smooth transition to adult mental health services where necessary.

Chapter Twelve

The Health and Well Being of Disabled Care Leavers

Julie Harris

Background

Research tells us that disabled children are more likely to be looked after than non-disabled children (Gordon et al., 2000). Government statistics show that approximately 2,400 disabled children are looked after away from home at any one time. I.e. the number of children looked after at 31 March with a need code of child's disability (N2) by placement, in England (DoH, 2002). In 2002, 965 (approximately 40%) of these young people were in foster care and 1,320 were looked after in residential schools or children's homes. The figures show that a child who is looked after primarily by way of being disabled (see below) is more likely to be placed in residential care than foster care in comparison with the general looked after population, of which 66% are in foster care (children looked after by local authorities, year ending 31st March 2002). (These figures exclude young disabled people using short break services).

It is likely however that the figures for looked after disabled children are an underestimate because local authorities record only the primary reasons for being looked after. Thus, a disabled child looked after because of abuse or neglect, for example, will not be registered under the disability need category (DfES, 2004). Service providers categorise disabled children variously as having 'special educational needs' (in education), which is used as a generic term, or 'disabled' (in the social care sector). Health services tend to use a specific diagnosis (DfES, 2004).

Definitions and approaches to providing services

Most services for disabled people use the medical model to establish the level of individual need and qualification for services. This is true also of the Children Act 1989, where disability is the primary reason for providing services. This means that services focus upon a person's impairment or medical condition and any limitations arising from it and plan individual

services accordingly and this has important consequences for the way in which disabled people receive services (Morris, 1998).

Disabled people themselves prefer to define disability in a way that identifies a whole range of needs, *some* of which may arise from impairment, but which in the main, arise from their right to equality of opportunity and access, to inclusion, self-determination and independence. In this chapter the term 'disabled' is used to describe the experience of facing significant barriers to social inclusion caused by society's response to impairment. This approach focuses on the removal of those barriers by encouraging services to respond to individuals as whole people.

The use of the medical model not only limits the supports and services available to disabled people but can also inhibit the development of understanding of the disabled experience through research. Information gathered relating to type and level of impairments accomplishes very little in terms of establishing need. In the research and policy review, *Gone Missing* (1995) Morris suggests that when exploring and analysing the experience of disabled children in some form of service provision it would be useful to gather:

- *Factual information about the child's impairment/ and or health.*
- *Information based on children's disabling/enabling experiences. Disabling experiences may be exclusion from mainstream education; abuse; family breakdown; failure to meet care needs within the family/community setting.*
- *Information about children's needs. These needs are likely to fall into five categories: communication; mobility; emotional; educational; health. Information would have to be based on assessments of individual children's needs and would only be of real use if these assessments were need-led rather than service-led. These needs are likely to be related to both impairment and disabling/enabling experiences.*

(Morris, 1995: 36)

Definitions of leaving care

There appears to be much confusion about who should be categorised as a care leaver, arising partly because non-disabled care leavers and young disabled people have always been treated as separate and distinct policy groups (Priestley et al., 2003). Inconsistencies in the management of information, poor information sharing and co-ordination between services has resulted in disabled care leavers' eligibility for services under the CLCA 2000 being totally obscured. This situation may also be symptomatic of an underlying confusion and ambiguity around resource and funding responsibilities for young disabled people in transition.

All young people who are looked after by the local authority at age 16 (and have been so for a period of thirteen weeks since the age of 14) are entitled to support under the Act regardless of any impairment or medical condition, the services that they use, their destination on 'leaving care' or their eligibility for continuing support from adults services.

Young disabled people becoming eligible for aftercare support on reaching the age of 16 will be in a variety of service locations which may include:

- Residential establishments, run by education, health, social services or the independent sector (residential schools, care homes).
- Foster care.
- Secure units.
- Short break units and respite centres.
- Health care settings.

Although young people using respite or short break services for periods of less than one month continuously and returning to parents or someone with parental responsibility in between, are not eligible, there will be young disabled people placed full time (or for periods of more than four weeks continuously) in short break centres who will meet the CLCA 2000's qualifying criteria.

Transitions to adulthood

Transition is a term used to describe the progress from childhood; a stage characterised by contained boundaries set by adults, to the flexible boundaries of adulthood. The process takes place over a period of years and is marked by a maturing identity and sense of self, the development of decision making skills, increasing responsibility and growing autonomy. In practical terms transition often involves the transfer from school into further education or work and financial independence; a move away from the family home and often to new relationships as partners or maybe as parents.

Research undertaken with young disabled people shows that they have very similar aspirations to their non-disabled peers, want paid employment and the means and resources to live independently, wider social networks and to feel that they are contributing to society (Hendey and Pascall, 2002). Participants identified the support and care of their parents as being key to their ability to live independently. They also benefited from their parents' high expectations of them to achieve in education, their ability to provide material and financial resources, to fight for services and to advocate on their behalf. The research also identified that 'lack of support beyond the family also presented some respondents with an impossible barrier to independent adulthood.'

Transition planning

Transition is also used to describe the complex statutory framework within which services provide support to young disabled people moving from children's to adult services, either in health or social services and also the progression from school to adult life for young people with special educational needs.

The experience of 'transition' has been the focus of considerable attention in recent years. Research has brought to light a wealth of issues including poor planning and co-ordination between agencies; poor information to young people and their families and carers causing anxiety and uncertainty; and a tendency for planning to focus on moves between services rather than the issues of concern to young people. Further evidence has pointed to resource-led decision making (resulting in a higher risk of being moved into residential or nursing home provision) and lack of proper involvement in decisions that affect their lives (Beresford and Sloper, 2000; Bignall and Butt, 2000; Hendey and Pascall, 2002; Heslop et al., 2001; Hussein, et al., 2002; Morris, 1999b, 2001; Simons, 1998). There is also evidence to suggest that many young people with learning difficulties leave school without any transition planning (Heslop et al., 2001).

Transitions for young disabled people leaving care

Little is known about outcomes for young disabled people who are leaving or who have left care, as data relating to disability is not routinely collected as part of the annual monitoring returns required of local authorities reporting outcomes for care leavers. With a few notable exceptions the disabled care leaving experience has been overlooked in research, campaigning and policy addressing the needs of care leavers (Morris, 1999a; Priestley et al., 2003; Harris et al., 2000).

One research project that did focus specifically on disabled care leavers (Rabiee et al., 2000) identified that issues arising for the non-disabled population of care leavers such as poor outcomes in education, employment and accommodation and poor preparation for adult life etc. (Broad, 1998; Stein, 1997) were also experienced by, and carried an additional significance for, young disabled people. It identified that for many:

- Transitions happen abruptly with little planning or information.
- There are few opportunities for further education or training that lead to real employment outcomes.
- There are few options for supported accommodation or independent living and decisions about living situation are often based on resources rather than on need.
- The transition to adulthood can mean little more than a transfer to adult services.
- Transitions tend to happen later for young disabled people, who often do not leave school until 19.
- Young people living with parents or long term foster carers benefited from higher levels of advocacy and more information about options than those reliant on service providers to support them through transition.
- Care leavers labelled with mild to moderate learning difficulties may not be eligible for adult disability services and are more likely to receive mainstream aftercare services. These services however feel inadequately resourced to meet their needs effectively.
- Aftercare services are unlikely to provide services to disabled care leavers who are eligible for support.
- Aftercare services work to a definition of independence that may not reflect the wishes or needs of disabled care leavers.

Independent living and personal assistance

This last point indicates an important difference between the non-disabled and disabled leaving care experience. Quite rightly, much attention has been drawn to the failure of the looked after system to prepare young people adequately for adult life, a contributing factor to the 'compressed and accelerated' transitions experienced by many care leavers (Stein, 1997). Aftercare services often concentrate on the development of the skills necessary for young people to achieve the important goal of independent living and their own accommodation.

The notion of 'independent living' has different connotations for disabled people referring to self-determination and ability to direct and control their own lives, often through the purchase of personal assistance. This is made possible through the use of direct payments, enabling the individual to employ assistants, determine and manage their own support needs (Community Care (Direct Payments) Act 1996). It is important when supporting disabled care leavers that the term 'independence' is not used to describe the degree to which someone is able to 'do things for themselves' (Priestley et al., 2003) or that assumptions are not made about goals and aspirations, which may differ considerably for disabled care leavers and centre on identifying their own support needs, making their own decisions, going out with their friends, managing personal assistance to help them access further education, training or employment opportunities and independent living. This is an important consideration in pathway planning for young disabled people, which, through the use of person centred approaches (see below) should build upon the wishes and aspirations of the young person. Notions around disability, transition and independence may also be culturally determined and research shows that minority ethnic groups may have different expectations (Hussain, Atkin and Ahmad, 2002).

The use of personal assistance can be a very effective and enabling tool for young disabled people, providing it is self-directed. The introduction of direct payments for 16 and 17-year-olds (Carers and Disabled Children Act 2000) is an important recognition of the 'right to adulthood'. There are issues around direct payments however, such as the level of take-up and concerns around young people not having the information they need, particularly around the practical arrangements (Joseph Rowntree Foundation, 2003). The management of personal assistance requires the range of skills, administrative and interpersonal that are involved in becoming an employer, which young people need support and training to develop.

The remainder of this chapter provides a brief overview of research indicating the factors that impact upon the health and well being of young disabled people as they start to develop an adult identity; the current policy framework and new initiatives aimed at improving outcomes, as well as some of the challenges that remain if we are to finally dismantle these barriers to equal opportunity and social inclusion. In doing so, it suggests the kind of support that leaving care services can provide to enable disabled care leavers claim their right to autonomous and fulfilled adult lives.

Accessing health care and managing transitions

Young disabled people may well have specific health needs arising from a medical condition or impairment for which they may need specialist or therapeutic services.

Whereas these services may be relatively easy to access as a child, they can suddenly cease on leaving paediatric services when young adults can hit a health services vacuum. In these circumstances the transition to adulthood can be marked by deterioration in a health condition that can even, perhaps, shorten life expectancy (Morris, 1999b).

For other young disabled people, whose continuing health needs mean that they will continue on into adult health services, different issues may arise. A childhood characterised by continuous medical supervision and intervention may result in young people reacting against unwanted dependency and expressing a desire for the freedom and independence experienced by most adolescents. Young people may need support and encouragement in continuing with medication or treatments that, if disregarded could have implications for longer-term health and quality of life (Morris, 1999b). There are indications that young people respond well to peer mentoring schemes, whereby they can spend time with young disabled adults who have experienced similar feelings and frustrations but who can provide positive examples of persisting with treatments and managing health effectively

and increasing independence over the longer term. Morris also points out that young disabled people may hold particularly difficult associations and memories of medical treatments, being in pain or living in hospital environments where other patients, sometimes friends, may have died etc. These young people may need considerable emotional support to enable them to continue accessing the health care they need.

Research shows that disabled people experience considerable difficulty in getting their general needs met with regard to dental health, eyesight, sexual health etc., and that accessing the primary health care services can be a problem. GPs and other professionals may sometimes demonstrate reluctance to accept disabled people either because they have inadequate knowledge of a medical condition or impairment or because of the financial and resource implications. Sometimes health professionals have insufficient understanding of health conditions. A report by Morris (2004) describes the difficulty that people with physical impairments have in accessing mental health services.

Access to good health care and the successful management of health in adult life is reliant on having the right information. Morris (1999b) uses the following illustration of how this can be the key to developing autonomy, taken from research exploring the experiences of young people with sickle cell disorder or thalassaemia:

> . . . *finding out about their illness was a way of asserting their autonomy and often – especially for boys – a means of signalling their independence from their parents. Acquiring information also gave the illness meaning, independent of self, and this enabled the young person to maintain a valued self-image . . .*
> (Atkin and Ahmad, 1998)

The management and control of physical health may be an important tool in effecting positive transitions for young disabled people and enabling them to maximise their opportunities for independence as adults.

Emotional health and welfare

The notion of well being is inextricably bound up with emotional as well as physical health and successful transitions will be dependent on how far an individual is emotionally supported to fulfil their full potential as human beings.

Little is known about outcomes for young disabled people leaving care. Outcomes for the non-disabled population of care leavers, are however, well documented (Broad, 1998; Stein, 1997) and there appears to be a correlation between the through care experience and difficulties experienced in early adult life with low levels of self-esteem and self-confidence, drug and alcohol related and mental health issues (Saunders and Broad, 1997).

Research over the last decade has provided new insight into the childhood experiences of disabled people. We know that they are likely to spend a disproportionate amount of time in the company of adults and be excluded from the normal social relationships of childhood (Priestley, 1998), are more likely to be looked after than non-disabled children (Gordon et al., 2000) and are more likely to have experienced abuse and neglect than non-disabled children (Morris, 1999a, 1999b; Westcott and Cross, 1996). We are also learning more about the experiences of disabled children living away from the family home (Morris, 1995, 1998; Abbott, Morris and Ward, 2001). Although there is still not enough known about these experiences and their subsequent impact on adult life, a participant in the *Gone Missing* research (Morris, 1995) gives us an indication of some of the concerns:

> . . . life at home . . . was difficult and my family needed support. But my experiences in the care system were not positive. In fact I would say I was further 'disabled' by what happened to me . . . Important issues of grief, separation and loss, were never addressed and no attempt was made to work with me in sorting out my past, for example by doing life story work. There were child abuse issues, too, that were simply overlooked. The multiple placements and lack of natural contact with my natural family resulted in feelings of rejection and grief that I have not been able to resolve even after years of therapy as an adult.

Young disabled people are likely, as other care leavers, to have issues that remain unresolved to be carried through into early adulthood, including those of family separation, displacement and feelings of rejection and loss. These issues are likely to be compounded by the disabled experience in which children may have encountered discrimination, bullying and exclusion. Black young disabled people and those from minority ethnic groups are likely to suffer double discrimination (Baxter et al., 1990; Hussain, Atkin and Ahmad, 2002) and these young people report that low expectations by education professionals can result in inadequate preparation for adult life (Bignall and Butt, 2000).

When asked about health issues young disabled people themselves have tended to identify a much broader range of issues than those associated with impairment or medical conditions (Rabiee et al., 2001) and expressed concerns that planning for transition does not cover the issues that are important to them (Heslop et al., 2001).

Understandably for adolescents, one of these issues is finding out about sex and sexuality, meeting people and having relationships. The *Whatever Next* research highlighted an assumption on behalf of professionals that disabled people do not have the same sexual needs and feelings as non-disabled people, despite the fact that many of the young people interviewed made it clear that the subject was high on their agenda. Moreover, the timing of information giving with regard to sex was determined by professionals rather than by the wishes or needs of the young person. Relationships between service users were difficult to continue under the constant eye of adult surveillance and in some services, were forbidden altogether. Other problems could arise when young people changed services, leaving behind boyfriends or girlfriends, with no independent means of maintaining contact and continuing the relationship.

The loss of friends, generally, when young people move services can result in sudden and traumatic isolation, as is demonstrated by the story of Stephen (Rabiee at al., 2001) who communicated his thoughts and feelings to the adults in the service, through his friend Charles, who interpreted his movements and signs. The importance of this friendship however was overlooked in the plans for Stephen to take up a place at college after school and Charles, as a significant figure in Stephen's life, was not included in the transitional planning.

An individual's emotional health and well being and their ability to form a positive adult identity are reliant on being listened to, involved and feeling valued. Again, young disabled people report their feelings about being talked over, excluded from important meetings and generally not being involved in decision making about their own lives (Rabiee at al., 2001). Although this has often represented an area of concern to disabled and non-disabled children alike who use statutory services, the disabled experience may carry added significance due, in some cases, to the failure of services to communicate with young people who use alternative methods to speech. This can arise from the inadequate provision of communication equipment, and funding responsibilities in this regard can be unclear. It may also indicate a failure to train staff appropriately in communication skills and to select staff with the qualities of patience required for relationship building.

Research indicates that the experience of disabled young people in transition and their families is generally characterised by poor information giving about options and possibilities (Heslop, Mallet, Simons and Ward, 2001) and this can impact directly on the well-being of young people. In some circumstances, for example, an absence of information can lead to young disabled people withdrawing from services altogether (Rabiee et al., 2001). Black and Asian young people and their families are likely to be further marginalised by providers failing to meet different language and communication needs (Chamba et al., 1999).

The opportunities available to disabled people as adults necessarily determine the nature of transition. Research shows that despite a desire for paid employment, limited opportunities for further education and real training lead to very poor employment outcomes. Many college and work placements are often little more than care placements (Morris, 1999a; Rabiee et al., 2001); and opportunities for supported employment are few (O'Bryan et al., 2000). There is a lack of suitable, accessible housing provision and the costs, particularly for those wishing to work or needing personal assistance to do so, are often prohibitive (Hendey and Pascall, 2002).

A research project auditing the health needs of care leavers in general (Saunders and Broad, 1995) asked young people to identify what they felt were the primary determinants of health. The most important factors were identified as: feelings about life, housing, close personal relationships, care experience and depression. It is difficult to conceive therefore, that the level of exclusion experienced by young disabled people from the fundamental opportunities of life, accepted as rights by the majority population, could have anything other than a detrimental effect on the emotional health and well-being as they approach adulthood. The *'Whatever Next?'* researchers encountered some young people to whom adulthood, in reality, meant little more than a change in services (Rabiee et al., 2001) and it is clear that the risks of not receiving support based on whole-needs approaches is that the transition to adulthood is simply never made.

The way forward in policy

The legislative and policy framework within which looked after and transition services are delivered to young disabled people is complex and too comprehensive to begin to describe in full here. The following therefore summarises the key initiatives that should be instrumental in effecting positive outcomes for this group.

As part of the *Modernising Children's Services* agenda, development has already taken place under the *Quality Protects* programme to 'ensure that children with specific social needs arising out of a disability or a health condition are living in families or other appropriate settings in the community where their assessed needs are adequately met and reviewed' (Objective 6).

The *Choice Protects* review launched in 2002 aims to improve placement choice and stability to looked after children and part of its remit will be to consider the factors that influence placements for disabled children. The vulnerability of disabled children in care to abuse and neglect was highlighted by the multi-agency guidance *'Working Together to Safeguard Children'* (2001). The National Working Party on Child Protection and Disability (2001) is also taking steps to address the issue. The report *It Doesn't Happen to Disabled Children* (NSPCC, 2004) makes recommendations aimed at creating systems and processes to protect disabled children and promote their rights to 'safe and effective care'.

The *National Service Framework for Children* (NFS) is to sit alongside the *Framework for the Assessment of Children in Need*, setting national standards across health, social services and education with the aim of modernising services and improving partnership working. There will be specific standards for services for young disabled people that promote inclusion, influence societal attitudes, provide multi-agency services and seamless transitions and promote young people's involvement in individual care planning and in service development and evaluation. The Children Bill, addressing those issues raised in the Green Paper *'Every Child Matters'* around children at risk, should integrate key services for young people bringing together Social Services, Education, Health and Connexions to provide comprehensive and seamless services and improve information sharing processes.

Key initiatives to improve social inclusion for disabled people include *Valuing People*, the Government's strategy for providing new opportunities for children and adults with learning difficulties, and *Removing Barriers to Achievement*, the strategy for tackling those who have a statement of educational need. The extension of Direct Payments under the *Carers and Disabled Children Act* to 16 and 17-year-olds is a further very welcome step in recognising young disabled people's rights to self-determination and providing opportunities for developing the skills that are needed to successfully direct personal assistance.

The Disability Discrimination Act 1995 Part 3 requires that all disabled people have the same access to goods and services as non-disabled people and by 2004 service providers should have made 'reasonable' physical and permanent changes to premises to create access and all services including housing, leisure, transport, education, health, social services and youth services should have undertaken the appropriate reviews.

Conclusion: the way forward in practice

Developed under *Valuing People: a new strategy for learning disability for the 21st Century*, person-centred planning is a tool to enable service users and practitioners to engage together in individual planning in a more meaningful way. It essentially aims to put the person at the centre, involving family and friends as partners in the process. It should reflect the things that the person views as important to their life and future and identify the support that they need to enable them to make a valued contribution to the community. It is human rights based and through a shared commitment, engages the participants in a process of continual listening, learning and action, helping the person to get what they want out of life.

There are many different styles and approaches to person centred planning which reflect a variety of needs, and these present a valuable opportunity in the development of pathway planning for disabled care leavers. Guidance and training should be available locally and young people, parents or carers should be able to access training to enable them to lead in the planning process. Self-advocacy schemes can be extremely helpful to young disabled people in supporting them to develop the skills and confidence to direct their lives in this way.

If pathway planning is to be dovetailed with transitional planning in an effective way it is advisable for leaving care support services to involve themselves with young disabled people at a slightly younger age than with their non-disabled peers. Attending the first transitional review at 14 years for those young people who are likely to be eligible for leaving care services at 16 will enable practitioners to plan ahead and be aware of any assessments, future plans and arrangements for support, thus eliminating duplication at a later stage. Leaving care services, or those delivering services on their behalf, should take account of the later transitions that occur for young disabled people, by maintaining support until the minimum age of 25 years.

Young disabled people will be eligible for the full health and development assessment under the CLCA 2000 (Regulation and 4(a)) within three months of becoming eligible or relevant. This should be a holistic assessment following the Department of Health guidance *Promoting the Health of Looked After Children* (DoH, 2002b; Appendix 4 Adolescence and Leaving Care 11–18). The young person should be given the opportunity to give their views on their health and identify the issues that are important to them.

The role of advocacy/self advocacy

In order for a young person to be able to develop a positive image of themselves as a disabled person it is essential that they be introduced to and understand the concept of the social model of disability. Peer and self help groups can be very supportive in providing opportunities for young people to identify with others of their own age who perhaps have similar impairments or health conditions, and shared experiences.

Young disabled people can often lose touch with those who act as natural advocates for them – particular staff within services, friends or carers, when they change services and so it is important that they be offered independent advocacy, particularly if they have communication needs. Self-advocacy groups have proved particularly successful in helping young disabled people to develop a sense of self-value and confidence in speaking out and can provide opportunities for socialising and leisure. It is important that young disabled people have contact with others who successfully manage their own support though personal assistance and can demonstrate the importance of self-determination in leading happy and fulfilled lives.

In sum then the above research and practice development evidence suggests that in order to maintain health and well-being in the transition to adult life young people may also need the following:

- To be supported by staff who have the patience, time and empathy to learn their method of communication. In some circumstances this may require specific skills.
- To be supported by staff who have received disability equality training and are committed to the social model of disability.
- Information that is presented in appropriate formats and enables them to make choices.
- Opportunities for education and training that lead to real employment opportunities.
- Physical access to meetings and venues.
- Communication aids and up to date equipment.
- Help in managing and maintaining relationships with family.
- Help in making and maintaining friendships.
- Help with sex, sexuality and relationships.
- Access to transport that enables them to access leisure and develop a social life.
- Support in developing decision-making and independence skills (including the use of person centred approaches and direct payments).
- Access to continuing specialist or therapeutic health services after paediatric services cease.
- Support in managing health needs arising from an impairment or medical condition, including information about health.
- Counselling and psychological support services.
- Opportunities for leisure in the community and spending time with friends.

Overall, health issues cannot be viewed in isolation because a young person has needs arising from impairment or a medical condition. They must always be understood within the context of the wider disabled experience of facing discriminatory barriers in the physical environment and in social attitudes, and the impact that experience has on a person's overall well-being. By adopting the social model, listening to disabled people and children and developing a broader understanding of the disabled experience, service providers can assist and support disabled people in deconstructing these barriers.

There has perhaps been a tendency in the past for mainstream aftercare services to assume that the needs of disabled young people are adequately met by disability services and adult provision and are therefore not within their field of concern. There is reason to believe, however, that this is not the case and that young disabled people suffer from an absence of holistic approaches in the support they receive as they approach adulthood. There is little evidence to date to suggest that services assess and meet their needs as young people, who want the same opportunities for achieving independence as any other young people. These include; going to college, having paid employment and contributing to society in meaningful ways, making friends and having a social life, forming relationships and achieving the kind of life goals and aspirations we all share. What the evidence does suggest is that a vacuum of support awaits these young people, with services each side of the divide, seemingly unprepared and under-resourced to meet their whole needs.

However, the arrival of the CLCA 2000 has the potential to radically impact upon and improve transitional outcomes for young disabled people leaving care by giving them the entitlement to consistent, long term and whole-needs based support right through into adulthood. However, the effective provision of these services present significant structural and practical challenges to all those service providers with statutory responsibilities to support transition. Arrangements will vary considerably depending on local arrangements and cross agency agreements but the responsibility must ultimately rest with those charged in delivering aftercare support to ensure that young disabled people's entitlements to health and well being support under the CLCA 2000 are fully realised.

Chapter Thirteen

Ways Forward

Introduction

This chapter pulls together the implications of the research studies presented here and in so doing it focuses on policy, practice, and theoretical developments and highlights and discusses ways forward in the leaving care field. A key theme addressed in this chapter is how young people leaving care, and other groups of young people facing social exclusion, can become more socially *included* and receive relevant, effective and more accessible services to improve their health and well being. At the beginning of this book we defined social exclusion and saw that it can be described as having four main elements. These are poverty or inadequate income; exclusion from the labour market; service exclusion; and exclusions from social relations.

This chapter begins by introducing the elements of a basic model for greater *social inclusion* as a way of providing the context and logic for the more focused policy and practice based recommendations that follow. After providing that model it then focuses on ways of improving the health and well being of young people facing social inclusion and introduces a framework for improving the health and well being of care leavers. Once that framework is presented the chapter is structured under the headings suggested by the young people in the last part of the book, namely:

- Earlier interventions.
- Better preparatory work for more independent living.
- Improved health and social care services in the community.
- Improved service delivery.

Social exclusion and improved health and well being

A model for greater social inclusion of young people

It is argued here that if only some of these recommended practices and policies are introduced or, where they already exist, built on, then this will have considerable impact on all young people who may go into care or leave care

including those 7,000 young people described earlier in Part Two. Figure 11 provides a basic model of social inclusion and supports.

The young people had very mixed experiences of health and social care services, ranging from 'excellent' to 'poor,' whether from education or health and social care services or informal care from their own families, partners, and friends. It is also the case that many, if not the majority, of these young people and their families have been let down, at various times, by both these potential sources of support.

A framework for improving the services and supports needed in education, personal and lifestyle areas in order to improve the health and well being of socially excluded young people is shown as Figure 12.

Research in the looked after and leaving care field points to the critical importance of wide-ranging strategic health and well being interventions. These range from improving early year's preventive services, family support, education services, foster care and residential care services, to the provision of leaving care services.

In the framework these different life-stages are highlighted, from early years through to teenage years. These are grouped under the aforementioned headings; earlier interventions; better preparatory work for more independent living; improved health and social care supports in the community; and improved service delivery, underpinned by a commitment to inter-agency work and engagement with the young person.

What is meant by earlier interventions?

In the health and well being research study it was found that young people wanted more regular health assessments, conducted in a more friendly and young person centred way and from an early age, with a greater emphasis on *mental health and emotional well being*. This involves greater inter-agency work, particularly if the child or young person is looked after or being cared for by extended family or family friend. This would

Figure 11: A basic model of social inclusion services and supports

Social Exclusion	Social Inclusion	How?
Poverty or exclusion from adequate income or resources	More adequate income	Education, support and advice from peers and professionals
Exclusion from the labour market	Inclusion in the education/training/labour markets	Training, education, and support from peers and professionals
Service exclusion	Mainstreaming accessible services/information	Services including health, social services, and education to be more flexible and responsive
Exclusion from social relations	Become more involved with friends, in activities, groups, joining in, participation as a citizen	Resilience work/ help from projects, counselling, creation of local pressure groups

Figure 12: A service framework for improving the health and well being of young people facing social exclusion.

Individual and family life stages from pre-school to teenage years	Improved service delivery	Examples of services and supports
• Earlier interventions	→	Family Support
	→	Education
	→	Resilience work
	→	Social services
	→	Health promotion
• Preparation for independence	→	Parenting
	→	Peer support
	→	Benefit agency
• Improved supports in the community	→	Accommodation
	→	Voluntary organisations
	→	Connexions
	→	Social Services
	→	Education
	→	Personal advisers
	→	Resources
	→	Planning
	→	Training

help prevent so many slipping through the net. The young people who had been abused, or had experienced physical violence, needed much more support at an earlier stage, in many cases even if this meant removal, for a time at least, from their own home. In other words the young people felt that if there had been more support for and from their birth families earlier on, they would be healthier now. Similarly, for those with their own child, young people needed better services to enable them to look after their children appropriately. The main earlier interventions recommended were:

- **A bigger emphasis on sexual education** in relation to parenting, relationships and sexual advice through provision of education and support.
- **Improved and relevant education services**, for example in personal and social education, about assertiveness, life and social skills as well as inclusion programmes for young parents and excluded young people.
- **More relevant and accessible information to be made available for those in, leaving or after care** on a whole range of health and related issues, bearing in mind the particular needs of this group.
- **Non stigmatising parenting skills classes or drop ins**, preferably staffed by local women, who could empathise with their personal circumstances and be locally based.

For example, to help others in the future the young mothers from MBLCS recommended slightly 'older' young women (i.e. about 18–20 years of age like themselves) coming to the children's home, foster placement or school to tell them what it is really like to be a young mother. They felt they would have listened to them and taken more notice of them and maybe either not have had a child so young or at least be more aware of the responsibilities involved. Other earlier interventions include:

- **Responsive counselling and mental health services** without having to wait months for an appointment.
- **Professionals valuing and respecting care leavers.** In many ways the term 'resilience-led practice' (Gilligan, 2001) offers a way of working which values the child/young person and placement continuity for those in care contributing to young people's education.

'Promoting resilience' for children and young people is one approach to helping protect vulnerable young people against the effects of some of the stresses they face (Gilligan, 2001). It can help to counteract the risk factors that contribute to poor health and well being. According to Rayner and Montague (2001):

In the resilient child someone left an invaluable imprint that told the young person, no matter what, they were valued, that they could influence their circumstances and that others have invested high expectations in them so they had still more incentive to survive competently.

Gilligan's key resilience areas also apply here namely:

- **Helping young people stay connected** to key people including family and friends.
- **Getting the most out of school opportunities and experiences** and having further opportunities to return again to education if necessary.
- **Emphasising the vital role of adults** – carers, mentors, social workers – in young people's lives.

Let us now move on to the second 'preparation for independence' phase.

What is meant by better preparation for more independent living?

The research findings point to the need for better preparation for leaving care around a range of important practical and emotional issues such as those concerning accommodation, training and self-awareness. In particular the young people wanted:

- **More information around health and well being issues**, as they affect young people facing social exclusion.
- **Greater political literacy and increased understanding of holistic notions of health** as it may affect them including poverty, accommodation, isolation, and deprivation.
- **Greater emotional literacy regarding improved life and social skills training** while in care.
- **Staff to receive further training** to include working with young people, black and ethnic minorities, young men, bisexual, gay and lesbian young people and those with special needs.

For example, some staff should be made more aware of the specific needs of young black people and be trained in meeting the needs of these young people in culturally sensitive ways. Staff should be trained about basic awareness issues such as food, diet, skin and hair care as well as religion and culture, whereby Holy days, festivals and other celebrations should be promoted and observed:

- **Practice needs to be set within an organisation's anti-discriminatory policy**, and not simply left to individual interpretation.
- Young people would like to see **more comprehensive and reliable leaving care and tenancy support teams**, who don't break appointments, let them down or 'dis' them.
- The young people think there should be **training/awareness for teachers** so they can better support and understand them in the school environment.
- Develop new and build upon existing **good health programmes for boys and young men**, especially around health issues (physical, mental, sexual, emotional), what is it like to be a parent, the responsibilities as a father, parenting skills, emotional literacy, alternatives to crime, education and training and employment.
- **More specific programmes** could be prepared around topics such as, anger management, positive parenting, being a father, as well as discussing issues around responsibility for actions, becoming more involved as a member of the local community and making and sustaining positive relationships.

For example, much more work can be done to build up young people's self-esteem and confidence, promote education, improve training and employment opportunities and provide positive role models or mentors from their local community and better integration within the local community. And finally:

- **Improved practical skills**. Further develop and improve all the skills needed for leaving care such as life and social skills, budgeting, cooking, nutrition, and financial advice and planning.

Specific work is needed to support refugee children and asylum seekers leaving care and strategies need to be put in place. The following 'good practice' strategies are endorsed:

Strategies for supporting refugee children and asylum seekers leaving care (adapted from Richardson and Joughin, 2000)

Listen to the child. It is important to hear what the children are saying and not only what you want to hear.

Ask – do not assume. Each individual has their own unique experiences and social and cultural context.

Pace your approach accordingly. Avoid temptation to find out everything because it is needed for assessment work (some things can wait – have you checked?).

Consider language barriers. Use interpreters. The initial open communication is crucial to the success of the relationship. It is important to check with the young people first. They need to be allowed some choice, because different social and political groups may have difficulties relating.

Be clear of your role. Explain the differences between the different professional groups and why the children might come into contact with them.

Be clear about communicating the legal position. CLCA 2000 and Home Office immigration and asylum requirements.

Keep the line of communication open and frequent. This helps in building trust and continuity.

Share. Let them experience the new context through yourself. Norms of different societies, as well as similarities and differences within a new and past context, can be shared without having to include personal issues.

Encourage support. Allow anyone they identify as a friend or support to accompany them and to join your discussions if they should choose to do so.

Whatever the circumstances, show respect. As the young people have lost a great deal, this gives them back some sense of self-worth and motivation to succeed in the new context. Giving information on plans for them, keeping appointments, etc. are important to the young people as a measure of respect from others in a place of authority.

Let us now turn to the recommendations about the nature of improved community supports needed for care leavers, and other young people facing social exclusion and living away from their home and family.

What is meant by improved health and well being services in the community?

What is meant here is the need for a range of ongoing health and social care services post-CLCA 2000 that are based on individual needs assessments and Pathway Plans. This list of recommendations is divided between those provided by social care agencies, and those provided by health agencies. The emphasis here is on practical recommendations, especially since the policy issues relating to mental health have already been discussed earlier in this book in Vostanis' chapter.

Whilst it is acknowledged that health and well being *needs* always outstrip their *supply*, this must not be an excuse for poor services being delivered by a poor corporate parent in an inflexible way. In any case many of the following recommendations are not resource laden but more about engagement with young people, service planning and priorities. Some of the young people have specialist needs such as those arising from atrocities in war, or being a refugee, an asylum seeker, an abductee returning to this culture after years abroad, or adult survivors of child sex abuse, and others. Therefore whilst it is the case that the young people in the research study had different needs, they also had similar needs and it is these common needs, which apply to all or most care leavers which are reproduced here.

Social care. The young people in the health and well being research study told the research team what they would like social care agencies to do:

- **Provide local drop-ins and support groups** run by local people who understand local issues and are part of the local community.
- **Provide positive adult role models/mentors** in the community for friendship, advice, guidance and help.
- **Prioritise urgent repairs** to be carried out by local authorities and housing associations as a priority just as 'older tenants' do.
- **Provide continuity of and longer-term support workers** until they can get by without support.
- **Offer impartial benefits advice** and improved benefit rates.

- Provide further support for **developing existing programmes for young women**, pregnant or with children.
- **Recruit local women** to be mentors/advisors/befrienders for young women.
- **Offer support with multiple issues**, including housing, repairs, finance, budgeting, social and life skills as well as training, education (especially support whilst at college) and employment.
- **Provide more services** to families, partners and support workers.
- **Re-appoint good staff wherever possible**, for example when a contract comes to the end, seeking to re-appoint that person or replace as soon as possible.
- **Support existing and develop new peer education** projects.

Health agencies. The young people told the research team what they would like health care agencies to do:

- Understand that black and minority ethnic young people value services from **specialist counselling services for black and minority ethnic young people.**
- **Provide better support for teenage parents** such as non-stigmatising drop-ins, family centres, support groups run by peers and friendly staff.
- **Promote health promotion discussion forums.**

For example, at one of the projects (a Foyer project) the young people wanted to have discussion groups or focus groups to look at and talk about risky behaviours, drug use, alcohol use, etc., in safety and in confidence. They also wanted to invite people in to give them clear and sound advice about issues that affect them.

- Continue/encourage young people's involvement and offer **a mutual support group**.

For example, topics such as safer drug use, the affects of alcohol, sexually transmitted diseases, contraceptive advice, child sex abuse, rape, diet and healthy eating, weight issues, education and benefit advice were suggested:

- **Local mentors** were valued for advice, help and friendship.
- **Making time and support.** Services and professionals offering young people the time and support to make informed choices are likely to be used and respected more.

- The provision of more **counselling and appropriate mental health services** is vital.
- **Specialist health and maternity staff** with a greater understanding of young people's life experiences and needs were highly rated.

Furthermore, as Lawson writes, drawing on her experiences as a mental health specialist working with young people leaving care:

> ... *(these young people) are not asking for expensive services – they are asking for a basic ground level accessible and relevant service ... A user friendly service on all tiers (i.e. front-line, counselling and specialist) could easily be incorporated into the current system.*
>
> (Lawson, 2004)

Teenage pregnancy

The government's *Teenage Pregnancy Unit* and national strategy to prevent teenage pregnancy are well established, with significant commitment at national and local levels. The message from our health and well being research, however, is that prevention strategies must take account of the reasons *why* many social excluded and vulnerable young women are *choosing* to become pregnant in their mid-teenage years.

Most of the young women who had become pregnant felt that 'traditional' sex education, focusing on methods of contraception, would not have prevented them from becoming pregnant. For others motherhood was seen as a way of helping the mother's emotional problems, providing a counter to 'risky behaviours' and bringing love, attention and another emotional focus into their lives. This finding has major implications for prevention strategies targeted at children from abusive or neglected backgrounds. It suggests that early interventions to improve the self-esteem and coping strategies of these vulnerable young people may help them to make a more informed choice about pregnancy. Other findings that some young women said they chose to become pregnant, as a genuine informed choice, also points to a need for much better health and social care supports if health and well being inequalities and cycles of poverty are not to continue.

The final dimension concerns the manner in which services and supports are both planned and delivered by health and social care agencies. What follows are recommendations by the young people about the improvements that are needed.

What is meant by improved service delivery?

The term 'improved service delivery' means the ways that services are delivered by single agencies, and engage with young people, as well as the way they are delivered across different agencies, wherever possible 'cross-cutting' through assessments of need. The agencies concerned include all health departments, especially mental health, social services, housing departments, benefits agencies, education departments, the youth agencies and all voluntary agencies. Self-help and support for young people by young people is also included here since peer education and peer supports were so consistently called for. As we have seen social exclusion is built up out of a multitude of interlocking factors, making problems difficult for a single agency to tackle alone. For example, the experience of living in local authority care can make a young person the target of bullying in school, which in turn may lead to that person disengaging from education, often without qualifications, and drifting into low-paid work that continues the cycle of poverty and exclusion. Or a young person's inability to deal with the stress and anger caused by their own experience of abuse may produce behavioural problems.

Health and social care services need to unpack these interlocking problems and address them, in a variety of ways, if they are to improve the health and well being of socially excluded young people.

Listening rather than judging

When the young people interviewed felt they had been labelled a 'problem teenager' or had been greeted with scepticism or with patronising attitudes, they had seldom received the help they needed and had seldom returned. There was not only a self-evident ring of truth about holding to this position but often a high level of sensitivity about self-presentation, self-esteem and feelings of rejection. It was equally clear, on the other hand, that whenever young people had been listened to and their views had been respected, they quickly recognised the difference and showed far more willingness to seek professional help again. The more effective and engaging services were the ones where the young people were asked their views, involved in decisions about what to do next and empowered to find their own solutions.

Based on this and other studies findings, *The Children's Society* compiled guidance for health professionals on how to build this type of participative approach into healthcare services. The findings also have major implications for all professional training, and for the work on occupational standards being done by *TOPSS* and *Healthwise* (the national training organisations for the social care and health sectors respectively).

Staff continuity and reliability

As well as stressing the importance of a respectful and participative approach, the young people also sent clear messages about the need for professional continuity and reliability. For these young people who have often been let down by adults or have seen too many adults come and go in their lives, a professional who 'stuck around' for them, who was reliably 'there for them', had often made all the difference. Staff recruitment and retention remain critical areas warranting even further investment and attention.

Stress and anger management

As we saw in Part III, and from other health and well being research about care leavers, many care leavers experience chronic stress, and for some, it had led to mental health problems, suicidal feelings, anger and violence. Many chose to continue smoking, although fully aware of the health risks, because it was their way of coping with stress, and a significant number said they used drugs (predominantly cannabis) or engaged in 'binge drinking' for the same reason.

Yet help with stress and anger management was largely only available to young people through the youth justice system, or in some areas through school exclusion projects. Some of the young people who wanted to learn how to cope could not use these services and were taking out their stress on themselves or on people around them. The young people themselves consistently called for more open access to *youth counselling* services. A key recommendation here is that there should be open access to courses or classes designed to help young people deal with stress and anger. Had such help been available to them from an early age, perhaps through their school, they would have been able to develop healthier coping strategies. However, because many of these young people had disengaged from school, alternative sources of help in dealing with stress and anger may be needed.

Helping and learning from each other

The young people in the study identified several ways in which they thought they could be better supported in improving their own health and well being. Most of these focused on building their capacity as individuals to find answers, to acquire resilience, and to learn from people who had been in similar situations. They suggested that the following services would meet their needs more effectively:

- *'Drop-in' and 'one-stop-shop' types of help and advice services.* When the young people could obtain all the help they wanted in one place they felt much more positive about seeking help and more in control of their own health care.
- *Peer education and support.* As we have seen many of the young people trusted other young people similar to themselves as reliable sources of information and advice, especially about 'health' issues such as drugs, alcohol and sexual behaviour. This may also carry some risks, about poor role models. They were also attracted by the idea of young people's support groups, where they could discuss their problems, including any difficulties they were having with the services they were using.
- *Mentors.* Similar to peer education many care leavers were attracted by the idea of having a mentor, perhaps someone only a little older than themselves who had been through similar experiences. The young people were less concerned about the type of expertise such mentors might provide than about the fact that they would be able to go to them for support when they were depressed or unmotivated.
- *Targeted services* tailored to the specific characteristics of different groups. For example, some of the young people were particularly complimentary about a counselling service for black and minority ethnic young people. The same approach could be used to encourage young asylum seekers, both male and female, to seek the help they need. The finding that young men generally are much less likely to seek health advice could be used as the justification for developing gender-specific health promotion programmes for young men.

Support for children as victims

Most of the young people in the study had at some time in their lives been the victim of violence, intimidation or emotional or sexual abuse, often sustained over several years. Many reported regular thefts and damage to property, and some experienced long-term domestic violence. Many of those who had been involved with social services when they were younger said that they had not received sufficient help and support at the time. However, as they moved into adulthood, they found that there was no obvious source of support for young people who were victims of crime. Those who did not report their experiences often received no services or support.

Multi-agency work

The young people needed focused, friendly and accessible services delivered at the right time for young people and in a convenient venue, and which should be inclusive and reflect the diversity of the local community, and which are vital in order to engage and support care leavers. At a multi-agency level this involves:

- **Better planning and liaisons** between and across agencies and quicker and more effective referrals.
- **Personal information** about young people only being given and shared on a 'need to know' basis with the agency which takes the lead responsibility to avoid each young person saying the same stories again and again to different staff.
- **Confidentiality** is of paramount importance to young people. Professionals working with young people should make explicit their 'confidentiality criteria' so a young person can decide if they wish to tell/share with a professional.
- **Non-judgemental attitudes** are essential for effective work with young people. This should be an essential criterion in staff recruitment.

Monitoring health and well being policies and services

It is vital that leaving care policies introduced by local authorities are monitored and checked. The *National Leaving Care Benchmarking Forum* (Rainer, 2004) has specific health and well being benchmarking indicators and standards, as one of its range of benchmarking indicators. These are well thought through and add considerably to our understanding of effective ways to promote good health and well being amongst care leavers. These health indicators, each of which have detailed standards set against them, are as follows:

- *The local authority has a health policy for looked after children and care leavers that meets its duties as a corporate parent.*
- *Care leavers should be encouraged and supported to have their physical, emotional and metal health needs regularly assessed and monitored. This will be recorded as part of a reviewing process.*
- *Care leavers have access to clear information about their health and about healthy lifestyles.*
- *Health and social care providers must establish formal partnership agreements and protocols to agree joint working relationships, points of referral and identify how care leavers can access health service provision.*
- *Specific formal links are established and developed with Child and Adolescent Mental Health Services (CAMHS) and Adult Community & Mental Health Services – including arrangements for transition to adult services.*
- *Care leavers mental health needs are regularly reviewed and monitored to ensure that services are designed and planned to meet their needs.*
- *Health and social care work together with care leavers to develop a programme of positive action of health and leisure initiatives designed to promote improved health outcomes.*

(Rainer, 2004)

Health and responsibility

Whilst children and young people leaving care need to take responsibility for their own health and well being (some would say this can be a burdensome sole responsibility imposed at too early an age), the legal responsibility for a child is that of the child's parents. However, prior to becoming an adult, this responsibility would also have been the child's parents/carer and/or the local authority acting *in loco parentis*. Health and well being can also be a shared responsibility within a family, a personal responsibility and confidential matter (in relation to medical treatment), and a public responsibility in terms of behaviours which affect others. For example this could include being violent to another or promoting risky behaviours by others (e.g. substance misuse). One key question is whether young people facing social exclusion can argue that not only are the health and well being problems they face not of their own making, but that others have some responsibility for resolving them? Alternatively, can it be argued that if young people are fully responsible for their actions and behaviours that it is solely up to them if and how they address them? This author argues that whilst some of these may be unclear moral questions, there is an *overriding public duty of care* here by the state to provide appropriate health and well being assessments and services for care leavers. Indeed, this duty as laid out in the primary legislation, requires local authorities, in consultation with the young person, to carry out comprehensive, informed health and well being assessments and action plans for all those young people entitled to services under the CLCA 2000.

Health and well being and the CLCA 2000

The key issue emerging from the research evidence presented here is whether the CLCA 2000 carries enough resources, and local will (competing with other modernisation initiatives), training, staff and inter-agency planning and agreements to deliver the vital inter-agency partnerships that underpin the implementation of this Act. Research evidence in this field has consistently highlighted the need for a more graduated period of transition from childhood to adulthood for young people leaving care than is often the case.

The implications from the research evidence here about services for care leavers starting from different baselines are enormous and problematic in terms of the implementation of the CLCA 2000. An analogy about different trains (as leaving care services) and tracks (as organisational mechanisms) may help to make the point, in particular the different services provided by slower trains and those provided by the more powerful express trains. Simply put, since the legislation, the slower trains still arrive at the station, mostly, and they are improving and getting slightly faster. However, they never catch up with demand, whilst the faster, better equipped express trains deal better with increased demand. Meanwhile whilst the faster trains also never fully meet demand, they always or mostly leave the station ahead of the slower train and always arrive at the destination first. If the young person misses the faster express there is also very likely to be another express train

behind it, in accord with the timetable but if they miss the slower train, they may be stranded for some time.

Policy comments

According to the research findings presented here whilst many (not most) services for care leavers are improving, the pace of change is very slow, especially for the lower performing and more hard-pressed leaving care teams, and further change for them is largely dependent on continued external funding. Longer-term investment, especially in terms of planning and service delivery after the end of ring-fenced *Quality Protects* funding in 2004, has already become problematic, and a return to the inadequate pre-investment days is beginning to have its effect.

In addition, circumstances are changing significantly for public sector employees. The average time a public employee is spending in each job is decreasing, and staff are increasingly expected to perform a wider range of roles as part of their career development. On top of all this, the health and social care sectors are continuing to experience severe recruitment and retention problems. Ongoing government reviews of public sector employment need to identify the kind of investment and infrastructure required to ensure adequate levels of staffing for vital health and social care services. It will be equally important for the future effectiveness of services that any further funding and service development is based on the sorts of 'what works' findings presented here and elsewhere in order that they lead to more effective and reliable services and outcomes.

Additionally, year-on-year increases in the numbers of children entering the looked after system, across all local authorities, is also a part of a wider trend which impacts on young people leaving care, in terms of resources, and needs. Greater use of other more creative models of family support, for example supporting children in need to remain living within an assessed kinship care placement, are recommendations previously made by this author (2001) as well as by the *Fostering Network* and *BAAF*. There will be other changes, most notably those needed to be made about foster care (Verity and Broad, 2003), residential care and family support services which should all improve services for children at risk and children looked after. Young people leaving care were not the focus either of the green paper *Every Child Matters* (DfES, 2003) or the Children Act 2004. Nevertheless, proposed changes seek to improve substantially the safety of children looked after and the quality of services they receive. This should eventually feed through to services for young people leaving care. Contrary-wise it is also likely that with the renewed emphasis being given to child protection, that young people leaving care will be *less* of a priority group for local authorities.

Whilst examples may well exist, there were no reports here of initiatives by Primary Care Trusts (PCT) focusing on delivering health and well being needs to care leavers-often the provision stops at the earlier 'looked after' stage. Therefore, it is of the highest priority that both at the national strategic level, NHS and DfES joint protocols and guidance are developed, and that at the regional level that CAMHS (see earlier chapter by Vostanis), local authorities and PCTs work more closely together. Examples of nurses and health promotion staff being appointed by local authorities to work with 'looked after' children's services are worthy of further research and practice dissemination.

National health and well being indicators and assets

As argued by Bradshaw (2002) and as is already the situation in America, there is a need in the UK for national health and well being indicators to be introduced. These would apply to children, young people and families. In America indicators are collected annually both to establish the health and well being of children/young people, but also rate and compare the capacity of different states to provide health and well being services to children and families in need. There are also strong indications that these are used to target and improve services by examining which services make what impact on, for example, young people (teenagers) in need. Also the use of this approach enables data about all children and families' health and well being to be collected, which could resolve the current problem in the UK whereby such data, when collected at all, is collected on a much more random and occasional basis.

One American study examining 300 programmes for improving the mental and emotional well being of young people, and having a resonance here from the two research studies' findings concluded:

- *Measures of mental and emotional well being tend to be related to each other, suggesting that programs aimed at improving one aspect of well being may have positive effects on others.*
- *Links have been found consistently between teens' well being and environments that are emotionally positive and warm and that provide support for developing adolescent autonomy.*
- *Longstanding depressive illnesses and behaviour disorders which have their origin in childhood are much more difficult to treat as a young person.*
- *Living in a supportive low-risk environment has a positive effect on young people's health and well being.*
- *. . . positive experiences in one area (for example, in the family, among peers, at school, through youth community service, or at work) may lessen the effect of negative experiences in other areas.*
- *Also, multi-component strategies seem more appropriate than narrow, single component strategies.*
- *. . . programs designed to improve functioning in one area may have a positive effect on mental health and emotional well being even when other areas remain relatively unchanged.*

(Zaff et al., 2002)

As part of a government's commitment to recording and improving the health and well being of the nation, this author is convinced of the merit of collecting health and well being indicators in the UK as a matter of course and policy, rather than continuing the limited ad hoc arrangements.

Improving the health and well being of care leavers

The evidence presented in part three of this book spelt out the deep-seated links between the earlier, often abusive lives, and the present, often-difficult lives, concerns, needs and experiences of 57 care leavers. A particular emphasis was given to focusing on current health and well being issues, including those relating to relationships and life-styles. The impact of past abuse, bullying and physical violence, and parents' emotional 'coldness' or indifference towards them, on the young people's current lives, levels of self-esteem, self-worth, health and well being and resilience, is an especially powerful theme of that study. This is not to say that many of the young people often succeeded every day in managing to put earlier abusive relationships behind them. These young people often demonstrated enormous measures of resilience in getting on with the often-complicated day-to-day demands. As we have seen they valued and often needed trusted friends, some family members, responsive social care services. Having analysed and presented the research findings, and that of others, the challenge is now with local and central government agencies and adults who work with young people to respond to the concerns and recommendations in this book. At the policy level social services departments, health authorities, education, housing departments and voluntary organisations need to plan and work together much more closely. Increased levels of targeted funding would also make an enormous difference. The limited recognition of the potential 'impact on children of adult behaviours,' something we have evidenced here, is also an important conclusion elsewhere (NSPCC, 2001). The same report also noted, as we have, the lack of consistent attention given to the specific health needs of black and minority ethnic children and young people. Funding for establishing additional counselling services for black and ethnic minority young people is one of many clear recommendations made here (also see Ince, 2004).

Formally, and as we have seen, health and well being are recognised in the CLCA 2000, and guidance is available, but there is still a long way to go to provide holistic health and well being services that go beyond the partial 'medical model' of health care for care leavers. It is also important to note that multi-agency social inclusion work which involves social services children's departments and health agencies, often experiences difficulties in getting 'health on board' (Atkinson et al., 2001). In part this is due to the multitude of government initiatives that need time, and attention, as well as a lack of resources, but it may also be to do with lack of understanding about and genuine commitment to, multi-agency work, especially where shared budgets are involved.

Conclusion

The evidence presented in this book describes the health and well being needs of young people facing leaving care and facing social exclusion and the good work being done which makes a difference. It then spelt out the deep-seated links between their earlier and current health and well being needs and included discussion of the importance and impact of earlier relationships on their present life-styles. The impact of *earlier* childhood abuse, bullying and physical violence, and their parents' emotional 'coldness' or indifference towards them, on the young people's *current* lives, levels of self-esteem, self-worth, health and well being and resilience, was an especially powerful leitmotif calling for holistic services. This is not to say that many of the young people try and often succeed in putting earlier abusive relationships behind them, and get on with their lives, providing they had trustworthy mates, helpful family and friends, and help and support available, and a good measure of resilience, when needed. The term 'social exclusion' was used to identify both levels of need and flag up the types of interventions needed for a fully integrated social inclusion agenda.

Based on the evidence available to date, this author has serious reservations about the extent to which the health and well being needs are placed sufficiently high enough on wider social inclusion *funding* agendas compared with the social inclusion *rhetorical* agendas to make the differences required within the timescale demanded. What must *not* happen is that either the momentum for change, or the recognition that care leavers and other young people facing social exclusion need, as a matter of urgency, a range of funded and flexible health and social care services to become more socially included, are lost.

A combination of health targets, funded incentives, DfES initiatives and inspections, staff training, as well as anti-poverty lobbying and campaigning are all likely to be required to produce even the most basic improvements across all authorities. The Foyer Federation's report (2001) about young people's health needs points to the need for funded cross-agency health focused partnerships to be introduced. The introduction of investments in the widest range of funded social inclusion measures is a major priority and will have a major impact on young people's health and well being. If the aim of greater social inclusion for all children and young people is becoming much more fully recognised as a policy goal, and receives the highest funding priority, then this author is confident that these young people's health and well being will improve.

Appendices

Appendix 1: Terminology and service entitlements for eligible, relevant, and former relevant children in the Children (Leaving Care) Act 2000

Groups of children under the Children (Leaving Care) Act 2000	Definition	Entitlements
Eligible children	Children aged 16 and 17 who have been looked after for at least 13 weeks since the age of 14 and who are still looked-after.	<ul><li>All the provisions of the looked-after system</li><li>Personal advisor</li><li>Needs assessment</li><li>Pathway Plan</li></ul>
Relevant children	Children aged 16 and 17 who have been looked after for at least 13 weeks since the age of 14, and have been looked after at some time while 16 or 17, and who have left care. Additional groups of relevant children are those who: <ul><li>Would have been relevant children but for the fact that on their 16th birthday they were detained through the criminal justice system, or in hospital.</li><li>Have returned home but the return has broken down.</li></ul>	<ul><li>Personal advisor</li><li>Needs assessment</li><li>Pathway Plan</li><li>Accommodation and maintenance *Section 23B(8)*</li><li>Assistance to achieve the goals (e.g. educational goals) agreed and set out in the Pathway Plan</li><li>The responsible authority must keep in touch</li></ul>
Former relevant children	Young people aged 18–21 who have been either *eligible* or *relevant children*, or both. If at the age of 21 the young person is still being helped by the responsible authority with education or training, they remain *former relevant children* to the end of the agreed programme of education or training even if that takes them past the age of 21.	<ul><li>The responsible authority must keep in touch</li><li>Personal advisor</li><li>Pathway Plan</li><li>Assistance with employment</li><li>Assistance with education and training</li><li>Assistance in general</li><li>Vacation accommodation for higher education or residential further education if needed</li></ul>

Bibliography

Abbott, D., Morris, J. and Ward, L. (2001) *The Best Place to be? Policy, Practice and Experiences of Residential School Placements for Disabled Children*. York: Joseph Rowntree Foundation.

Acheson, D. (1998) *Independent Inquiry into Inequalities in Health*. London: The Stationery Office.

Action on Aftercare Consortium (1996) *Too Much Too Young: The Failure of Social Policy in Meeting the Needs of Care Leavers*. Ilford: Barnardo's.

Action on Aftercare Consortium (2004) *Setting the Agenda: What's Left to do in Leaving Care?* London: AOAC.

ADSS (2004) *Briefing: Policy Bulletin Number 29 – Transitions at 18*. Kent: Association of Directors of Social Services.

Aggleton, P. (1996) *Promoting Young People's Sexual Health: A Compendium of Family Planning Service Provision for Young People*. London: Health Education Authority.

Allard, A. (2002) *A Case Study Investigation Into the Implementation of the Children (Leaving Care) Act 2000*. Unpublished MSc thesis, London: London School of Economic and Political Science.

Allen, M. (2003) *Into the Mainstream: Care Leavers Entering Work, Education and Training*. York: Joseph Rowntree Foundation.

Anderson, L., Vostanis, P. and Spencer, N. (2004) Health Needs of Young Offenders. *Journal of Child Health Care*. 8, 149–64.

Anthony, D. and Collins, G. (2003) *Mental Health Needs Assessments in Prisons*. Leicester: De Montfort University.

Atkin, K. and Ahmad, W. with Al-Falah, (1998) *Ethnicity and Disability: The Experience of Young People with Sickle Cell Disorder or Thalassaemia*. Leeds: Centre for Research in Primary Care, University of Leeds.

Atkinson, M., Wilkin, A. and Kinder, K. (2001) *Multi-Agency Working: An Audit of Activity*. Slough: National Foundation for Educational Research/Local Government Association.

Barber, J.G., Delfabbro, P.H. and Cooper, L.L. (2001) The Predictors of Unsuccessful Transition to Foster Care. *Journal of Child Psychology and Psychiatry*. 42: 785–90.

Barnardo's North West (1999a) *Manchester Leaving Care Service Annual Report 1998/99*.

Barnardo's North West (1999b) *Manchester Leaving Care Service Annual Report 1999/2000*.

Barn et al. (forthcoming) *Issues Facing Black Care Leavers*. (working title)

Bartley, M., Blane, D. and Davey-Smith, G. (Eds.) (1998) *Sociology of Health Inequalities*. London: Sage.

Baxter, C., Poonia, K., Ward, L. and Nadirshaw, Z. (1990) *Double Discrimination. Issues and Services for People with Learning Difficulties from Black and Ethnic Minority Communities*. London: King's Fund Centre/Commission for Racial Equality.

Benzeval, M., Judge, K. and Whitehead, M. (Eds.) (1995) *Tackling Inequalities in Health: An Agenda for Action*. London: Kings Fund.

Beresford, B. and Sloper, T. (2000) *The Information Needs of Chronically Ill or Physically Disabled Children and Adolescents*. Social Policy Research Unit, University of York.

Berridge, D. and Brodie, I. (1998) *Children's Home Revisited*. London: Jessica Kingsley.

Bibini (2000) *Annual Report 2000*. Manchester: Bibini.

Biehal, N., Clayden, J. and Byford, S. (2000) *Home or Away? Supporting Young People and Families*. London: NCB/JRF.

Biehal, N., Clayden, J., Stein, M. and Wade, J. (1992) *Prepared for Living? A Survey of Young People Leaving the Care of Three Local Authorities*. London: NCB.

Biehal, N., Clayden, J., Stein, M. and Wade, J. (1995) *Moving on: Young People and Leaving Care Schemes*. London: HMSO.

Big Step (2002) *The Health of Young People in Care and Leaving Care in Glasgow*. Glasgow: Big Step.

Bignall, T. and Butt, J. (2000) *Between Ambition and Achievement: Young Black Disabled People's Views and Experiences of Independence and Independent Living*. Bristol: The Policy Press.

Boeck, T. (1999) *Social Exclusion: A Presentation of the Theory and an Introduction to the Research*. Leicester: Department of Social and Community Studies, De Montfort University.

Bonnerjea, L. (1990) *Leaving Care in London*. London: Borough's Children's Regional Planning Committee.

Bradshaw, J. (Ed.) (2002) *The Well Being of Children in the UK*. London: Save the Children.

Appendix 2: Terminology and service entitlements for qualifying children in the Children (Leaving Care) Act 2000

Groups of children under the Children (Leaving Care) Act 2000	Definition	Entitlements
Qualifying children and young people over 16	Any young person aged under 21 (under 24 if in education or training) who ceases to be looked after or accommodated in a variety of other settings, or privately fostered, after the age of 16. This includes: • Young people who leave care after October 2001, at or after the age of 16, but do not qualify as eligible children • Young people who left care before October 2001	• The same benefits as under section 24 before amendment In addition, • The responsible authority must keep in touch with local authority care leavers as they think appropriate in order to discharge their functions under sections 24A and 24B • Local authority care leavers are entitled to assistance with education and training up to the age of 24 (a) Local authority care leavers are entitled to vacation accommodation for Higher Education courses or residential Further Education courses if necessary

Appendix 3: Comments about mental health research findings

The research findings sought in the health and well being research study about mental health issues, particularly those associated with the nature, extent and levels of psychiatric illness were unsatisfactory and incomplete. The research team found that many team staff 'flagged up' mental health issues as a problem, and most were particularly frustrated about the non-availability and poor access of mental health services. Yet very few young people reported to us that they currently or recently had specific 'mental health' problems.

This is not to say therefore that none of these 57 young people did have such problems. It is more likely that young people with mental health problems did not respond to our invitation to participate, or attend meetings, and subsequent interviews. Also mental health issues are quite subtle ones, in terms of assessment, definition, and planning. The conclusions that can be drawn from this research about incidents of 'mental health' is that the young people used the term 'mental health' in a very fluid way. For example when young women were reporting current depressive experiences, or recalling being in care as 'affecting my mental health' or 'it did my head in'. By drawing on young people's perspectives and definitions, therefore, it is not possible to produce precise figures about 'mental health' from this study. However, we do know from other studies that this is a key issue for many vulnerable young people (detailed in, for example, the *Bright Futures* Report, from the Mental Health Foundation, 1999). The minority of young people who told us about their current mental health concerns, discussed them primarily in the context of their previous in-care experiences, and to a lesser extent, as a side effect of occasional drug taking. Also, what the young people did vividly describe to us, were the effects of depression, being isolated, and lonely.

British Youth Council (1996) *Never Had it so Good.* London: BYC.

Broad, B. (1991) *Punishment Under Pressure: The Probation Service in the Inner City.* London: Jessica Kingsley.

Broad, B. (1994) *Leaving Care in the 1990s.* Kent: Rainer.

Broad, B. (1997) The Inadequate Child Care Legislation Governing Work With Young People Leaving Care: A Research Based Review. *Childright*, Sept. 139: 17–8.

Broad, B. (1998) *Young People Leaving Care: Life After the Children Act 1989.* London: Jessica Kingsley.

Broad, B. (1999) Improving the Health Needs of Children and Young People Leaving Care. *Adoption and Fostering.* 23: 1, 40–8.

Broad, B. (2003) *After the Act: Implementing the Children (Leaving Care) Act 2000.* Children and Families Research Unit Monograph No. 3, Leicester: De Montfort University.

Broad, B. (2005 in press) Young People Leaving Care: Implementing the Children (Leaving Care) Act 2000? Children and Society.

Broad, B. (Ed.) (2001) *Kinship Care: The Placement Choice for Children and Young People.* Lyme Regis: Russell House Publishing.

Broad, B. and Fry, E. (2002) Sustaining Supported Lodgings: A Golden Opportunity for Growth. in Wheal, A. (Ed.) op. cit., 105–14.

Broad, B. and Robbins, I. (forthcoming) The Well Being of Unaccompanied Asylum Seekers Leaving Care.

Broad, B. and Saunders, L. (1998) Involving Young People Leaving Care as Peer Researchers in a Health Research Project: A Learning Experience. *Research, Policy and Planning.* 16: 1, 1–9.

Broad, B., Hayes, R. and Rushforth, C. (2001) *Kith and Kin: Kinship Care for Vulnerable Young People.* London: NCB/Joseph Rowntree Foundation.

Brunt, S. (1999) *Improving Children's Health: A Survey of 1999–2000 Health Improvement Programmes.* London: NSPCC.

Buchanan, A. and Brinke, T. (1999) Are Care Leavers Significantly Dissatisfied and Depressed in Adult Life? *Adoption and Fostering,* 23: 4, 35–40.

Callaghan, J., Pace, F., Young, B. and Vostanis, P. (2003) Primary Mental Health Workers Within Youth Offending Teams: A New Service Model. *Journal of Adolescence.* 26: 185–99.

Callaghan, J., Young, B., Pace, F. and Vostanis, P. (2004) Evaluation of a New Mental Health Service for Looked After Children. *Clinical Child Psychology and Psychiatry.* 9: 130–48.

Callaghan, J., Young, B., Richards, M. and Vostanis, P. (2003) Developing New Mental Health Services for Looked After Children. *Adoption and Fostering.* 27: 4, 51–63.

Centrepoint (2004) *Income and Outcome: Simplifying Financial Support for 16–19 year olds.* London: Centrepoint.

Chamba, R., Ahmad, W., Hirst, M., Lawton, D. and Beresford, B. (1999) *Minority Ethnic Families Caring for a Severely Disabled Child.* Bristol: The Policy Press.

CHAR (1995) *Planning for Action: The Children Act 1989 and Young Homeless People: A Black Perspective.* London: CHAR.

CHAR (1996) *Inquiry Into Preventing Youth Homelessness.* London: CHAR.

Children and Young People's Unit (2001) *Strategy for Children and Young People.* London: CYPU.

Coleman, J. (1997) *Key Data on Adolescence.* Brighton: Trust for the Study of Adolescence.

Community Care (2003) Race Equality Legislation Has Yet to Make Enough Impact. *Community Care.* 29 May.

Corlyon, J. and McGuire, C. (1997) *Young Parents in Public Care.* London: NCB.

Corlyon, J. and McGuire, C. (1999) *Pregnancy and Parenthood.* London: NCB.

DEE (1999) *Preparing Young People for Adult Life.* A Report by the National Advisory Group on Personal, Social and Health Education, London: DEE.

DEE (2000) *Sex and Relationship Guidance.* London: The Stationery Office.

Denscombe, M. (1998) *The Good Research Guide.* Buckingham: Open University Press.

Der-Kevorkian, G. (1996) *Health Promotion Report on Health Issues Concerning Young People Aged 15–21 Leaving Local Authority Care in Northamptonshire.* Northampton: NHA.

DfES (2003a) *Every Child Matters.* London: HMSO.

DfES (2003b) *The Children Act Report 2002.* London: DfES.

DfES (2004) *Disabled Children in Residential Schools:* London: DfES.

DHSS (1980) *The Black Report. Inequalities in Health: Report of a Working Group Chaired by Sir Donald Black.* London: DHSS.

DHSS (1984) *Report of the House of Commons Social Services Committee (the Short Report).* London: HMSO.

DHSS (1985) *Reviews of Child Care Law.* London: HMSO.

DHSS (1987) *The Law on Child Care and Family Services.* London: HMSO.

Dimigen, G., Del Priore, C., Butler, S., Evans, S., Ferguson, L. and Swan, M. (1999) Psychiatric Disorder Among Children at Time of Entering Local Authority Care: Questionnaire Survey. *British Medical Journal.* 319: 675.

DoH (1991) *Children in Public Care.* London: DoH.

DoH (1992) *Health of the Nation.* London: DoH.

DoH (1995) *Health of the Young Nation.* London: DoH.

DoH (1998a) *Our Healthier Nation.* London: DoH.

DoH (1998b) *Quality Protects: Transforming Children's Services.* London: DoH.

DoH (1999a) *Government Objectives for Children's Social Services.* London: DoH.

DoH (1999b) *Me Survive Out There.* London: DoH.

DoH (1999c) *Promoting Health for Looked After Children: A Guide to Healthcare Planning, Assessment and Monitoring.* Consultation Document, London: DoH.

DoH (2001a) *Children Looked After by Local Authorities Year Ending 31 March 2000.* London: DoH.

DoH (2001b) *Children's Taskforce.* London: DoH.

DoH (2001c) *The Children (Leaving Care) Act 2000.* Regulations and Guidance, London: DoH.

DoH (2001d) *Working Together to Safeguard Children.* London: Stationery Office.

DoH (2002a) *NHS Plan Improvement, Expansion and Reform: The Next 3 Years Priorities and Planning Framework 2003–2006.* London: DoH.

DoH (2002b) *Promoting the Health of Looked After Children.* Guidance, London: DoH.

DoH (2002c) *Social Service Performance Assessment Framework Indicators 2001–2002.* London: DoH.

DoH (2003a) *Children Looked After by Local Authorities Year Ending 31 March 2002.* London: DoH.

DoH (2003b) *Guidance on Accommodating Children in Need and Their Families.* Local Authority Circular (13), London: DoH.

DoH, External Working Group (2003) *Getting the Right Start: the National Service Framework for Children, Young People and Maternity Services.* London: DoH.

DoH/DfEE (2000) *Guidance on the Education of Children and Young People in Public Care.* London: DoH/DfEE.

Douglas, A. (2004) From Care to Where? *Care and Health.* 18: 18–9.

First Key (2001) *The Children (Leaving Care) Act 2000.* Seminar, Leeds: First Key.

Fostering Network (2000) *Rights of Passage.* London: Fostering Network.

Fostering Network (2003) *Leaving Care and After: A Survey of Foster Carers Views About the CLCA 2000.* London: Fostering Network.

Foyer Federation (2001) *Working Together to Promote Better Health for Young People.* London: Foyer Federation.

Franklin, C. and Corcoran, J. (2000) Preventing Adolescent Pregnancy: A Review of Programs and Practices. *Social Work.* 45: 1, 40–52.

Garnett, L. (1992) *Leaving Care and After.* London: NCB.

Gilligan, R. (2001) *Promoting Resilience: A Resource Guide on Working with Children in the Care System.* London: BAAF.

Gordon, D., Levitas, R., Pantazis, C., Patsios, D., Payne, S., Townsend, P., Adelman, L., Ashworth, K., Middleton, S., Bradshaw, J. and Williams, J. (2000) *Poverty and Social Exclusion in Britain.* York: Joseph Rowntree Foundation.

Gordon, D., Parker, R. and Loughran, F. (2000). *Disabled Children in Britain: A Re-analysis of the OPCS Disability Surveys.* London: The Stationery Office.

Gosling, R. (2000) *The Health Needs of Young Refugees in Lambeth, Southwark and Lewisham NHS Trust.* London: South London Community Health Trust.

Hagell, A. (2002) *The Mental Health of Young Offenders.* London: Mental Health Foundation.

Hai, N. and Williams, A. (2004) *Implementing the Children (Leaving Care) Act 2000: The Experiences of Eight London Boroughs.* London: NCB.

Harman, J., Childs, E. and Kelleher, K. (2000) Mental Health Care Utilisation and Expenditures by Children in Foster Care. *Archives of Paediatrics and Adolescent Medicine.* 154: 1114–7.

Harris, J. and Broad, B. (forthcoming) Improving the Outcomes for Young People Leaving Care.

Harris, J., Rabiee, P. and Priestley, M. (2002) Enabled by the Act? The Reframing of Aftercare Services for Young Disabled People. In Wheal, A. (Ed.) *The RHP Companion to Leaving Care.* Lyme Regis: Russell House Publishing.

Hayman, C. (2000) *The Foyer Federation Directory.* London: The Foyer Federation.

Health Advisory Service (1995) *Together We Stand.* London: HMSO.

Health Education Authority (1998a) *Tackling Inequalities: Young People and Health:* London: HEA.

Health Education Authority (1998b) *Unintended Teenage Conceptions.* London: HEA.

Health Education Authority (1999) *Young People and Health*. London: HEA.

Heaven, P. (1996) *Adolescent Health*. London: Routledge.

Hendey, N. and Pascall, G. (2002) *Disability and Transition to Adulthood: Achieving Independent Living*. Brighton: Pavilion Publishing.

Heslop, P., Mallet, R., Simons, K. and Ward, L. (2001) *Bridging the Divide: The Experiences of Young People with Learning Difficulties and Their Families at Transition*. Bristol: Norah Fry Research Centre, University of Bristol.

House of Commons (1998) *The Health of Children Looked After by Local Authorities*. London: HMSO.

Hussain, Y., Atkin, K. and Ahmad, W. (2002) *South Asian Disabled Young People and Their Families*. Bristol: The Policy Press.

Ince, L. (2004) *Fighting Back: Promoting Resilience Among Children and Young People of African and Dual Heritage Backgrounds*. Children and Families Research Unit Monograph. No. 4, Leicester: De Montfort University.

Institute for Public Health Research and Policy (2000) *Inequalities in Health*. paper by Dr. Chrissie Picken, Bury and Rochdale NHS: Lancashire.

Jackson, S., Ajayi, S. and Quigley, M. (2003) *By Degrees: The First Year*. London: NCB.

Jenkins, J. (2001) Overview of the Legal Position of Grandparents as Kinship Carers. In Broad, B. (Ed.) (2001) op. cit.

Jones, L. and Allebone, B. (1999) Researching Hard to Reach Groups. *International Journal of Inclusive Learning*. 3: 4, 353–62.

Joseph Rowntree Foundation (2003) *Direct Payments for Young Disabled People*. Findings No. 553, York: York Publishing Services.

Lader, D., Singleton, N. and Meltzer, H. (2000) *Psychiatric Morbidity Among Young Offenders in England and Wales*. London: Office for National Statistics.

Lawson, C. (2004) Mind the Gap. unpublished paper adapted from article in *Keynotes*. 30, 4–6.

Lewis, H. (1999) *Improving the Health of Children and Young People in Public Care: A Manual for Training Residential Social Workers and Foster Carers*. London: NCB.

Loney, M. (1983) *Community Against Government*. London: Heinemann.

Lupton, C. (1985) *Moving Out: Older Teenagers Leaving Residential Care*. Portsmouth: SSRIU, Portsmouth University.

Madge, N. (1997) *Abuse and Survival: A Fact File*. London: NCB.

Manchester Health Authority (2000) *Manchester Health Improvement Programme 2000/01*.

Manchester Health Authority and Manchester City Council (2000) *Children's Services Plans 1997–2000, A Strategic Framework*. Manchester, MCC.

Manchester Healthy City Initiative (2001) *Teenage Pregnancy in Manchester: Annual Report 2000–2001*. Manchester: MCC.

Manchester Sexual Health Forum (1999) *The Manchester Sexual Health Strategy for Young People*. Manchester: MCC.

Manchester, Salford and Trafford Health Authority (2000) *Health and the Young: Public Health Report*. Manchester: MST Health Authority.

Marsh, P. (1999) Leaving Care and Extended Families. *Adoption and Fostering*. 22: 4, 6–14.

Mather, M., Humphrey, J. and Robson, J. (1997) The Statutory Medical and Health Needs of Looked After Children. *Adoption and Fostering*. 21: 2, 122–31.

McCann, J.B., James, A., Wilson, S. and Dunn, G. (1996) Prevalence of Psychiatric Disorders in Young People in the Care System. *British Medical Journal*. 333, 1529–30.

McLeod, E. and Bywaters, P. (2000) *Social Work, Health and Inequality*. London: Routledge.

Meadows, S. and Dawson, N. (1999) *Teenage Mothers and Their Children: Factors Affecting Their Health and Development*. London: HDA.

Meltzer, H., Gatward, R., Goodman, R. and Ford, T. (2000) *Mental Health of Children and Adolescents in Great Britain*. London: Office for National Statistics.

Mental Health Foundation (1999a) *Bright Futures: Promoting Children and Young People's Mental Health*. London: Mental Health Foundation.

Mental Health Foundation (1999b) *The Big Picture: Promoting Children and Young People's Mental Health*. London: The Mental Health Foundation.

Minnis, H. and Devine, C. (2001) The Effect of Foster Carer Training on the Emotional and Behavioural Functioning of Looked After Children. *Adoption and Fostering*. 25: 44–54.

Minnis, H., Pelosi, A., Knapp, M. and Dunn, J. (2001) Mental Health and Foster Carer Training. *Archives of Disease in Childhood*. 84: 302–6.

Minty, B. (1999) Annotation: Outcomes in Long-term Foster Family Care. *Journal of Child Psychology and Psychiatry*. 40: 991–9.

Monaghan, M. and Broad, B. (2003) *Talking Sense: Messages From Young People Facing Social*

Exclusion About Their Health and Well Being.
London: The Children's Society.

Morris, J. (1995) *Gone Missing? A Research and Policy Review of Disabled Children and Young People Living Away From Their Families.* London: The Who Cares? Trust.

Morris, J. (1998) *Still Missing? Vol. 1: The Experiences of Disabled Children and Young People Living Away From Their Families.* London: The Who Cares? Trust.

Morris, J. (1999a) *Move On Up: Supporting Young Disabled People in Their Transition to Adulthood.* Essex: Barnardo's.

Morris, J. (1999b) *Hurtling into a Void: Transition to Adulthood for Young Disabled People with Complex Health and Support Needs.* Brighton: Pavilion Publishing.

Morris, J. (2004) *One Town for my Body Another for my Mind: Services for People with Physical Impairments and Mental Health Support Needs.* York: Joseph Rowntree Foundation.

National Statistics (2003) *The Mental Health of Young People Looked After by Local Authorities in England.* London: HMSO.

Nicol, R., Stretch, D., Whitney, I., Jones, K., Garfield, P., Turner, K. and Stanion, B. (2000) Mental Health Needs and Services for Severely Troubled and Troubling Young People, Including Young Offenders, in an NHS Region. *Journal of Adolescence.* 23: 243–61.

NSPCC (2001) *Improving Children's Health (2) An Analysis of Health Improvement Programmes 2000–2003.* London: NSPCC.

NSPCC (2004) *It Doesn't Happen to Disabled Children: Report of the National Working Group on Child Protection and Disability.* London: NSPCC.

O' Bryan, A., Simons, K., Beyer, S. and Grove, B. (2000) *A Framework for Supported Employment.* York: Joseph Rowntree Foundation.

Parsons, K. (2000) *Accommodation Issues Arising From the CLCA 2000.* In Wheal, A. (Ed.) op. cit.

Payne, H. (2000) The Health of Children in Public Care. *Current Opinion in Psychiatry.* 13: 381–88.

Peckham, S. et al. (1996) *Teenage Pregnancy: Prevention and Programmes.* Southampton: Institute for Health Policy Studies, University of Southampton.

Phillips, J. (1997) Meeting the Psychiatric Needs of Children in Foster Care. *Psychiatric Bulletin.* 21: 609–11.

Picken, C. (2000) *Inequalities in Health.* Lancashire Institute for Public Health Research and Policy.

Priestley, M. (1998) Childhood Disability and Disabled Childhoods: Agendas for Research. *Childhood.* 5, 207–23.

Priestley, M., Rabiee, P. and Harris, J. (2003) Young Disabled People and the 'New Arrangements' for Leaving Care in England and Wales. *Children and Youth Services Review.* 25: 11, 863–90.

Quinton, D. and Rutter, M. (1984) Parents with Children in Care: II. Intergenerational Continuities. *Journal of Child Psychology and Psychiatry.* 25: 231–50.

Rabiee, P. Priestley, M. and Knowles, J. (2001) *Whatever Next? Young Disabled People Leaving Care.* Leeds: First Key.

Rainer (2004) *Care Leavers Health Needs Service Standards.* National Leaving Care Benchmarking Forum, London: Rainer.

Randall, G. (1988) *No Way Home.* London: Centrepoint.

Randell, G. (1989) *Homeless and Hungry.* London: Centrepoint.

Rayner, M. and Montague, M. (2001) *Resilient Children and Young People: A Review of the International Literature.* Victoria, Australia: Children's Welfare Association of Victoria.

Richards, A. (2001) *Second Time Around.* London: Family Rights Group.

Richards, A. and Tapsfield, R. (2003) *Funding Family and Friends Care: The Way Forward.* London: Family Rights Group.

Richards, M. and Vostanis, P. (2004) Interprofessional Perspectives on Mental Health Services for Young People 16–19 Years. *Journal of Interprofessional Care.* 18: 115–28.

Richardson, J. and Joughin, C. (2000) *The Mental Health Needs of Looked After Children.* London: The Royal College of Psychiatrists.

Roy, P., Rutter, M. and Pickles, A. (2000) Institutional Care: Risk from Family Background or Pattern of Rearing? *Journal of Child Psychology and Psychiatry.* 41: 139–49.

Royce, D. (1995) *Research Methods in Social Work.* Chicago: Nelson Hall.

Rutter, M. (1985) Resilience in the Face of Adversity: Protective Factors and Resistance to Psychiatric Disorder. *British Journal of Psychiatry.* 147: 598–611.

Saunders, L. and Broad, B. (1997) *The Health Needs of Young People Leaving Care.* Leicester: De Montfort University.

Scottish Executive (2003) *Supporting Young People Leaving Care.* Consultation paper, Edinburgh: Scottish Executive.

Select Committee on Health (2000) *Minutes of Evidence, March 23*. London: Health Committee Publications.

Shelter (2002) *Review of First Year of Housing Act 2002*. London: Shelter.

Shucksmith, J. and Hendry, L.B. (1998) *Health Issues and Adolescents*. London: Routledge.

Simons, K. (1998) *Home, Work and Inclusion: The Social Policy Implications of Supported Living and Employment for People with Learning Disabilities*. York: Joseph Rowntree Foundation.

Smith, K. and Leon, L. (2001) *Turned Upside Down: Developing Community-based Crisis Services for 16–25-year-olds Experiencing a Mental Health Crisis*. London: Mental Health Foundation.

Smith, R., Monaghan, M. and Broad, B. (2003) Involving Young People as Co-researchers: Facing up to Methodological Issues. *Qualitative Social Work*. 1: 2, 191–207.

Social Europe (1993) *Social Exclusion, the Concept and the Context*. (supplement 4), Luxembourg: European Union.

Social Exclusion Unit (1999) *Teenage Pregnancy*. London: The Stationery Office.

Social Exclusion Unit (2000) *Social Exclusion Model*. taken from web page of Social Exclusion Unit, London: Cabinet Office.

Social Exclusion Unit (2003) *A Better Education for Children in Care*. London: SEU.

Social Services Inspectorate (1997) *When Leaving Home is Also Leaving Care: An Inspection of Services for Young People Leaving Care*. London: DoH.

Social Trends (2002) *Social Trends 2001–2002*. London: HMSO.

Stein, M. (1997) *What Works in Leaving Care*. Essex: Barnardo's.

Stein, M. (forthcoming) *Overcoming the Odds: Resilience and Young People Leaving Care*. London: Joseph Rowntree Foundation.

Stein, M. and Carey, K. (1986) *Leaving Care*. Oxford: Basil Blackwell.

Stein, M. and Wade, J. (2001) *Helping Care Leavers: Problems and Strategic Responses*. London: DoH.

Stein, M., Sufian, J. and Hazelhurst, M. (2001) *Supporting Care Leavers: A Training and Resource Pack for People Working with Young People Leaving Care*. First Key: London.

Stephenson, P. (2002) *Billy*. London: Harper Collins Entertainment.

Stone, M. (1990) *Young People Leaving Care: A Study of Management Systems, Service Delivery and User Evaluation*. Westerham: Royal Philanthropic Society.

Thompson, N. (1994) *Anti-discriminatory Practice*. London: Macmillan.

Utting, W. (1997) *People Like Us: The Report of the Review of the Safeguards for Children Living Away From Home*. London: The Stationary Office.

Verity, P. and Broad, B. (2003) *Moving Foster Care Centre Stage: An Agenda for Action*. Children and Families Research Unit Monograph No. 2, Leicester: De Montfort University.

Vernon, J. (2000) *Audit and Assessment of Leaving Care Services in London*. London: National Children's Bureau.

Voice for the Child in Care (2004) *Start with the Child, Stay with the Child – the Blueprint Project*. London: VCC.

Vranken, J. (1995) *The Use of Models for a Better Understanding of Social Exclusion and Social Integration*. Collective Paper issued from the Seminar on Social Exclusion Indicators. Brussels: European Commission Directorate General Xll Science, Research and Development.

Wade, J. and Biehal, N. et al. (1998) *Going Missing: Young People Absent from Care*. Chichester: Wiley

Ward, H., Jones, H., Lynch, M. and Skuse, T. (2002) Issues Concerning the Health of Looked After Children. *Adoption and Fostering*. 26: 8–18.

Ward, J., Henderson, Z. and Pearson, G. (2003) *One Problem Too Many*. Home Office Research Study, No. 260, London: Home Office.

Wellings, K. (1999) *Promoting the Health of Teenage and Lone Mothers: Setting a Research Agenda*. London: HEA.

Wellings, K. et al. (1996) *Teenage Sexuality, Fertility and Life Chances*. DoH.

West, A. (1995) *You're on Your Own: Young People's Research on Leaving Care*. London: Save the Children.

Westcott, H. and Cross, M. (1996). *This Far and No Further: Towards Ending the Abuse of Disabled Children*. Birmingham: Venture Press.

Wheal, A. (2001a) *Family and Friends who are Carers: A Framework for Success*. In Broad, B. (Ed.) (2001) op. cit.

Wheal, A. (2001b) *Family and Friends who are Carers*. In Wheal, A. (Ed.) op. cit.

Wheal, A. (Ed.) (2001c) *The RHP Companion to Foster Care*. Lyme Regis: Russell House Publishing.

Wheal, A. (Ed.) (2002) *The RHP Companion to Leaving Care*. Lyme Regis: Russell House Publishing.

White, S. (2004) Research into Practice. *Community Care*. 22–28 April, 49.

Who Cares? Trust (1997) *Who Cares about Health?* London: The Who Cares? Trust.

WMCCC (2002) *Review of the Implementation of the Children (Leaving Care) Act 2000.* Birmingham: Birmingham Social Services.

Wrate, R. and Blair, C. (1999) Homeless Adolescents. In Vostanis, P. and Cumella, S. (Eds.) *Homeless Children: Problems and Needs.* London: Jessica Kingsley.

Wyler, S. (2000) *The Health of Young People Leaving Care.* London: the Kings Fund/Oak Foundation.

Wylie, T. (1997) *Invest in Futures: A Blueprint for Young People's Social Inclusion.* Leicester: NYA.

Young People's Health Network (2001) *Newsletter No. 11.* Spring, London: HEA.

Zaff, J., Calkins, J., Bridges, L. and Geyelin, M.N.G. (2002) Promoting Positive Mental and Emotional Health in Teens: Some Lessons From Research. *Child Trends.*